His thoughts turned to the woman who had sat across from him tonight with her flashing eyes and high-spirited look. There was something about her...a strength of spirit that seemed to speak to him without words, a sense of knowing things about her he had never been told—as if they had been acquainted for years.

He was being drawn to Juliana St. Clair and felt powerless to do anything about it. He thought about his future, how it had seemed so bleak just a few short weeks ago. And now?

He sighed. Now? Now he knew only this. He loved Juliana St. Clair.

God help him, he loved her. He wanted this woman, this stubborn, beautiful woman in his life. Forever.

Palisades...Pure Romance

Titles and dates are subject to change.

Palisades.
Pure Romance.

FICTION THAT FEATURES CREDIBLE CHARACTERS AND

ENTERTAINING PLOT LINES, WHILE CONTINUING TO UPHOLD

STRONG CHRISTIAN VALUES. FROM HIGH ADVENTURE

TO TENDER STORIES OF THE HEART, EACH PALISADES

ROMANCE IS AN UNDILUTED STORY OF LOVE,

FROM BEGINNING TO END!

A PALISADES HISTORICAL ROMANCE

WESTWARD

AMANDA MacLEAN

PALISADES

WESTWARD
published by Palisades
a part of the Questar publishing family

© 1995 by Amanda MacLean
International Standard Book Number: 0-88070-751-8

Cover illustration by George Angelini
Cover designed by David Carlson
Edited by Paul Hawley

Printed in the United States of America

For information:
QUESTAR PUBLISHERS, INC.
POST OFFICE BOX 1720
SISTERS, OREGON 97759

95 96 97 98 99 00 01 02 — 10 9 8 7 6 5 4 3 2

To my mother,
Elizabeth,
with love.

The LORD will guide you always;
he will satisfy your needs in a
sun scorched land
and will strengthen your frame.
You will be like a well-watered garden;
like a spring whose waters never fail.

ISAIAH 58:11

Prologue

∽✦∾

Stonehaven Plantation
Spring 1830

Tired and distraught, Richard St. Clair opened the diamond-paned doors leading from the library and stepped onto the wide porch overlooking the terraced gardens. He stood for a moment, leaning against the intricately carved porch rail. Drawing a ragged breath, he tried to steady himself.

Richard gazed across the wide expanse of lawn with its borders of lilacs, azaleas, and camellias. In the distance, new fields of cotton and corn stretched to the banks of the Mississippi, the lush foliage of new growth gleaming in the sun. Normally, this scene delighted the master of Stonehaven. But on this April morning it provided a nearly unbearable contrast to the dark sickroom where his beloved wife, Anne Marie, had just closed her eyes in death.

Then his gaze rested on his daughter, eight-year-old Juliana. Beside the gazebo under the cascading branches of a weeping willow, she stood near an easel, engrossed in an art lesson with her tutor, Maurice Dupree. The child held in her hand a palette dabbed with a profusion of colored oils. Even from this distance Richard could see his daughter's delight.

Watching Juliana, his heart ached. How could you tell a child she would never see her mother again?

His thoughts turned again to Anne Marie. Why hadn't he realized what bearing another child would do to her? Though delicate in stature, she had seemed invincible with her iron will and indomitable spirit. Eight years ago she had delivered their first child, Juliana, with ease. Then came the others, three altogether, never living to draw a first breath. Each miscarriage had taken a greater toll on his wife.

But this pregnancy had seemed different. His wife had said so from the beginning, her thin face beaming. "It must be another girl, Richard. And a healthy one. I can feel her turning somersaults inside." And husband and wife had embraced, barely able to contain their joy. "Her name will be Callasandra—Callie—after your mother. Promise me, if anything happens to me, Richard, that you will call her Callie."

"Nothing will happen to you, darling," he'd said. But Anne Marie hadn't answered. She had just smiled softly and touched his hand.

Later on Anne Marie's limbs had begun to swell and her skin had taken on a gray pallor. Then came the pain and bleeding. The doctor ordered her to bed. She lasted through nearly nine months—long enough to bear the infant. But not long enough to see baby Callie for the first time. And not long enough to say goodbye to Juliana, the child who spent hours on end outside the sickroom door, lonely for her mama.

Now Anne Marie was gone. And Richard was left to tell Juliana her mother was dead.

With a determined stride, he left the porch and walked toward Juliana and Dupree.

"Papa, look!" Juliana turned toward her father, her face a wreath of smiles.

For a moment Richard couldn't speak. How she reminded

him of his wife! Juliana had her mother's delicate loveliness—hair the color of burnished copper and eyes with the sparkle and depth of a mountain pond. Her face was still that of a cherub, but held the promise of shape and tilt that would someday turn into that of a stunning woman.

"Papa, I'm learning to paint!" Juliana, still smiling, beckoned her father to draw nearer. "Come, see. It's wonderful!"

Richard stepped closer to look over her shoulder at her work. He was surprised at what he saw. The canvas held no discernible shapes. None of the stick drawings of houses and trees he expected. Instead she had placed dabs of color, light and dark, in obscure but beautiful patterns. He looked up in surprise at the tutor, Dupree, an artist he had hired from New Orleans, who nodded in understanding.

"Why, darling," he said, "it's wonderful." Then unable to resist, he added, "What is it?"

"It's light," Juliana said simply. "It's the sunshine and shadows on everything I see." She looked steadily at her father, as if expecting something from him.

Richard nodded. "That's nice," he said.

Juliana, looking disappointed, dabbed more paint on her canvas.

"Dupree," Richard then said, turning his attention to the tutor. "Would you give me a few minutes alone with my daughter?" Dupree nodded, picked up his things, and walked back toward the main house.

When he was gone, Richard put his arm around Juliana's shoulders. "Honey, I've got something to tell you."

The little girl didn't stop painting. And she didn't look up at her father.

"Juliana." Richard paused, searching for the right words. "I don't know how to say this to make it any easier. Mama's gone.

She died just a few minutes ago."

Juliana dabbed more paint onto the canvas, her brush moving faster. "I don't care," she said. Her lower lip started to quiver.

Richard squeezed her shoulders tighter. "Honey, I'm sorry."

Juliana didn't answer. Furiously, she jabbed her brush into the paints and swept it across the canvas. Gone were the glorious colors, the sunshine colors. In their place came the colors of shadows—deep, dark, frightening shadows.

Then the child threw down her brush and sobbed in her father's arms.

⚬₰₰⚬

"I tell you, Richard, that highfalutin artist Dupree is a waste of time—not to mention a waste of your money." Gray-haired Caleb Benedict climbed the stairs to Stonehaven's wide porch. Richard trailed slightly behind him. The two men had just walked to the main house from the stables, past the gazebo where they saw sixteen-year-old Juliana painting at her easel, lost in concentration.

Caleb turned to peer through his spectacles at his dead sister's husband. "Dupree is filling your daughter's head with thoughts that will do her no earthly good. Juliana told me yesterday she wants to be an artist someday." The man practically spat the words. "Talks about gallivanting all over the countryside to paint what she sees." He shook his head slowly and set his lips in a look of disgust. "In my opinion, young women should be taught the rudiments of running a household—things that will make them useful when they marry. You've spent a fortune on your daughters' schooling—teaching them to read classics and to speak French. When will they ever use such skills? Tell me that, Richard. And of what use will Juliana find her painting? I dare say, you'll be sorry someday that you filled her head with such nonsense."

Richard kept his voice even. "You're right about one thing, Caleb. Those are just your opinions. How I educate my daughters is my business, not yours."

In the past he had trusted Caleb implicitly: Caleb Benedict, not only his dear Anne Marie's brother, but a man with years of experience as a lawyer and politician. For the past twelve years, Caleb had served as a U.S. senator and moved among Washington's elite. Richard and Anne Marie had made him godfather to Juliana, and after Anne Marie's death, Richard had asked him to be Callie's legal guardian as well. Lately, however, the man had grown secretive and difficult. It was only out of respect for Anne Marie's memory that Richard allowed him to spend time at Stonehaven.

Caleb went on. "Word has it that you've overextended yourself, Richard. People are talking."

Richard bristled. Caleb had hit a sensitive spot.

"They say—"

"I don't care what people say, Caleb."

But the older man wasn't about to be so easily dismissed. "They say you're land-hungry."

Richard didn't answer. There was no use arguing with the man. Besides, there was truth in what he said.

"Word is you're biting off more than you can chew." Caleb leaned forward, peering into Richard's eyes. "There's nothing wrong with expansion. Believe me, I agree with you on that." His voice took on a gentler tone. "But son, you can't expand and face crop failures at the same time."

"Stonehaven has known no crop failures."

"You can't predict the future, Richard." Caleb turned toward the fields and gestured widely. "All that could be gone in one season. In one month. You know it as well as I do. But it seems you just keep building anyway…trying to make Stonehaven into something it was never intended to be."

"Don't worry about my business, Caleb. I do appreciate your concern. But everything will be fine."

For a moment neither man spoke; then Caleb rubbed his beard, as if wondering whether to go on. Finally he said, "Carlisle over at the Natchez bank says you've taken out a sizable loan against Stonehaven."

Richard could feel his anger rising to the surface. "It's always been my assumption that my business—anyone's business—at that institution is confidential."

"Carlisle and I are old friends. He spoke to me as a family member."

"He spoke out of turn."

Neither man noticed that Juliana had left the gazebo and now stood on the stairs leading up to the porch. As she listened to their words, she noticed how the late afternoon's lengthening shadows moved toward where her father and Uncle Caleb stood talking. Before they finished speaking, darkness had fallen across them both, stretching to where she stood.

Shivering, Juliana turned away and quickly moved back into the sunlight.

&⤳

"Where is the best light?" Twenty-year-old Juliana had just finished setting up her easel and was dabbing blue, yellow, and red paints onto her palette. She brushed a strand of auburn hair from her face as she looked up at her tutor. "I don't mean right here." She gestured toward the gardens and fields nearby. "I mean out there. Anywhere. Everywhere."

Dupree smiled, the wrinkles on his ancient face deepening. "I knew what you meant. I'm just surprised you haven't asked me before."

Juliana waited for him to continue. When he didn't, she went on. "You've told me about the artists who travel with different tribes—those who've recorded the Mandans, the Comanches, even the Paiutes. You've told me how they sketch and paint the people and the land. And you've said that in the West the light has a wonderfully intense quality—unequaled anywhere."

Dupree nodded.

She laughed softly. "The West is a big place. Where is that perfect light found?"

"I suppose it's a matter of opinion, Juliana. Perfect light can be found almost anywhere." He looked thoughtful. "But several years ago I spent time in northern Mexico, a province called New Mexico, and I've never forgotten what I saw. There are certain times of the day, or maybe seasons of the year, when conditions are just right. Sometimes it happens after a storm. Usually in the mountains. Around a place called Fort La Sal is where I saw it. A golden light—a renaissance kind of light—seems to cause the landscape to almost shimmer. I had heard about it, but didn't believe it until I saw it firsthand." Dupree's wrinkled features grew soft as he remembered. "For an artist, it is something akin to perfection." Then he shrugged. "Maybe not everyone would see it that way. But I did. And I'll never forget it."

"I want to go to New Mexico. To Fort La Sal."

"I have no doubt that you will somehow find your way there."

Juliana nodded and began painting. "I will go," she said. "I don't know when. Or even how," she added with a laugh. "But I will go."

Twenty-four-year-old Juliana sat in the rich leather couch in the downstairs library at Stonehaven. Callie, now sixteen, sat beside her, holding her sister's hand. Across from them, behind their father's massive burled-oak desk, sat their uncle, U.S. Senator Caleb Benedict, reading their father's will and final instructions to them.

It had been only two days since Richard St. Clair's fatal heart attack. Their grief and shock were still raw. It seemed too soon to deal with their father's business, but Uncle Caleb had insisted, saying their financial situation was precarious at best and they had to act quickly.

"As you may be aware," the elderly man said, removing his spectacles after he finished reading the legal document, "your father made some errors in judgment in recent years. Because of that, nearly everything I just read to you is invalid. I mean to say, though your father left the estate to you, there will be nothing of value after the creditors take what's owed them."

Juliana caught her breath. She heard a small cry from Callie and squeezed her sister's hand.

"Your father died heavily in debt. He borrowed against Stonehaven extensively several years ago, and when the crops failed this past fall, he couldn't make the payments."

Juliana and Callie remained silent, waiting for their uncle to go on.

"Creditors had been hounding him. He was about to lose Stonehaven." The old man sighed sadly. "I tried to warn him—but never mind about that." He shook his head. "Now that your father's gone—there's no way to save the plantation. There's too much owed against it. I'm sorry, girls. I know this is an added burden to what you already carry."

Then Caleb cleared his throat and rubbed his beard nervously.

"There is something else we need to discuss. That is, we need to make plans, definite plans, for your futures." He sighed and shifted uncomfortably in his chair. "As I just read from your father's will, Juliana, you are of legal age and are free to do as you wish. However, Callie, because you are but sixteen years, I have been given legal responsibility for your well-being."

"That can't be true." Juliana was incredulous. "Papa didn't say that in the will."

"The issue of Callie's guardianship was recorded in an earlier document. Your father never saw need to change the terms." He shuffled through the papers on their father's desk.

Juliana and Callie looked at each other, then back to their uncle.

"Ah, yes. Here it is," he said. He picked up his spectacles and began to read.

Juliana listened in dismay. Caleb was right. Her father had indeed given him legal responsibility for Callie.

"When was this written?"

"It says here, 1830."

Juliana felt her cheeks turning hot in anger. "That will was made when Callie was an infant...and I was only eight years old. Why didn't Papa change it when I came of age?"

The old man shrugged. "I don't know why your father did most of the things he did."

Callie's face paled, making her freckles stand out darker than usual. She took an even tighter grip of Juliana's hand. Her voice shook when she spoke. "Well, now that we know the terms of the will, Uncle Caleb, what do you have in mind?"

Again their uncle cleared his throat and looked nervous. "This is a difficult situation. Very difficult. I've thought a great deal about what would be best for you both, and you must understand I do have your best interests at heart. You must be cared for." He hesitated. "So I've come up with a plan, an equitable plan."

"Go on," Juliana said.

"I've taken the initiative to seek a position of employment for you, Juliana." He hurried on before she could respond. "And I'm happy to report I have received enthusiastic responses from those I contacted. You can well imagine, families in these parts have been impressed with the education afforded you by your father."

"You're speaking of a position as governess—"

"Of course. With your education, you're perfect—"

Juliana's voice turned to ice. "I'm perfectly capable of finding my own employment."

"Of course you are, dear," Caleb said with a patronizing smile. "But we don't have time to waste. I have many contacts in the county. With my influence, you will be interviewed by only the finest families and have the opportunity of placement in a good, solid household."

Juliana's cheeks again flamed red-hot. She found herself speechless with anger. How dare Caleb step in and attempt to run her life?

"And for you, Callie—" He turned toward the younger sister. "I have made inquiries on your behalf as well, although in an entirely different vein." Again he cleared his throat, then took off his spectacles, pulled his handkerchief from his pocket, and proceeded to clean them. "I...ah...made inquiries about suitable prospects for your marriage."

"Marriage?" both young women cried in unison.

"Is that so shocking? Many young women are married by sixteen." His eyes narrowed as he stared at Callie, as if challenging her to disagree.

Callie's face had turned even paler. "But Uncle Caleb, I'm not in love with anyone."

He waved his hand as if dismissing the whole notion. "Love? That comes after years of marriage…not from some romantic look across a room when you're sixteen." He paused, then went on. "I'm pleased to tell you I've found someone who is eager to take you as his wife—"

Callie jumped to her feet. "I won't marry anyone against my wishes." She stared at her uncle. "You can't make me."

"You will do as you are told, Callie St. Clair," Caleb said sternly. "As will you, Juliana," he added, his thin lips fixed in a straight line.

Juliana stared at her uncle. Her eyes narrowed. "I believe you'll see that we are quite capable of taking care of ourselves, Uncle Caleb."

For a moment no one spoke. Callie turned her tear-stained face toward her sister. Her expression showed admiration mixed with hope.

Caleb laughed, a short brittle sound. "Take care of yourselves?" He practically spat the words. "And how do you propose to do that? You're penniless. You have nowhere to go."

Juliana's smile was cool. She measured her words, then spoke softly. "You've greatly underestimated us, Uncle." She said no more, though she could see he waited for her to go on. Then she stood and took Callie's hand to lead her from the room.

"You come back here!" Caleb Benedict sputtered. "I'm in charge of your affairs. I order you to come back and sit down. You must hear what else—"

Callie interrupted. "—hear what else you have planned for us? I don't want to hear any more." She began to cry again as she followed her sister.

21

At the highly polished mahogany doors Juliana turned gracefully and met Caleb's eyes with a steely gaze. "Don't worry about Callie and me, Uncle. You no longer need to concern yourself with us."

"And what's that supposed to mean?"

Neither sister answered. Juliana squeezed Callie's hand as she pushed open the door. Then Juliana turned once more to face Caleb, who was still seated behind Richard's desk. His face was purple with anger. He turned to stare out the window.

Callie pulled Juliana through the doorway, and arm in arm the two young women climbed the winding staircase to their rooms.

One

❧

The moon slipped from behind silver clouds, briefly lighting the wide upstairs hallway of the big house at Stonehaven Plantation. Juliana St. Clair moved silently along the thick oriental carpeting, her heart pounding with each creak of the wooden flooring beneath her.

Along the walls, life-sized portraits of generations of St. Clairs stared mutely from within their ornate, gold-carved frames. Grandparents and great-grandparents, long deceased, the women in satins and lace, the men in high starched collars, all gazed down with sightless eyes, looking aristocratic and grand.

Juliana touched her bright auburn hair and adjusted the plaits at the nape of her neck, stuffing them inside her hat, an old felt her father had worn when inspecting the fields. *I'm probably the only St. Clair woman who ever dressed in boys' clothing,* she thought, looking down at her breeches, vest, and homespun peasant blouse with a wry smile. She'd purchased them as a lark from a traveling gypsy years ago, never suspecting they would someday be useful.

As she moved along the hallway, Juliana glanced at portraits at the top of the wide spiral staircase leading to the foyer. They were of her parents, Anne Marie and Richard St. Clair, done by her old tutor, Dupree. On the left was her mother, with her fine patrician bearing and look of soft hope. Then Juliana's gaze moved to her father's face. Hot tears filled her eyes as she studied its expression of merriment and determination. And strength. Always his strength. *He may have misjudged his business investments, but no one could ever accuse him of being weak.*

Even now, barely a week after his funeral, it seemed that the halls of Stonehaven were still alive with his booming voice, his humor, his giving spirit. How could such a man be gone?

"Goodbye," Juliana whispered, touching the canvas. "I'll miss you, Papa." Then she brushed away her tears and moved quickly to Callie's door.

As she stepped from the thick carpeting to the polished cypress floor, her footsteps echoed down the hallway. Juliana caught her breath, listening for sounds of Caleb or one of the servants coming to investigate.

Moments passed. She breathed easier in the silence of the still-sleeping household.

Opening Callie's door, Juliana peered across the room to the high four-poster bed. Her sister slept peacefully in the moonlight, her unruly red curls splayed across the pillow.

"Callie! Wake up!" she whispered, as the moon again slid beneath the clouds. She shook her sister's shoulder.

Callie opened her eyes. "Wh—" she began, confused.

Juliana lightly placed her fingers on Callie's lips. "Sh-h-h. Don't make a sound."

Callie nodded sleepily, her eyes showing she understood.

"Where are your things?"

Callie pointed to the wardrobe. "They're in there," she whispered. "Some small satchels and a carpetbag."

"Good. Hurry now. Get up and get dressed. There's a sharp breeze rising off the Mississippi. Dress warmly. And take your cloak. You'll catch your death if you don't."

The moonlight again streamed through the windows and cast a glow in the room nearly as bright as dawn. Juliana could see Callie's face break into a wide smile.

"I'd rather die of a chill than look as silly as you do." Callie laughed quietly. "You look more like a dockhand than the mistress of Stonehaven." She suddenly looked sad. "I'm sorry, Julie. I didn't mean to—"

Juliana interrupted. "Don't apologize. Neither of us can undo what's been done. And certainly crying over Father's misfortune won't change anything."

"But it's just so unfair—"

"Don't think about it now, Callie. We've got a great adventure ahead—better than we can imagine. Let's concentrate on the future, not the past." Juliana forced gaiety into her voice. She didn't want Callie to know she couldn't bear to think of their loss.

"Well, I still think you look like a dockhand," Callie teased as she sat up in bed.

Juliana glanced down at her drab trousers. Callie was right. Her clothes were a far cry from the lace and organza frocks she had worn before their father died.

But she had chosen her outfit carefully and had warned Callie to do the same: Two young women traveling alone to the frontier needed to be careful not to attract undue attention. Juliana had reached her twenty-fourth year and knew she was more than capable of caring for herself and Callie. But she also knew the dangers that lay ahead.

"You will do well to dress as I have." Juliana playfully tousled her sister's red curls. "Hurry now, Callie. We need to get to the river before daybreak."

Callie stood. The tilt of her chin was stubborn, even in the pale light. "I've taken your advice, Julie, but only to a point. I refuse to wear trousers. Instead, I've picked for my ensemble..." she whirled to the wardrobe and pulled out a plain brown skirt and homespun blouse similar to Juliana's. "And to make sure I'm in the very height of fashion..." She rummaged in her wardrobe a few moments, then held out a pair of sensible boots for her dainty feet. "Dashing, don't you think?"

Juliana grinned. "*Chic*, my dear. Simply *chic*."

As her sister dressed, Juliana sat on the padded seat of the deep double-bay window and gazed out at the moonlit grounds of Stonehaven. She wanted to memorize the look of it: the towering oaks with their ivy-covered trunks and sweeping branches filled with trailing moss, the deep green pines and jaunty magnolias.

She sighed and let her gaze move east toward the river where the riverboat owner she had contacted in Natchez said he would await their arrival.

How she would miss the only home she had ever known! Her father had built Stonehaven in 1817. He had been so proud of the way it sprawled comfortably amid the gently sloping hills and age-old shade oaks. In the summers the bright flowering azaleas, camellias, and japonicas lined the walkway that was paved, as he often boasted, with stone slabs brought from Europe as a ship's ballast.

The look of Stonehaven was both majestic and inviting, its great white pillars standing tall and imposing on the front portico and smaller double pillars on either side of the massive colonial door. Even the interior design reflected her father's touch. The floors were made of thick cypress boards, and hand-carved woodwork framed each door. Floor-length windows with solid mahogany frames opened as doors from the front parlor on the west wing and the library on the east wing to an outside porch that wrapped around the house.

Juliana let her gaze sweep to the long drive, lined with wrought-iron lamps, winding to a main road that led east to the Mississippi River. And though she couldn't see them from the window ledge where she sat, she pictured the terraced gardens behind the house, the brick slave kitchen and slave quarters, and of course, Stonehaven's acres of cotton, tobacco, and corn.

Callie broke into her thoughts. "Jules, I'm ready." Callie stood behind Juliana, looking through the windows at the same moonlit scene. Her usually exuberant voice was soft, as if she could read Juliana's thoughts.

Callie sighed. "Let's go. It makes me sad to see Stonehaven looking so beautiful in the moonlight."

"I know, Callie. I know."

"I'd rather have it raining." Callie's voice was subdued. "Then it wouldn't be so hard to leave."

"Nothing would make it easy. Not rain. Not anything." Juliana took her sister's hand in hers. "Take a good look anyway, Callie. Memorize every old crooked oak. Notice the way the moonlight dances on the magnolia leaves. Remember the sounds of the crickets and mockingbirds with their night songs. Fill your heart with it, Callie." Juliana hugged her sister, and the two of them stood staring out across the lands of Stonehaven.

"I'm coming back someday, Juliana."

"I feel the same way."

"You don't know what I mean." There was a trace of bitterness in Callie's voice. "This place belongs to us. Father would never have let Stonehaven slip from his fingers the way Caleb said. It belongs to the St. Clairs—not to the bank."

"I'd like to believe that, too, Callie. But it's simply not true. Caleb has been quite clear about it. Father made some investment mistakes. Terrible mistakes."

"Think about it, though. We have only Caleb's word. What if he's wrong?"

"I wondered the same thing in the beginning. But I examined the books. The numbers are accurate. Believe me. There's no mistake. Stonehaven's no longer ours." She reached for Callie's hand. "I'm sorry. That's just the way it is."

"But what if you overlooked someth—"

Juliana interrupted, her voice sharp. "I didn't, Callie." Then she softened her voice, noticing Callie's sad expression. "Don't fill your head with empty hope. It's not worth it."

"I'll come back, though, Jules. Someday I'll come back." Callie's jaw had a stubborn set. "I will," she finished with a toss of her red curls.

A few minutes later Juliana and Callie slipped silently down the winding staircase, through the leaded glass side doors to the gardens, then past the slave quarters to the stables. They slowly pushed open the stable door, then let their eyes become accustomed to the darkness.

"It's all right, Darley," Callie called softly to the spirited Arabian that had belonged to their father. "Come here, girl." She rubbed and patted the horse's neck for a moment, then led her from the stall.

Juliana saddled the big gray, Sir Galahad, that had been hers since childhood, then fastened a carpetbag to either side of the saddle. She instructed Callie to do the same with her satchels.

Juliana, swinging into her saddle, laughed softly as Callie tried to balance the weight of the bags on the back of her horse. "I feel sorry for Darley—I think you've packed half of your wardrobe into those two satchels."

Callie sniffed as she cinched the bags into place then mounted Darley. "I've brought only necessities."

"Three party frocks?" Juliana knew her sister well. "Lacy pantaloons, even your straw hat?"

"And what of it? I don't plan to sit on the back of a horse—or on a wagon bench staring at the behinds of oxen—forever. If you hadn't stuffed your carpetbags so full of paints, brushes, and sketchbooks, you could've done the same, Jules."

"Actually, I did bring my green velvet. It was the last thing Father gave me. I couldn't bear to leave it behind."

"You chose well." Callie said simply, her voice suddenly sad.

Juliana knew Callie's thoughts had touched on the pain of their father's death. She felt tears begin to well in her own eyes and quickly blinked them away. It was too hard to dwell on it now. Their father would have wanted them to be strong. And she would be. For him. For Callie. For herself. She squared her shoulders and rode on.

By now they were approaching the slave quarters again. Juliana motioned for her sister to move Darley closer to Sir Galahad so they could speak without being heard.

"Did you remember to bring Mother's jewelry?"

Juliana nodded, then patted one of the saddlebags. "It's here."

They neared the slaves' small houses. A dog's bark was followed by a distant baby's cry. A mother's soft voice singing something that sounded like "sleep, baby Jesus boy" carried through the night. Juliana felt strangely comforted by the sweet, deep sound.

She put her finger to her lips, motioning to Callie that they shouldn't speak until they were farther from the shanties. As soon as they had ridden past a grove of cottonwoods by an open field, Juliana brought the gray to a halt, waiting for Callie to halt Darley beside her.

Callie looked pale in the moonlight. "I'm still worried that

Caleb might come after us. That he'll bring charges against us."

"For stealing you away?"

Callie nodded.

"I think he'll be relieved. We're no longer his concern."

"You're wrong, Juliana. You've felt all along that he's had our best interests at heart. I think you're too easy on him."

"What do you mean?"

"His plans for us were based on reasons we don't know about—even the marriage he'd planned for me wasn't simply to see me 'taken care of.'"

"You're thinking the worst of him. I really think you're being unfair, Callie. He wanted to see us cared for—me as a governess placed with a good family, you in a marriage to a worthy man."

"Worthy?" Callie sounded as if she would choke on the word. "You see only the good in people. You're not realistic." Then she was quiet a moment. "I just hope the way you see things—and people—doesn't put us in danger."

"Don't worry about something we have no control over, Cal." Juliana thought about Callie's original question. "As for Caleb following us—I see no reason for him to. We've done nothing illegal." Juliana suddenly shivered, hoping she was right.

They reined the horses toward the road leading to Greenville landing, then kicked them into a gallop and rode on through the moonlit night without speaking.

As they rode Juliana thought about her sister's worries. Callie's concerns were based on what she thought was the treachery of their uncle. Juliana knew their present danger was much more real than what Uncle Caleb might or might not do.

She sighed and turned to look at her sister. Callie, covered now, just as Juliana was, with an old woolen cape and heavy boots on dainty feet, had also placed over her curls one of their father's battered field hats. It was fastened by a narrow leather ribbon tied under her chin. What a contrast to the luxury they both had known. Their lives, until now, had been filled with the finest gowns and jewels, trips and lessons, soirées and concerts. Richard had seen to it that his daughters had the best of what this world had to offer. Now it was gone.

Juliana understood the journey ahead. She had read accounts of emigrants heading West. Dupree had told her of his own hair-raising experiences. But Callie had no idea of the dangers, the difficulties.

Juliana watched as Callie rode out ahead of her. Juliana was afraid for the thousandth time about her sister's safety in the rough land they were heading into. Callie was headstrong, and Juliana worried that she might endanger herself—or them both—by her outspoken and stubborn ways.

The sisters rode in silence for nearly an hour. As the pale gray of dawn began to creep across the eastern sky, Juliana urged Sir Galahad to a full gallop. "We need to move faster," she called out to Callie who still rode several yards in front of the gray. "I told the captain we'd be there by sunup."

Several minutes passed, then Juliana spotted the Mississippi through the distant mist. Soon they halted their horses on a rise above the Greenville landing.

Juliana looked down at the riverboat, lying still and ghostlike in the ashen light. Even from a distance it looked as if it had seen better days. Barrels and crates were piled on its deck. Near a single lantern at its stern, some men sat talking, their coarse voices carrying on the breeze to the hilltop from where Juliana and Callie watched.

Callie looked up at Juliana, her freckles looking dark against her pale skin. "This is it?"

Juliana nodded slowly. "It must be. It's the only one there."

"How long will we be on it?" Callie's voice sounded small.

"It'll take us about three weeks to get to St. Louis. Then from there another several days on the Missouri to Westport."

Callie sighed. "Then we'd better get started." She stiffened her shoulders, pulled the oversized hat over her flame-colored curls, and spurred the bay down the cliff.

Suddenly touched by her sister's bravery, Juliana kicked Sir Galahad into action. "Hey, wait!" she called after Callie, and the sure-footed gray galloped down the hill toward the barge.

CHAPTER

Two

For three weeks the riverboat steamed slowly along the muddy waters of the Mississippi. Though the November air was chilly, Juliana and Callie spent most of their time on deck, glad to be out of their cramped quarters. When the captain had first shown them to their "stateroom," Callie promptly declared that it was half the size of the kitchen pantry at Stonehaven. Juliana had agreed. The room was barely the length of its two narrow bunks. And as they hung their clothes on hooks above their bunks, Callie had wrinkled her nose in disgust at the stained and smudged walls. "You'll see worse than this before we get to New Mexico," Juliana had said in quiet admonition. Callie had shrugged, muttering under her breath, "Well, I may have to live with dirt, but I don't have to like it."

The days passed swiftly, one day melting into the next as the paddle wheel at the boat's stern moved them north. Because the riverboat carried more freight than passengers, the two young women kept mostly to themselves. They were the only females on board, and Juliana kept a wary eye out for any inappropriate advances from the crew.

"Have you noticed how the deckhands watch us?" Callie

asked one of their first mornings on board.

"Ignore them, Callie," Juliana reminded her sister more than once. "And keep near me. Don't even go below to check on the horses—unless we're together." Callie nodded, but Juliana knew her sister well. If Callie had a mind to take a midnight stroll or feed the horses at five in the morning, she would act first and be surprised at the consequences after it was too late.

And Juliana could indeed see the looks the crew gave Callie. She became determined to see to it that Callie had activities enough to keep her nearby and occupied.

Juliana insisted that her sister join her in reading a guidebook on traveling to the Southwest. Her old friend and teacher Maurice Dupree had left it to her when he died just two years before. He had also left her his journals from his travels to the province of New Mexico, which gave Juliana and Callie his first-hand accounts, insights, and advice for traveling on the Santa Fe Trail.

So the young women spent hours on the riverboat's deck, taking turns reading from the guidebook and Dupree's journals about the supplies they would need, about the dangers, the beauties, the adventures ahead.

They also began a list of what they would buy when they reached Westport, figuring the needed barrels of flour, coffee, and cornmeal. Of course they would buy a side of salt pork, a Dutch oven, an iron skillet, tinware, and a porcelain-covered coffee pot.

"It's going to be frigid cold, Julie. I insist on buying a counterpane," Callie said the day they first spoke of their plans. "And how will we keep dry? I insist on keeping dry."

Juliana sighed, "Callie, we're going to be roughing it. You can't *insist* on anything. This isn't Stonehaven. You can't just stomp your foot and have a servant see to your every comfort."

Callie put her chin in the air. "Well, you can rough it all you want. I intend to keep dry and warm. I want to get the very best wagon we can buy—no broadcloth top—I want heavy canvas, linseed-oiled. The book says that's the very best. That's what I want."

"We'll take what we can get, Callie. We may not have a choice."

Callie went on as if she hadn't heard. "And no bag-of-bones oxen either. We need to make sure they're the best. Listen to this." She began reading to Juliana from Dupree's account of the mishaps of a fellow traveler who thought he'd bought his team for quite a bargain, only to have them take sick and die along the trail. The poor fellow had nearly met disaster himself because of his folly.

"Of course I agree with you about the oxen," Juliana said, with growing exasperation. "Safety is one thing. Unnecessary insistence on comfort is quite another."

"Just wait till you're sopping wet and chilled to the bone, Juliana St. Clair. With a smelly wet woolen cloak over your shoulders. Then you'll wish you had listened to me." Callie tossed her red curls and set her lips in a line.

More than once, as they figured the expenses, Juliana silently thanked her father for having the foresight to give her and Callie their mother's jewels. Some of it had already paid for their riverboat passage. The rest would more than cover the costs of their trail supplies if she could convince Callie it wasn't wise to spend unnecessary money for items of comfort.

She also feared for the jewels' loss through theft or her own carelessness. Their small stateroom had no lock, only a latch. So she carried them with her, tucked in a leather tobacco pouch of her father's inside a small satchel in which she kept her journals, sketch pads, and charcoals. She reasoned that keeping the bag

35

constantly by her side wouldn't cause undue suspicion because she obviously needed her supplies nearby as she wrote in her journal or sketched.

As the days wore on, when she and Callie weren't poring over the guidebook or Dupree's journals, Juliana spent hours sketching scenes along the river, plantations on its banks, deer stooping for drinks of water at its shallow shores, the odd array of rough-looking passengers picked up at landings along the way.

While Juliana drew with her charcoals, Callie often wrote in her journal, sometimes looking sad, even angry, as she worked. Juliana asked her only once, "Cal, do you want to talk about it?" Callie's eyes filled with angry tears, but she only shook her head an emphatic no.

Juliana instinctively knew that for all her sister's airs of self-assurance, she was scared inside, dealing with the still-fresh pain of losing everything that had been dear. "I'm here if you need me," Juliana said, and touched her sister's arm. But Callie, as she too often did, turned away and stared out at the muddy waters. Minutes later she was the laughing, seemingly carefree spirit she had always been. Juliana wished she knew how to help Callie, how to touch the wound deep inside that needed healing. But then, she had been touched by fresh loss herself. How could she help Callie when she was having a difficult time dealing with her own sadness and pain?

One morning several days later, the boat pulled into a small landing just a day south of St. Louis. A lone passenger stood waiting to board.

The man glanced toward Juliana as he walked along the boarding plank. In the briefest of moments, his gaze seemed to embrace her. Juliana quickly averted her eyes.

Beside her, Callie drew in her breath. The exchange hadn't gone unnoticed. "He's dashing, Julie," she whispered. "And did you see the look he gave you?"

Juliana shushed her. "Don't be silly."

"Mmm. Mmm. He's a nice change from the ruffians who usually board."

"You just behave yourself, Callie." But fascinated, Juliana continued to watch the man as he moved from the landing to the boat and back again, carrying aboard two more heavy trunks and several pieces of baggage. She admired his strength as he shoved the trunks into place. His skin was the color of buckeye, tanned as if he lived outdoors. His dark hair hung loose to the shoulders of his greatcoat, and he walked with a long, confident gait, his heavy-soled boots accenting each step. But it was his expression that puzzled her. It held either great insolence or great assurance, or maybe both. And it seemed, for just a moment, that his eyes glinted the color of gun metal.

"You're staring," Callie whispered.

Juliana turned quickly back to her sketch pad, feeling her cheeks flush.

Within minutes the steamboat backed away from the landing and swung a wide arc to again head north. Juliana purposely lost herself in her work. She sensed, however, that he continued to watch her.

That evening, just before the dusk anchoring, Callie retired early to their small stateroom to freshen herself before supper. "We're invited to dine at the captain's table tonight. I must present myself properly for eating at his table —even if it's beans on tin plates," she said with a sniff of affectation.

Alone, Juliana leaned against the rail and stared out across the darkening waters of the Mississippi. She thought about the journey ahead. She was following a childhood dream planted in the fertile soil of her mind by the old master Dupree. For years she had imagined painting the golden meadows and majestic mountains of New Mexico. Now, within months, she would be there.

She and Callie would start a new life. Maybe build a ranch and settle in the high country. It was frightening to consider the work ahead, the obstacles that might get in her way, the dangers they might encounter.

Juliana took a deep breath, marveling at the feel of the dusk air against her face, the smell of the river, and silhouettes of weeping willows against a silver-streaked sky.

She thought again of New Mexico, and as she did, she lifted her chin in determination.

Her mother was dead. And now her father. She had lost the family's home and land holdings. There was nothing left. Nothing but her dream.

Nothing, no one, would stop her from seeing to it that she and Callie had the chance to live their own lives. Dream their dreams.

She needed no one's help to make that a reality, Juliana thought to herself. She would count on no one but herself—her wit, her charm, her intelligence. *For Callie's sake. For my own. I alone will make it happen.*

She gazed into the still-silver sky, wondering if there was a God and whether he would help her. Then she smiled to herself, feeling suddenly silly. Oh, for the naive comfort of being a tiny child again, whispering bedtime prayers, believing that Someone "up there" actually existed. And cared.

No. Her life, for better, for worse, was up to her to create. Again the thought rang indelibly in her mind: *I alone will make it happen.*

"Miss?" A resonant voice broke into her thoughts.

Juliana turned to see the passenger who had boarded earlier. He touched his hat and nodded in greeting.

His courtliness impressed her. The woolen cape that covered her homespun breeches and shirt was less impressive than that of a servant. She hardly expected to be addressed with gestures reserved for a lady. She smiled.

"I realize I'm being quite bold and perhaps presumptuous in approaching you this way," he began, his voice deep and sincere, "but I couldn't help noticing when I boarded—you were sketching, were you not?" His dark eyes held hers in a fixed gaze.

Juliana nodded.

He smiled. "Ah, I thought so." He sounded genuinely delighted. "I would love to see your work."

Juliana tilted her head. "Sir?"

"How thoughtless of me. We've not been introduced." He laughed softly and doffed his hat, looking truly embarrassed. "Matthias Graves, at your service." Then he bowed and, taking her hand in his, held her fingers to his lips, though a bit too long, she thought.

Juliana felt herself flush and pulled her hand away.

A fleeting shadow of irritation crossed his face, then quickly disappeared. "I'm sorry—," he began.

"No. Don't apologize." Juliana suddenly felt ashamed for her lack of social graces on his behalf. When gentlemen visiting Stonehaven had kissed her hand, she had smiled and accepted their behavior as natural. Why should the actions of this man— Matthias Graves—seem too familiar? She smiled warmly to make up for her blunder. "My name is Juliana St. Clair."

"I'm pleased to meet you, Miss St. Clair." He hesitated a moment. "It is *Miss* St. Clair?"

"Yes. It is." She smiled again, this time at his transparency.

For a moment neither spoke. The steamboat moved into a steep and narrow channel with overhanging foliage. Juliana could see a landing ahead, probably where they would anchor for the night.

She remembered his original question about her sketches.

"Are you an artist, Mr. Graves?"

He threw back his head and laughed. "Oh, no, Miss St. Clair. Hardly." He laughed again. "No. I simply appreciate fine art. I've traveled abroad and have studied the works of the great masters. I enjoy the artistic endeavors of others. That's all." He glanced at the carpetbag. Her sketchbook was beside it.

"May I?" He reached for the pad.

Again Juliana felt a hint of displeasure at his boldness. But she opened the book to a drawing she had worked on during the afternoon.

Matthias studied it for a time without speaking. "This is fine work," he said quietly. "What you've done with darkness and light is powerful."

Juliana appreciated his observation. "Not many people notice the contrasts."

They spoke for a time about art and artists in the Old World and in the New. Juliana was delighted to find that he had met George Catlin and Karl Bodmer on his travels in the West. Juliana told him of her desire to sketch and draw in New Mexico.

They exchanged a few parting pleasantries, then Matthias tipped his hat and strolled over to another group of passengers.

❧

"Juliana!" Callie whispered from her bunk. "Julie, wake up!"

Juliana groaned in her sleep, then squinted through the darkness at her sister. "What's wrong?"

"I hear a noise." Callie's voice sounded younger than her sixteen years. "There. I hear it again."

"I don't hear anything, Callie."

Callie was quiet a moment. "I hear creaking outside our door. Like someone walking by, then stopping. Then the floor creaks again. Then it stops."

"It's probably your imagination." Juliana turned over to go back to sleep. They would be landing in St. Louis the next day and boarding another boat, and they needed to be refreshed for the long day ahead. "Go back to sleep, Cal."

"No. There. I hear it again."

This time Juliana caught her breath. Maybe she did hear footsteps. But she listened carefully, hearing only her heart pounding in her ears. It must be just her imagination—and Callie's—working overtime.

"Did you hear it?" Callie whispered loudly.

"I don't think it's anything to worry about," she whispered back. The steamboat, still tied to the night landing, swayed slightly as a brisk breeze caught the craft, rocking it like a child's toy. "Maybe it's just the wind causing this old bucket to sway and creak." Juliana hoped to soothe Callie's fears, and her own, with her words.

She relaxed again, pulling up her covers, and was about to fall asleep when the door latch clicked. Then, from the outside, it slowly lifted.

Callie gasped.

At the same time, Juliana leapt from her cot and sprang to the door. She pushed her weight against it, holding one foot tightly against its base. "Help me, Callie! Now! Get over here."

With a small cry, Callie joined her and the two of them braced their rigid arms against the door. They could feel a push of equal force from the outside. There was a masculine grunt followed by a drunken exclamation.

"I thought you said this'd be unlocked." The deep voice carried through the thin door.

"There ain't locks on any of these doors. Move over. Lemme try."

There was scuffling outside, then the door moved inward slightly. Juliana could feel herself sweating as she pushed against the new force with all her strength.

Then the sound of low, coarse laughter came from the other side of the door. "Them skinny little gals are holding the door." The laughter continued. "Can you figure that? They must think they can keep us out."

Juliana heard someone loudly clear his throat and spit. There was another push. She pushed back. Beside her, Callie panted as she threw her weight against the door.

"Hey, let us in. We just wanna get to know you all better. Nothing more. We promise."

"What're we going to do?" Callie's voice was frantic.

"We've got to get one of the beds over here. Blockade the door."

"But we can't let go long enough to get it."

"Maybe if we—"

Her words were interrupted by the sounds of counting. "One...two..." By the time she realized what it meant, it was too late. At "three," the door slammed in on them. Two men burst into their room with a howl of triumph.

In the first horror of the moment, Juliana, nauseated by the pungent smell of liquor and sweat, felt too stunned to move.

Callie's cry of distress, as one of the men grabbed for her, awakened her to action.

"What do you think you're doing? You get out of here right now!" She forced herself to speak with authority.

The nearer man laughed in her face. She flinched.

"Like I said earlier..." he grabbed Juliana's arm and twisted it behind her back as he spoke. "...we just want to get to know you better." Juliana tried to escape from his grasp, but his hand squeezed harder against the flesh of her forearm.

Suddenly, from the doorway, another voice spoke low, controlled, authoritative. "I suggest you boys find another way to occupy your time. I believe these young ladies don't want the likes of you in their stateroom."

The man holding Juliana spoke. "Says who?"

"Doesn't matter who." The voice rose, sounding cool though angry. "It just matters that you do as I say."

"Mister, we suggest you either join our party or be on your way. This ain't any of your business," hissed the man holding Callie.

"Yeah." The first man laughed coarsely. "You're welcome to join us."

The man in the doorway spoke slowly. "Don't make me say this again, boys. Let the women alone. Be on your way."

For a moment no one spoke. Juliana could hear Callie's ragged and fearful breathing.

There was the unmistakable click of a cocked pistol followed by silence.

Then the man behind Juliana laughed. "You think we're fools? You shoot—you'll only get one of us. And it just might be one of the young ladies here." He pulled Juliana between himself and the doorway. She could smell his fetid breath, feel its warmth on the back of her neck.

"I can see well enough," said the man in the doorway. "You want to take a chance? Means nothing to me either way."

Again there was silence. Then the man holding Callie finally spoke. "Come on, Billy. Let's go. These women ain't worth getting shot over."

There was grumbling from the one called Billy, then he let go of Juliana's arm. The two men shuffled from the room and down the hallway away from the girls' stateroom.

"Thank you," Callie said with a shaking voice to the man who had rescued them.

Juliana lit a candle and turned to also thank him.

Matthias Graves met her gaze. Leaning against the doorjamb he pulled his handkerchief from a vest pocket and slowly polished the pearl handle of his Colt. He dropped it back in the carved half-flap holster at his hip, then smiled at Juliana, his eyes kind. "I'm just glad I happened along," he said.

CHAPTER

Three

⌘

By noon the following day the riverboat had docked in St. Louis. Juliana and Callie wasted no time debarking with Darley and Sir Galahad in tow.

They walked along the St. Louis boardwalk with its saloons, inns, and blacksmith shops, mercantiles, chandlers, and liveries. Juliana was surprised at the number of furriers. She knew the heyday of fur trappers had passed, but dozens of shops with beaver pelts in window displays were still doing a bustling business. Here and there were gun shops; most prominent was the Hawken Brothers Gun Emporium in the center of town.

Hundreds of people milled about: dockworkers, shopkeepers, travelers with little children and the elderly, trappers, and here and there a stray Indian in buckskins. Music and laughter drifted from the swinging doorways of the saloons into the street and across to the docks. The smell of frying catfish hung in the air, along with the inviting sounds of clinking dishes carried from hotel restaurants. Carriages and wagons rumbled along the planked streets with drivers calling out "Haw!" or "Hee!" to their teams of horses or mules.

"Don't stare," Juliana reminded Callie, as her sister stood

gaping at the sights. Then she chuckled at her admonition. She caught herself nearly doing the same thing. She had never before seen sights and sounds anything like these.

"Let's check to see when the next Westport boat leaves, then find decent lodging." Juliana could only think of settling into a safe place to rest, someplace that would provide hot baths. She was exhausted after the previous night's terrifying events. Even after the danger was over, they had not slept, because Matthias had stayed to protect them from any further disturbance, making sure they were safe until they reached St. Louis.

Now as she and Callie walked along the boardwalk, Matthias Graves occupied her thoughts. His bravery on their behalf had impressed her. And as the three of them talked until dawn, she and Callie had confided in him about their escape from Stonehaven and Caleb Benedict and their plans to head west on the Santa Fe Trail. With a delighted expression on his handsome face, he told them of his destination—Fort La Sal, in New Mexico.

"I'll be joining a trading caravan in Westport," he said, handing her a card inscribed with the name of its leader—'Captain Parker James, Commerce of the Santa Fe.' "It is one of the few winter trains—perhaps the only year-round train—out of Westport. If you do not want to wait until spring for your journey, you may want to join us." He smiled. "If you are there before his train leaves—join us. Please." Then he looked into Juliana's eyes, his gray eyes luminous and warm. He went on. "I would escort you from St. Louis on, but I've got business here. I'm not sure how long I will be."

Later, as they parted company at the dock, Matthias took her hand and pressed it to his lips. "Promise me you'll contact Captain James and his wagon company when you get to Westport." She had nodded in agreement before turning to leave with Callie.

Callie's voice brought Juliana back to the present. "I hope we have time to exercise the horses before we get on the boat." She rubbed Darley's neck. "They've been cooped up too long—and so have we," she added, as she gazed wistfully to the open fields beyond the rows of boardwalk shops. Juliana readily agreed.

After jostling their way through the crowded streets and back onto the dock, they found their way to the *Ginny Lee,* a paddle-wheel scheduled for departure two days hence. The riverboat would carry them up the Missouri River, a major highway carrying travelers west into the wilderness.

The two young women were happy to find that the *Ginny Lee* was not a freighter but a modest passenger carrier catering mostly to families preparing to head west. It would take them to Westport, the beginning of the Santa Fe Trail, just south of St. Joseph, the take-off point for the Oregon Trail.

Juliana began to relax for the first time since leaving Stonehaven a week earlier. She had chosen a freight-carrying riverboat up the Mississippi because she figured her uncle would never think of looking for them there. And now they would be on a boat crowded with families—not the fashionable travelers of a posh Mississippi riverboat with its music and gambling, but people of modest dress and serious intent. She and Callie would fit right in. Even if Caleb had sent someone to look for them, he would be hard-pressed to spot them. She was sure that, even if he guessed their destination, he would never guess their route or their means of travel.

After two days of rest, complete with soaks in the hot baths that Juliana had dreamed of, and riding Darley and Sir Galahad through the golden autumn fields, Juliana and Callie gathered up their carpetbags and rode to the landing to board the *Ginny Lee.*

Callie also seemed more relaxed now that they were settled in their stateroom, cleaner and more spacious than their quarters on the Mississippi riverboat. She spent time visiting with other passengers while Juliana pulled out her sketch pad and lost herself in her art.

The first day on board, Juliana found herself watching an old trapper in fringed leggings and coat. His wife (at least she supposed the woman was his wife) was Indian, bronze skin with high cheekbones and strange light eyes. She wore a single thick braid down her delicate back. Her hair shone like a raven's wing reflecting the sun. They seldom spoke but sat quietly apart from other passengers, staring out across the river. Juliana drew them, working candidly and quickly. It occurred to her, after watching them for several days, that they communicated without words. Their eyes spoke for them. Even their facial expressions spoke of their love.

As she watched, she realized that the trapper wasn't old at all. His skin was weathered, but the lines around his eyes were squint lines, not wrinkles from aging. His beard was more sun-bleached than gray, and the fringed leathers he wore, though ingrained with dirt, seemed to fit him as naturally as a second skin.

And the woman—Juliana once heard the trapper call her Sun—was, at closer inspection, older than Juliana had originally thought. Her blue eyes seemed to hold a quiet wisdom, a serenity that Juliana thought must come from contentment—though she knew that Indians in a white world could surely not be content.

Once, Juliana looked away because of the depth of intimacy she observed between them. As she gazed out at the river, she wondered if she would ever find that kind of love, the kind that blends two people, two souls together without words.

Juliana was still lost in her thoughts of love when Callie approached her, breaking her reverie.

"Jules, have you heard anything about the war in New Mexico?" Callie asked breathlessly.

Juliana turned toward her sister quizzically. "What are you talking about?"

"I've just been in the dining room for tea. It's the only topic of conversation." Callie looked worried. "Really, Juliana. I think we need to find out more about it before we sign on with a caravan heading to New Mexico province."

"Callie, you heard Father and Caleb talking about the war last spring. I know you did—I was there with you many times. We all talked about it."

Callie shook her head. "The talk was about Mexico—not New Mexico. I remember Father saying something about an attack on our troops near the Nueces River in Texas. And that President Polk was thinking about sending troops to Mexico City and California. That's all. I never heard they actually went—until today. And I certainly never heard a word about New Mexico."

Juliana remembered hearing the events discussed throughout the summer, though they had seemed remote at the time. After her father's death, and the pressing affairs that followed, she had set aside any concerns for Mexican politics and her own government's positioning for war. Even as she planned their escape from Stonehaven, Juliana held to her father's belief that when and if a Mexican war happened, Mexico would fall like an overripe peach.

"Callie," she said, her voice calm, "we'll find out everything we can when we get to Westport. I know that civilian caravans won't be allowed into New Mexico if there's a war going on." She took Callie's hand. "Believe me. I won't place us in any unnecessary danger."

"What if there are no caravans heading to Santa Fe? What then?"

"We'll either wait it out in Westport until it's safe, or travel up the Missouri to St. Joseph and join a train bound for Oregon."

"But your heart's already set on New Mexico."

"Yes, Callie. It is."

That night at supper, Juliana discovered Callie was right. The discussion centered on the latest news of the Mexican war.

A pale, blond man was seated at Juliana's right and introduced himself as Seth Johnson. He said he'd heard that General Winfield Scott had proposed that two American armies be sent into Mexico—one to capture Mexico City, the second to seize the Mexican provinces of New Mexico and California.

"New Mexico?" Juliana asked.

Johnson peered at her with weak-appearing eyes. "Ah, yes. That's what this war's about. Land, land, and more land." He laughed. "There've been border disputes for years—Mexico pays no attention to our claims. And we don't pay a lot of attention to theirs. But the long and short of it is that for a long time we've wanted to get our hands on Mexico's northern provinces—including that prime land known as California. And, of course, the beautiful New Mexico."

"But what about the army that Scott wants to send to seize New Mexico?" Callie, who sat at Juliana's left, leaned forward to ask the question of Johnson.

"*Wants* to send?" Johnson said with a short laugh. "It's already done. Kearny's army of some sixteen hundred troops—dragoons, Missouri Volunteers, and artillerymen—marched into Santa Fe weeks ago and seized the province of New Mexico. Without firing a single shot."

"Are they still there? I mean, are they planning to stay—to occupy the province?" Juliana, after her initial concern, was beginning to feel that New Mexico would, in fact, be a safe destination.

"No," said Johnson, "It was a peaceful takeover. Then while Kearny was in Santa Fe, Kit Carson rode in from California. Told him that California had fallen to Frémont and Stockton." Johnson took a drink of coffee then continued. "So Kearny split his troops. Took some of the dragoons to California. But most he sent to Chihuahua. He even sent some Mormons to open a wagon route into California through northern Sonora."

"How is it y'all know so much?" An older man who had said he was from New Orleans leaned across the table. His question sounded like more of a challenge than a simple inquiry.

Johnson looked uncomfortable; beads of sweat appeared on his lip. Then he laughed lightly. "I've got kin with the dragoons. I heard from him regularly until he left with Kearny for California. I haven't heard anything since."

The conversation about the Mexican war continued. Someone said they'd heard that the troops heading to Chihuahua were suffering from the dreaded *vómito*. A large woman to Callie's left turned pale and covered her mouth with her napkin. Callie giggled, and Juliana poked her in the ribs to shush her.

Over dessert, Johnson leaned toward Juliana. "From your earlier questions I take it you're interested in New Mexico—perhaps even on your way there."

Juliana nodded as she stirred a spoonful of sugar into her coffee. "Yes. My sister and I planned to join a trading caravan in Westport." She took a dainty sip. "The recent takeover is a worry, though. Normally I pay more attention to the nation's affairs. But we recently experienced a death in the family—my mind has been on anything but wars—or rumors of war. I just want to make sure we're not heading into dangerous circumstances."

"Everything I've heard—firsthand, mind you, from my brother Jed—is that Santa Fe is dead calm. Jed wrote me that Kearny appointed a well-respected U.S. citizen and long-time resident of the region—Charles Bent—as governor of New Mexico. I've heard from others besides Jed that he's a good man."

"Ain't what I heard." An unkempt man from a nearby table

turned in his chair and grinned. "I ain't ever heard nothin' good about Charles Bent. He's well known in these here parts, you know. Word is that he's plumb crazy. Married himself a squaw. Can you imagine that?" The man laughed, half coughing as he did. "Married hisself a dirty ol' squaw."

Embarrassed, Juliana glanced quickly around the dining room to see if the trapper and his wife, Sun, were seated within hearing distance. She didn't see them and looked back to the coarse-talking man.

"That Charlie Bent's plumb crazy and a crook besides. If the folks in New Mexico don't know it now, they will soon. And I wouldn't mess with them Mexicans. Nosiree. I wouldn't mess with them Mojadas either. Not me. You mess with them, you end up bald. If you know what I mean." He laughed again and, with his fingers, made the sign of a knife slicing across the top of his forehead. He was still laughing as he turned his chair back to his own table.

Callie rolled her eyes at Juliana. "As if he knows anything about New Mexico."

Juliana glanced at her sister in surprise. *Callie thinks she knows anything about New Mexico?*

Callie caught her sister's skeptical look. She smiled. "I listened when Maurice Dupree told you about New Mexico—golden light, the Mojada, everything." Callie took a bite of chess pie, then raised her eyebrows in Juliana's direction. "You maybe never considered that New Mexico might be my dream as well as yours, Julie. What Dupree told you was contagious." She took another bite of pie. "I want to go, too."

Juliana squeezed her sister's hand. "Thanks for telling me, Callie. Somehow that may make our decision easier—if it comes to that."

"You mean if we have to decide whether New Mexico is worth the danger of going?"

Before Juliana could answer, Johnson turned toward them again and joined their conversation. "The man's wrong, you know…," he jerked a thumb toward the man at the other table, "…about Charles Bent. According to Jed, Bent is highly respected in New Mexico. He's married to a Mexican woman. His brother William's the one married to a squaw. Charles's wife, María, is from a well-connected political family in Santa Fe. If anyone could bring stability to the area after a U.S. takeover, it would be someone like Charles Bent."

Johnson took a sip of coffee, then looked thoughtful for a moment before going on. "You mentioned earlier that you're planning to join a trading caravan to Santa Fe. Make sure you check out the captain. Right now there may be illegal weapons and ammunition headed toward New Mexico. Santa Fe companies would be ideal shipping sources. Just be careful. Find out all you can ahead of time."

After a few more minutes of talking with the others at their table, Juliana and Callie excused themselves and headed for a stroll on the deck before retiring.

"Do you really think New Mexico's a safe place to go?" Callie asked, as they climbed the spiral staircase leading to the upper deck.

"We'll do as Johnson says as soon as we get to Westport. But I don't think we need to worry about the captain Matthias recommended. What is his name again? Oh, yes. James I think it is. Captain Parker James. We'll get other references about him, too. And before we join his train, we'll ask him about the political climate in Santa Fe. The caravans make several trips each year. I'm sure Captain James will know better than Seth Johnson whether the war is truly over."

The two young women walked in the silence of the night. In the distance an owl hooted mournfully. An answering call floated across the river. "Callie," Juliana finally said. "I've thought a lot about this since Father died—though I've not really spoken of it." She sighed, then stopped by the handrail and gazed up at the blanket of stars above them.

She could barely see Callie in the light from a lantern in the pilot's house above the deck. "We've taken our lives into our own hands by leaving all that was known to us since childhood—the safe, the secure. Even if you had chosen to marry the husband Caleb picked for you, your life would have been one of ease."

"If I had decided to take a position as governess with a good family, my life also would have been one of comfort. But we agreed we didn't want to do that. In fact, we both were sickened by the prospect of choosing the safety net Uncle Caleb threw out for us."

Callie nodded, understanding.

Juliana went on. "From the beginning we have chosen danger over the safety of the known. Look what happened to us on the Mississippi. We could have been hurt, maybe killed.. When I think about what could have happened—if Matthias Graves hadn't come along when he did..." her voice trailed off.

"I know," Callie agreed, her voice soft. "I don't like to think about it either."

Juliana's tone grew bolder. "My point is—we've already chosen. And we have no fear or we wouldn't have gotten this far. I don't want to deliberately place us in the middle of a war. But Callie, if you think about it, we could be in graver circumstances on the Oregon Trail, attacked by Indians, or contracting cholera."

She paused, then continued. "To me, New Mexico, after peacefully surrendering to American troops, is not high on my list of places to avoid because of danger."

"You sound more like you're trying to convince yourself than me." Callie laughed. "And I'm already convinced—I'd decided the same thing before we left Stonehaven. That was even before I knew of the Mexican War."

She too looked heavenward for a moment before continuing. Then her green eyes met Juliana's. "You're the strongest person I know, Jules. I'm not just saying that because you're my sister. After Father died and you stood up to Uncle Caleb the way you did—I figured right then and there that you could do anything you set your mind to. No matter what you decided, I knew the solution you picked for us would work." Callie laughed at the memory. "I secretly hoped that you'd plan for us to run away to deepest Africa. Or maybe someplace exotic like China. And I had no doubt that you'd get us there. And get us there safely."

Juliana squeezed Callie's hand as they headed back to their stateroom. "You're the best, Cal."

"I know," Callie said with a wink.

After the young women had closed and locked their door, a man walked slowly by, lingered near their door for just a moment, then moved on. Much later he stood on the deck, very near where Callie and Juliana had walked.

"Graves, that you?" A hoarse whisper floated out from the darkness.

Matthias Graves grunted an affirmative reply but didn't say more until the other speaker drew closer.

"Is everything taken care of?" The speaker now stood very near him. The two men shook hands. "I've been concerned about the arrangements."

"You worry too much, Johnson. And you talk too much. I heard what you said to the St. Clair sisters."

"You said I needed to convince them it's safe to travel to Santa Fe."

"You gave them too much detail." Graves's voice was angry.

"They didn't need to know so much."

"I thought I was pretty convincing."

"Yeah. The part about a brother in the dragoons." Graves laughed. "I do have to admit, that was a nice touch."

They were silent for several minutes. Then Johnson spoke. "Why do you want these women on the Parker train?" He waited for a moment, but when Graves didn't respond he went on. "And why do you want them in Fort La Sal?"

Still Graves said nothing.

Johnson persisted, not realizing his tone was becoming irritating to Graves. "Why the St. Clairs?" he pushed. "You've never gone to so much trouble to get a woman before. Why now? Why them?"

Graves's jaw worked as he tried to decide how much he wanted to tell Johnson. Nothing, he decided. One had to be careful whom one trusted with such delicate circumstances.

He laughed heartily as he thought about the powerful Senator Caleb Benedict, the young women's uncle. "You'll find out soon enough, *mi compadre.*" He brushed a strand of dark hair from his eyes. "Just trust me." And he laughed again.

Parker James stepped into the dark saloon. It was a warm and gusty Indian summer afternoon, and he was glad to get out of the relentless wind-kicked dust of the Westport streets.

As his eyes adjusted to the dim light, he glanced around the room, searching for U.S. Army Major Bennett Cookingham, the man who had sent word he needed to meet Parker in a place they wouldn't be noticed.

It had been two years since Parker had seen his friend, and he looked forward to the meeting. But he also knew Bennett wouldn't have contacted him in such a way if he didn't want something from him.

The men had been roommates at West Point, and after graduation had spent eleven years working together on special undercover assignments for the U. S. government. After chasing crooks throughout the country, Parker had decided he wanted a life of his own. His friend had made undercover work his career.

Parker took a seat near the back of the saloon to await Bennett's arrival. He pulled his worn felt hat low over his eyes and tipped back his chair. He remembered the excitement of his days working undercover, the camaraderie, the danger. No time since had matched it. But he didn't regret for a moment that he had turned his back on it all.

He had done it for Laurie. When they decided to marry, she had wanted him home with her in the little house in St. Louis they'd built together. No more traveling. No more danger. The year they had together before she died was filled with warmth and happiness. He carried the memory of her in his heart, just as he carried her likeness in the case of his gold pocket watch.

He looked up to see the grinning face of Bennett Cookingham across the room. Long-limbed and gangly gaited, eyes too big for his thin face, Bennett reminded Parker of a red-headed praying mantis. He grinned back as Bennett strode toward him and greeted him warmly.

"It's been too long, friend." Bennett fixed a penetrating gaze on Parker. "How are you?"

The last time the two had spoken was right after Laurie's funeral two years before. Parker had been nearly incoherent in his grief. And his friend had simply listened quietly, his presence bringing a welcome calm into the turmoil of Parker's raging emotions. Bennett had stayed as long as he could. When he left St. Louis, he'd urged Parker to return to the Army. But Parker had declined, not wanting to leave the place where he'd known such sweet and tender happiness with Laurie. It had been too soon.

"I'm much better. Someone said that time heals." Parker's voice reflected the sadness of his memories. "That's not entirely right—but time does ease the pain. I don't think anything will ever erase it completely."

The two talked for a few minutes about Parker's business venture, the Santa Fe trade he had begun only months earlier.

"It's going well," Parker told his friend. "There's a good market on both ends. In fact, business is so good that I'm thinking of adding another two caravans next year." He smiled. "You're not thinking of leaving the Army, are you? I could use a partner."

Bennett laughed. "You know me better than that." He settled back in his chair. "I don't know that I'll ever be ready to leave." Bennett's expression grew solemn. "How are things in Santa Fe—I mean, since it fell to Kearny? You've made one trip since the takeover—"

Parker interrupted. "How'd you'd know that?"

"You've forgotten—"

"Forgotten how good you are at following the whereabouts of people you're interested in? No, of course I haven't. I'm just curious about why you'd care about my activities." Parker felt irritated. He did not appreciate being at the microscope's opposite end.

"Don't get your feathers ruffled, James. We had our reasons."

"You always do."

"Let me begin again." Bennett sighed, then briefly glanced at the street outside the saloon's dusty window before continuing. There was a new wariness in his expression.

Bennett continued. "It's the events in Santa Fe we're watching, my friend, not you. You just happened to be in the right place at the right time."

"Mind explaining that?"

Bennett was silent a moment. "Let's just say an American who can freely travel into a newly acquired region of the United States is a valuable commodity."

"'Acquired' isn't the right word. It's not like we bought and paid for New Mexico." Parker looked hard at his old friend. "But, that aside, why do I feel you're about to disturb my hard-earned tranquility?" he drawled sardonically. "I know you too well, Bennett. You wouldn't plan a meeting like this just to talk about the recent events in New Mexico. What is it you're leading to?"

Bennett laughed, his demeanor lightening for a moment. "I've got an assignment for you, Parker. If you'll take it."

"You know I can't leave my trading company—even if I did want to join the Army again. Which, I might add, I don't want to do."

"For this job, you wouldn't have to."

Parker cocked his head, then removed his hat and ran his hand through dark blond hair. "Ah, yes. It's becoming clear to me. I can travel in and out of New Mexico without raising suspicion. You—or perhaps I should say, the U.S. government—want me to do something for you there. Something no one can know about. Or something you don't want the locals to know about."

"You're good, Parker." Bennett grinned. "You haven't lost your touch. But do you want to keep guessing? Or shall I spoil your fun and simply tell you?"

"Go on."

"As you know, Kearny made Charles Bent governor after New Mexico fell. Kearny warned him that though the region fell without a shot being fired, many people are hostile."

"I didn't see any hostilities when I was there."

"It's below the surface. More in political circles than economic. That's why you didn't see it. But believe me, Bent's got enemies. Dangerous, because they're unknown to him. He's liked in some quarters, but in others—" Bennett's voice broke off. He leaned forward, his eyes serious as he continued. "It's just a matter of time before someone strikes."

"Say it plainly, Bennett. You're trying to tell me that someone's out to get him. Kill him. Oust the U.S."

"It's not that simple. I don't think it's a matter of overthrowing the U.S. It's more a matter of local politics. To the New Mexicans there's a higher rule than that which comes out of

Mexico City—or Washington D.C. No. It goes beyond that. And it has to do with power, with land, with greed. And Charles Bent is caught in the middle of it all."

"Do you think someone wants to get rid of Bent? Maybe declare a new governor?"

Bennett nodded. "That's right. Probably someone who will grant lands to the right people for the right price."

Parker thought about his friend's words. "Do you know who this person is?"

"No. We don't. We only know that someone's moving to make it happen. We know that a powerful force in Santa Fe, the Oñate family, is behind it. We know they have chosen their 'heir apparent.' But we're not sure why they haven't made their move. We don't know what they're waiting for."

"Maybe the man isn't there."

"What do you mean?" Bennett looked at his friend intently.

"Maybe the man they've chosen to replace Bent isn't in Santa Fe."

"Go on."

Parker knew his friend had baited him into speculation. But it didn't matter, he could feel himself getting pulled in. It was unavoidable, probably in his blood. The intrigue of examining political maneuvers—even before they played out on stage—was hard to ignore. And to do so felt familiar, comfortable. Like the old days.

He went on, exploring the possibilities as he spoke. "If, as you say, it doesn't matter to the locals whether they are governed by the U.S. or Mexico, and they've not attempted to rebel against the U.S. takeover, it makes sense that they might want to replace Bent with a U.S. citizen—someone who would be accepted by Kearny, or any other American official. But more important, this person must be corruptible and willing to work with the Oñate family. Charles Bent is too honest. He's not their man." When Parker finished, he looked across the table at Bennett. He could tell by Bennett's pleased expression that he had hit the mark.

"Well done, Parker. Not a bit rusty either, I might add."

"Enough false flattery. You still haven't told me what it is you want me to do."

"We need you to warn Bent."

"You mean he hasn't been told?"

"Of course, he's been warned. But he's ignoring everything he's been told." Bennett shook his head. "Maybe it's because the man has lived in the region for so long that he feels impervious to the dangers around him. Or maybe he has false expectations of bringing peace among the various factions." He shrugged. "No one understands why he's done what he's done."

"What do you mean?"

"Bent moved his headquarters to Fort La Sal. That's in the center of the most hostile area in New Mexico."

"You're speaking of the Mojada." Parker was putting a few more of the missing puzzle pieces together. He felt a chill travel up his spine.

His friend nodded again. "The Mojada Indians, surrounded by the Oñate family rancho. Bent was warned about moving there. But he did it anyway."

"Maybe he was made to move against his will."

"That we don't know. At this point, it doesn't matter whether he went against his will or not. What matters is just getting him out."

For a few minutes neither man spoke. Parker knew what his friend was about to ask. "You want me to get him out," he said simply.

"Yes, we do."

"Why do you think I will succeed when others haven't been able to?"

"Because I know if anyone can do it, my friend, you can. You've got the perfect cover—your scheduled trip into New Mexico—and a caravan filled with bullwhackers and merchandise." Bennett gave him a lopsided grin. "Plus you're the craziest son-of-a-gun I know when it comes to moving Heaven and earth to see that a job gets done."

It was Parker's turn to smile. He regarded his friend with affection, remembering their partnership in other ventures. "If I agree, is there any way you could come along?"

"Do I look like a bullwhacker?" Bennett grinned again.

"You'd be passable."

This time Bennett didn't answer.

They talked in hushed tones through the afternoon and into the late evening, stopping only for steak and beans at suppertime. Before they parted, Parker had finally agreed to accept the mission. Bennett gave him a map of Fort La Sal, detailing the layout of the governor's house and the surrounding adobes. They spoke of plans to get Bent to safety until U.S. troops could be moved into place.

Before they walked from the saloon, Bennett draped his arm around Parker's shoulders. He again warned Parker about the secrecy of his mission. "Remember to trust no one. Bent's life is at stake. And very probably the lives of his wife and children—all those who are close to him."

Before Bennett mounted the tall chestnut tied outside the saloon, he turned again to Parker. "Your life will be in danger, too, my friend, should you be found out." He paused. "The Mojada are brutal. They stop at nothing to get their way. They torture and maim. Don't fall into their hands, my friend. Don't tell anyone about this mission."

A few days later, Parker sat in his office along the main street of the dusty frontier town of Westport. The carved wooden sign above his door read, "Parker James, Commerce of the Santa Fe." The place doubled as his home when he wasn't captaining a caravan bound for Santa Fe. Since Laurie died, his needs were simple, and his living quarters reflected that simplicity. Besides the scarred desk in the center of his office, his only other possessions included, in the adjoining room, a pot-bellied stove and a bed. Of course there were his books, or friends, as he often thought of them, neatly arranged on shelves that covered three walls.

The sun had risen into a glorious blue sky. The town was awakening to the bustle of traders preparing for journeys along the Santa Fe Trail. Though it was November, those seeking a spot in a wagon train bound for Santa Fe milled about, looking for space in a winter train. Parker's next caravan, scheduled for departure in ten days, would be the last winter train to head west taking the Santa Fe. He had already turned away those he considered to be casual travelers, saving room in the company for traders only, for those whose livelihoods depended on travel to New Mexico.

As Parker pored over the cargo list for the train, a light tapping at his door broke his concentration.

"Enter," he said without looking up, wanting to finish the last calculation.

The door opened quietly. There was a polite silence.

"Yes," he said, still ciphering the figures on the paper before him.

"Mr. James?" The voice was a woman's, soft, low, almost musical.

He looked up. Without realizing it, he caught his breath. Moving toward him was a woman of such delicate gracefulness that for a moment he was too stunned to speak.

It wasn't her clothing that spoke of her refinement. She was dressed like a man in leather breeches and a homespun shirt, not unusual for women in this frontier town. Maybe it was the way she stood against the sunlight that streamed through the window behind her, lighting her auburn hair, casting an ethereal glow around her slim frame.

He swallowed. "I'm Parker James."

She moved closer as he stood and accepted her outstretched hand of greeting. His response to the touch of her strong yet gentle hand surprised him. After Laurie, no woman had affected him so. He took a deep breath and nodded toward a chair where she could sit. He again seated himself behind the desk.

He looked into her eyes. They were the color of a mountain pond filled with flecks of sunlight. The kind of eyes a person could get lost in. It wasn't just her beauty that struck him. If he looked closely, the shape of her face seemed slightly imperfect, with lips perhaps a bit too wide. But the overall effect of her high cheekbones, soft dusting of freckles, and sparkle of life in her eyes, made her the most striking woman he had ever seen.

"May I help you?" he finally managed.

She smiled, her eyes lively, as if she knew his thoughts. "My name is Juliana St. Clair," she said in that low, breathy voice.

"I'm pleased to meet you, Miss St. Clair." He noticed she wasn't wearing a wedding band.

"Thank you," she said simply before going on. "Your trading company has been highly recommended to me. I understand it is the only winter train traveling to New Mexico."

Parker waited.

"My sister and I need to find passage to Santa Fe. We're looking for a reliable wagon company to join. We, of course, will buy our own outfit, pull our own weight—"

Parker interrupted before she could go on. "Miss, I don't run a passenger service."

The woman flushed visibly. "I understand that, Mr. James. I wouldn't expect to be treated like a passenger. But I've heard that you allow other people besides muleskinners and traders to travel with you." Her tone took on a more passionate turn. "We'd be no trouble. We simply need the protection that comes with traveling in a larger train."

"I'm sorry. As I said, I don't run a passenger train. You and your sister cannot join my caravan." Though looking at her, he thought he would like nothing better than to have this woman near him for the trip to Santa Fe. But what was he thinking? It was out of the question. It was far too dangerous. Especially now.

"New Mexico isn't a safe place for women to go—," he began.

"Why?" she demanded, her voice still low and controlled. "You mean it's safe for men, but not for women?" She laughed, almost as if baiting him.

"That's not what I meant."

"That's what you said, Mr. James."

"It's not safe for anyone."

"Then why are you going?"

"I run a trade caravan."

"You're telling me it's safe for a U.S. citizen to travel to New Mexico for purposes of trade?"

Parker nodded, sensing he was about to fall into a trap.

"But you're also telling me it's not safe for a U.S. citizen to travel to New Mexico for any other reason?"

He nodded again.

For a moment she was silent, then seemed to measure her words carefully when she again spoke. "I would believe you, Mr. James, except for someone who has told me otherwise. Someone

66

I recently met on the riverboat coming here, someone who says he knows you well."

"Who's that?"

"A trapper named Jeremiah Jones, and his wife, Sun. Jeremiah and Sun tell me they are planning to travel in your trading caravan all the way to Santa Fe."

It was true. Parker had known Jeremiah and Sun for years. More than just known. He smiled to himself. Those two were almost like members of his own family. They had caused quite a ruckus at his and Laurie's wedding. But his ties with Jeremiah were stronger than any highfalutin attitudes of the other guests. His ties with them were still strong enough to assure them a space in his train anytime they showed up ready to travel. They had sent word several weeks earlier about their intentions to return to New Mexico, joining his caravan to Santa Fe.

"They've lived in the wild. They know how to take care of themselves." He reached across the desk and took her hand in his, turning it palm upward. "You are not prepared for the hard work of taking a wagon and team over hundreds of miles. These hands, I daresay, have never known a day's work. I would guess by the look of them that you, Miss St. Clair, have been waited on by servants. You've been a pampered pet of a household that availed itself to your beck and call."

Juliana jerked her hand away.

"How dare you—"

He interrupted. "How dare I tell you the truth? Listen to me—it may mean your life, Miss St. Clair. This country is not for those traveling on whim, or simply to relieve the boredom of a pampered life. This country is only for the toughest in spirit and body. And very frankly, I don't think you have what it takes." He paused, letting his words sink in. "That's why I don't want you in my caravan."

The woman's eyes flashed. "How dare you speak to me in such a way? How dare you assume things about me and my background that are not only dead wrong, but are also none of your business?" She stood and stared at him, the light now gone from her eyes. No longer did they appear to be the color of a mountain lake on a sunny day. Now they looked more like the same lake in the midst of a storm.

Then, without further words, Juliana St. Clair turned with a flourish and left his office, slamming the door behind her.

It seemed to Parker that she took with her the morning's sunlight.

CHAPTER

In her fury, Juliana practically ran from Parker James's office. She had never before experienced the feelings this man stirred in her. When she first saw him, she felt that he was someone she had known all her life. The look of him, with his light brown hair, the boyish way it fell across his forehead, the intensity of his clear blue eyes, all seemed familiar and somehow dear.

Now this same man had turned into an unreasonable, rude, arrogant brute. She looked at her hands and thought of the accusations he had hurled at her. How could he assume anything about her life until now? How did he know she hadn't the gumption, the grit, to endure the hardships of trail life? Someday her hands would be covered with calluses. And she would be proud of every one.

She walked swiftly along the boarded walkway next to the dusty street, declaring to herself that she would not allow Parker James or anyone else to tell her what she could or could not do. What she was or was not capable of doing. No one had that right.

She could understand Parker James's reluctance to let her travel with his caravan if he simply said it was too dangerous for anyone to go into New Mexico right now. But he had already made room for the trapper and his gentle wife and for others she had met on the Missouri riverboat. Others who were not mule-skinners or traders.

No. It seemed to Juliana that Parker James simply thought her too soft. He clearly had made his decision based on that assumption alone. Juliana had gone to great pains to cover her genteel upbringing, but maybe it was more evident than she thought. That must have been James's reasoning. *His pigheaded reasoning.*

She rounded the corner, still moving swiftly in her anger. She looked up barely in time to avoid colliding with a well-dressed man heading the opposite direction. She saw a blur of gray pin-stripes and silk neck scarf before she looked up into the hand-some face of Matthias Graves.

"Juliana St. Clair! What a welcome sight you are on this fine morning." He touched her arm in greeting. "I was hoping I would see you."

"Mr. Graves," Juliana said, surprised to see him.

"Please, call me Matthias." He smiled. "In fact, call me Matt. All my friends do. And I would be honored if you would do the same. After what we went through together, I would consider us friends, wouldn't you?" He laughed lightly, seeming to enjoy sharing their common memory.

"Of course, Matt." Juliana was glad to see him again. "But please, call me Juliana."

Matthias nodded. "Then Juliana it is. I am honored." He took her elbow and lightly guided her across the street. "May I walk you back to your hotel?"

Juliana nodded. Her thoughts remained on the critical events that had just taken place in Parker James's office. On the river-boat Matthias had said he knew James. Perhaps if he could

70

vouch for her and Callie, James would relent. Besides, if there was danger ahead, it would be good to have a friend such as Matthias Graves in the same train.

"Matthias, I need to talk with you. Something has come up, and I need your advice. Maybe your help."

"It would be my pleasure to help you in any way I can, Juliana. I think you know that." His gray eyes were fixed on hers as he spoke. "I have noticed that you are bothered by something." He paused, looking around at the now bustling sidewalks. "Why don't we walk down to the river? It will be a bit more pleasant there. We can talk on the way." Once again he cupped his hand beneath her elbow, guiding her gently toward the pathway leading to the river.

Juliana felt a sense of relief and gratitude. Matthias had proven his trustworthiness that night on the riverboat. It was good to be with him again. She began to tell him of her conversation with Parker James and his refusal to allow her to join the caravan. She could see her anger reflected in his steely eyes as she related the venom contained in James's words. His clenched jaws worked as she spoke.

"You're right. The man is assuming you're some delicate plant grown in a southern hothouse. His actions toward you are biased. I don't blame you for being upset." He took her hand. "He has no idea of your strength and determination."

Juliana nodded, feeling somehow surprised at the intensity of his reaction.

"I will be traveling with colleagues in this same train. Any of us—all of us—can be at your disposal should you need us. Perhaps if Captain James realized that, it would make a difference."

They had reached an overlook above the river. Juliana looked down at the water, suddenly wanting to set up her easel and paint. Life had been less trouble when all she needed to think

71

about was her art. She watched as the sunlight danced across the water like a thousand tiny diamonds. Then she raised her eyes toward the remnants of an earlier morning haze still hanging in the boughs of the rock oaks, black willows, and sugarberry trees. The low-hanging branches cast a darkness across the water. Juliana trembled. The shadows. Always the shadows.

She took a deep breath before turning again to Matthias. For a moment she didn't want to speak, to break into the sounds of the river: the lapping waves against the beach; the croaks of the pond frogs and sounds from the foliage along the banks; the half-mournful, half-joyous wail of a mockingbird.

Seasons. Juliana didn't know why they suddenly came to mind. But around her was their evidence: golden cottonwood leaves casting off from their branches, katydids hollering their last hurrah of autumn, even the thin sun of a tilting earth spoke of time moving in its natural order. The cottonwood needed no wisdom to drop its leaves. Frogs needed no wisdom to know when to hibernate. The earth needed no wisdom to decide to tilt.

Her gaze followed a yellow leaf that drifted from a topmost branch of its tree, then was carried downriver by the gently moving water. The natural order of life for that leaf. How simple. How easy. Oh, that her decisions could be that easy. But they weren't. She alone needed to weigh the evidence about whether New Mexico would be a safe place for travel. She alone needed to decide whether to push aggressively to join the James caravan.

Juliana had made life-changing decisions for herself and for Callie based on her own wisdom. Yet how inadequate that wisdom seemed. For the second time in just a few days, she found herself wishing for a God who cared. Someone who would guide her, give her wisdom. Then perhaps she wouldn't feel so alone.

Standing beside her was a man she trusted, a man who knew the Southwest and its people, a man who had offered his help if she needed it.

She looked up at Matthias, then flushed when she realized he'd been watching her intently. "Do you know Captain James well enough to speak on my behalf?"

"We've had business dealings. I've used his freight line on two occasions. He seems to be a fair man. I think he'll listen to reason."

"Then I would like you to talk with him. Maybe a word from you will make a difference."

They talked for several minutes longer before heading back into town. Matthias told her more about New Mexico, his eyes taking on a dark passion as he spoke of the beauty of its mountains and the warmth of its people. He had been born there, he said, and though he had traveled throughout the world, the Fort La Sal area would always be home. As they parted at Juliana's hotel, Matthias said he would gladly speak to Captain James.

⤔

Parker James headed toward the livery where he saddled his Appaloosa, then mounted and headed to Shawnee Wells, a large flat field some fifteen miles from town. Wagons had already begun pulling into the area, staking out a place in the caravan while supplies were bought and trading goods were loaded.

Parker knew he would find Jeremiah and Sun camped at the river near the field. It had been too long since he had seen them. Urged on by the pleasant anticipation, he nudged the Appaloosa into a gallop.

A few minutes later, at the top of a rise, he spotted their camp.

Sun sat near a small fire chopping vegetables. She dropped what looked like wild onions a handful at a time into a Dutch oven she'd placed on a flat rock at the fire's edge. As Parker rode

73

closer, he could smell the pungent herbs she'd already added. And rabbit. He smelled fresh roasting rabbit. No one could make a better supper from one scrawny rabbit than Sun Jones. He'd picked the right night for a visit.

"Sunshine-o'-my-life," he called out, using his favorite nickname for her.

Sun looked up, her delicate face turning into a wreath of smiles at the sound of his voice. She ran to him as he dismounted, and he grabbed her into his arms and whirled her around, hugging her close.

"You put me down right now," she said, laughing. Her voice held the sound of the prairie winds, her laughter that of rushing waters. Just hearing her speak and laugh lightened Parker's heart.

He set her down gently on her moccasined feet and looked into her ageless blue eyes. "It's good to see you, Sun."

"And I am glad to see you," she said. "Why have you not come to see us sooner?"

Parker laughed. "As if I could find you. That husband of yours never stays in one place long enough to track."

Parker walked with her to the fire and seated himself. Sun picked up a knife and scraped a potato, then dropped it into the Dutch oven. She handed him a potato, nodding toward the pot. Sun always treated him like family. Maybe that was why he loved her.

Parker pulled out his Bowie knife and began to scrape the vegetable. "Where is the ol' coot, anyway?"

"You are meaning Jeremiah?" She smiled, reminding him, just as she usually did, that she respected her husband too much to go along with his joke. She looked toward the roasting rabbit. "My husband thought this one too skinny for our meal. He has gone hunting for another." She thought for a moment, her eyes bright. "It is a good thing, too. He had no idea that man-with-ahole-in-stomach would be joining us tonight."

Parker threw back his head and laughed. "Ah, my Sunshine. You've not lost your ability to keep me humble."

They talked and laughed together while working their way through the remainder of the potatoes, carrots, and wild turnips. Soon the conversation turned to the coming caravan trip.

"A woman told me this morning that she met you on a riverboat from St. Louis." Parker valued Sun's judgment and was curious about what she thought of the young woman, Juliana St. Clair.

Sun nodded. "I saw many women on the riverboat." She gave him a knowing look. "But I think I know which young lady you are talking about."

Parker ignored her implication. "Her name is Juliana St. Clair."

"Ah, yes. The young woman with hair like a sunset before a storm." Sun smiled, as if goading him on. "We spoke."

Parker shook his head slightly, deciding to ignore that comment as well. "She came to me to book passage on the caravan."

"And you told her no."

He cocked an eyebrow in Sun's direction. "How did you know?"

"I know you well, my son. Since your Laurie died, I've felt your sorrow. I know your grief."

"What does that have to do with my saying no to Miss St. Clair?"

"She has a spirit much like yours. When I spoke with her on the riverboat, I saw it. I thought of you." Sun paused. "I think you saw it, too. And you are afraid of what you saw."

"No. You have it all wrong. I said no because I feared for her life."

Sun looked at him, her blue eyes steady. "Feared for her? Why?"

"Juliana St. Clair is young and inexperienced in the ways of western travel. She has a younger sister with her." He shook his head. He could see Sun didn't believe him. "I don't want to coddle a couple of female greenhorns for eight hundred miles."

"Many women have traveled the trails alone. If they have the strength they need in here," she tapped her heart, "then they will make it." She looked at him thoughtfully. "I think you are afraid for you...not for her."

She stirred the stew with a wooden spoon, looked at him solemnly, but said nothing more about Juliana St. Clair.

❧

Later, after a sumptuous meal with Sun and Jeremiah, Parker untied his bedroll and spread it near the fire. Staring into the moonlit sky, his thoughts again returned to Juliana. He wondered about the events that had brought her to Westport. From the way she spoke, the way she carried herself, he knew she was genteel, highborn, probably from the South.

What would have brought a young woman and her sister to the frontier? No doubt she was running away from something. Or someone.

A long time ago he had believed in a personal God, a God who intervened in the lives of men and women, who guided them along life's pathway. A God who might bring a woman along a path that would cross his own. But now? He laughed at the thought. Now he believed there was no such intervention by a loving God. In fact, there was no such God.

After Laurie died, he had shaken his fist at the heavens. If her death was the work of the God who loved him, he wanted nothing to do with him.

He looked again at the stars, the thousands of pinpoints of fire scattered across the sky. Words long ago forgotten, perhaps from a verse that he and Laurie had read together, drifted into his mind, "For the invisible things of him from the creation of the world are clearly seen, being understood by the things that are made, even his eternal power and Godhead; so that they are without excuse."

No. He refused to believe that this sky, the earth around him, was the evidence of a living, loving God. But his last thoughts upon falling asleep were those of hope. Hope as bright as the spangled skies above him. Hope that he was wrong.

❧

The following morning, Parker had hardly sat down in his office when the door opened and Matthias Graves entered. He strode across the room and offered his hand in greeting.

"Good to see you again," Graves said, removing his hat.

Parker nodded toward the chair opposite his desk, and Graves seated himself with an air of assurance.

After speaking for a few minutes about the train's departure date, the placement of the three Graves wagons within the caravan, and other details of the trip, Graves locked his eyes on Parker. "I would like to speak to you on behalf of a young woman—Juliana St. Clair."

Parker raised his eyebrows, waiting.

"She was quite upset after speaking to you yesterday."

"Go on."

Graves studied his hands a moment before fixing his eyes again on Parker. "Ah…we hadn't planned to announce our intentions quite yet…you see, we wanted to wait until Juliana has met my family in Fort La Sal…but we are planning to be married." Graves smiled broadly, the proud intended. "Juliana didn't want me to say anything yet, of course...that's why she and her sister Callie are still traveling as a separate party. The real announcement will have to wait."

Parker felt strangely crestfallen upon hearing the news. "I see," was all he could manage.

"What I'm attempting to say here, James, is that I'd be much obliged if you would allow Juliana and her sister to travel with your caravan."

"Why didn't you make arrangements for their rig when you contacted me about yours?"

Graves smiled again. "We've only just decided to marry." He chuckled. "You know how fickle women are." He shook his head, still laughing lightly. "I wasn't sure I could convince her when I contacted you about passage for my wagons."

Parker didn't respond.

Graves went on. "If it's her safe passage that you're worried about...my men and I will be there to help her all the way across."

Parker thought of the spirited young woman who had stood before him the day before. Strange that today he thought of her as someone who didn't need—in fact, would disdain—anyone's help. But then Graves, her betrothed, obviously knew her much better than he.

Parker nodded slowly. "If you'll vouch for her, her rig can join."

Graves looked pleased. "Thank you, friend. Thank you." He seemed somehow over-zealous as he stood and pumped Parker's hand. Graves turned before opening the door to leave. "One more thing, James. No one knows of our betrothal. I'd appreciate it if you didn't speak of it. You know, a young woman traveling with her intended without a chaperone—" His voice dropped, and his dark eyes pierced Parker's.

"I understand," Parker said.

"I'm sure they'll be grateful." And he was gone, pulling the door shut behind him.

From his office window, Parker watched Matthias Graves cross the dusty street, and turn toward the hotel. A sadness settled over him that he could neither explain nor resist.

Of course he said yes," Matthias said to Juliana, as they walked to the river. He stopped and, taking her hand in his, gazed deeply into her eyes. "I explained to him that you and Callie are responsible, hard-working, reliable—"

Juliana laughed, interrupting him. "Enough, Matt. I understand what you're trying to say."

"He just needed to be reassured of your determination."

"You're a miracle worker—"

His eyes did not leave hers. "I can't think of anyone I'd rather help."

Juliana laughed again softly, but pulled her hand away. "And you've certainly done your share of helping two damsels in distress."

They strolled together down the walkway to the river. "Now, Juliana," Matthias said after a few minutes. "Now that we have you in the train, we'd better see to purchasing your outfit. We've got little more than a week. I'll go with you, if you like. I know a reliable wagon dealer and a good place to get your oxen. When do you want to start?"

"I have business I need to take care of first, Matt. But if you want to join Callie and me tomorrow morning, why don't we begin then?" Juliana suddenly felt more lighthearted than she had for weeks. Everything seemed to be falling into place. She believed in independence. But her father had also taught her to use the wisdom and talents of others when they were willing to give it. "Your advice will be welcome." She gave him a warm smile. "Thank you, Matt, for everything."

"You don't know what a pleasure it is for me to be at your disposal," he said, taking her arm as they headed back toward the hotel.

❧

Just as they rounded the corner and moved onto the rutted main street of Westport, Parker James stepped from his office. He immediately saw the couple—though they didn't see him—and stopped for a moment to watch their animated conversation, the way Graves leaned toward Juliana protectively, the way she looked up at him.

He felt a stab of jealousy, then immediately dismissed it. The woman was nothing to him. He had met her only briefly. Even then not a single pleasant word had been exchanged. And of course, all along, though she had kept it hidden, her mind and heart had belonged to someone else.

He turned away from them and headed for the livery. A ride across the fields on the Appaloosa would free his mind of unbidden thoughts of Juliana St. Clair.

❧

Juliana found Callie waiting for her in the hotel room.

"Cal, we've got to go now to sell the jewelry. We can't wait any longer."

81

Callie looked up from her reading. "Do we have to sell all of it?"

Juliana nodded. "I think even if we saved some for New Mexico we'd be sorry. They might not bring the price there that they will here."

"That's not what I mean."

Juliana looked at her sister quizzically.

"Julie, we've given up everything. Most of the time I don't even feel like a girl anymore." She glanced down at her plain clothes.

"I know, Callie."

Callie's clear green eyes met hers. "Can't we each just keep something that belonged to mother and father? To remember the good times at Stonehaven?"

"The most important thing is getting enough in exchange for them to buy the supplies we need." Juliana's voice softened. "I know it's hard. We've been through some really sad times. But, Cal, we have our memories. We don't need a ring or necklace of Mama's to remind us of the love we grew up with."

She sighed. "Callie, I'd like to say yes. But I really don't know what we'll need. We've got our rig to buy...and oxen, supplies, foods. Then there's buying property and building a house in New Mexico. I know it seems like we've got a fortune in jewels, but we also have a lot ahead of us to buy."

Callie turned her head toward the window.

"Cal, do you want to go with me to the pawn shop?"

Callie didn't turn to look at her. She just shook her head.

Juliana touched her sister's shoulder before leaving the room.

Clutching the carpetbag that held the jewelry, Juliana headed down the street toward a pawnshop she had spotted earlier. People jostled her along the crowded board sidewalks as they bustled in and out of the mercantile, the livery, the saddlers, the bank, restaurants, gambling halls, saloons, and inns. She felt vaguely uncomfortable as she looked around, noticing that men dominated the scene. A few gave her appraising looks, but she tried to keep her eyes straight ahead. Now and then she side-stepped drunks stumbling out of saloons or gambling halls.

Juliana made her way to a narrow street toward the east end of the town. The crowds thinned out and she heard her lone footsteps along the boarded walkway. When she came to the door of the pawnshop, a "closed" sign was displayed in the window. Not to be deterred, Juliana knocked once, then twice. There was no answer, so she knocked again.

"Yes?" A white-haired man raised the shade at the glassed door and peered out.

"I'd like to talk with you," Juliana shouted, unsure whether he could hear her through the closed door.

Nodding his head, the old man unlocked the door. He motioned for her to enter the shop, then shuffled to the one counter in the small room.

When he was in place, he eyed the carpetbag. "What can I do for you, honey?"

Juliana resented the familiarity, but she didn't want to antagonize him, so she said nothing. She opened her carpetbag and withdrew the small case containing the jewelry.

"I need to sell these," she said, pouring the contents on the counter. The diamonds and emeralds sparkled even in the dim light of the shop.

The old man moved slowly to the corner of the room where he lit a lantern, then carried it to the counter. He placed a jeweler's loupe to his eye and studied the jewelry piece by piece, lifting each to the light. Then, removing the loupe, he peered up at Juliana, not speaking for several moments. He quoted her a price.

Juliana was indignant. "That's only a quarter of what it's worth," she cried. The proceeds wouldn't buy even a wagon, let alone oxen to pull it.

The old man shrugged. "Take it or leave it. That's all you're going to get around these parts." He smiled, though not unkindly. "We don't get much call for finery here."

"Look at them again," Juliana urged, unwilling to give up. She picked up several pieces and held them to the light, turning them to show their fire. "Please reconsider. I know for a fact that these are worth thousands."

"Maybe to you, missy. Like I said, we don't have much call for—"

Juliana didn't listen. Fighting tears, she scooped up the jewelry, replaced it in the case, then once more dropped it into the satchel. Without a word she turned and left the shop.

She paid visits to two more pawnshops and received the same assessment of her mother's jewelry. The sale of every piece in the collection would not even bring enough to book passage for her and Callie to return to Stonehaven. Desperately sad, Juliana left the third pawnshop, satchel still in hand, and headed back to the hotel.

Later, Callie listened intently as Juliana laid out their dilemma. "Maybe Matthias knows a trader who'd be interested. He seems to move in circles different from the rest of these beargrease-smelling backwoodsmen," Callie said with an arrogant sniff.

Juliana grinned, feeling better. Callie had a way with words. "You're right," she said. "Let's go pay our friend a visit."

A short time later the two young women sat in the lobby of Matthias Graves's hotel. The proprietor had sent word to his room that he had guests waiting. After Matthias joined them, he listened intently as Juliana told of her attempts to sell her mother's jewelry.

"You two have been in some difficult circumstances since you left home," he said sympathetically, after Juliana had finished.

Juliana nodded, glad they had earlier told him of the circumstances that made them flee Stonehaven, glad too that they had come to him for help. Matthias Graves was proving to be a true and valuable friend.

"I know a trader who just might be interested," he said, his face solemn. "I'll need to see him first, though. He's not the easiest man to run down…or to deal with."

Juliana tried without success to read Matt's expression. It worried her that so much hinged on his success. "How soon can we see him?"

Matthias shook his head. "It depends on when—and where—I find him. I know his favorite campsite. I'll ride out to it this afternoon, see if I can find him there." He smiled into Juliana's eyes. "If I'm successful, the three of us can ride out to speak with him tomorrow."

❧

The following morning Juliana and Callie met Matthias at the livery, where they saddled Sir Galahad and Darley. Matthias mounted a sturdy chestnut and the three rode from town toward the trader's campsite.

The day was overcast and gray. A late fall drizzle hung in the air, stinging Juliana's face as they rode. She was glad she and Callie had thought to wear their heavy coats. She remembered Maurice Dupree telling her of the fickle weather this time of year—the same that they would face during the nearly eight hundred miles on the trail—if, of course, they were able to sell the jewelry and go. She knew they might face several days of Indian summer, purple-skied, hot and clear. Or they could be beset by intense and sudden storms building from nowhere. Juliana shivered as she rode, wondering again what the weeks ahead would bring.

It took less than an hour to get to a rise where they could see the campsite in the distance. A sense of excitement struck Juliana as she saw the trader's big Conestogas in the center of a grassy area, his campfire sending smoke into the gray sky, a small *remuda*, or herd, of mules, oxen, and saddlehorses grazing nearby.

She glanced over at Callie, who rode beside her on Darley. Callie's cheeks were red from the cold, her eyes bright with the same excitement that Juliana felt. If all went well with the trader they were about to meet, they would be buying their own rig to ready for the trip to Santa Fe.

Matthias halted the horses at a worn and weathered Conestoga. After the three had dismounted, he led the young women to a tent at the rear of the wagon.

"Zeb, we're here," he called out near the flap that served as the tent's doorway.

There was no answer.

"Zebulon Reed!" he shouted again.

Again no answer.

Matthias sighed and pulled back the tent flap. Before averting her eyes, Juliana caught a glimpse of a disheveled figure lying prone on a dirty cot. Callie wrinkled her nose and rolled her eyes as the smell of whiskey wafted from the tent.

"Zeb, hey Zeb! Wake up, you old fool." Juliana heard Matt say in exasperation. There was an answering groan. "Get up!"

Juliana and Callie looked at each other in dismay as they listened to the sounds of a creaking cot followed by scuffling about the tent. Then came more groans of protest, punctuated now and then by Matt's sharp voice.

Finally, a still disheveled-looking man stumbled, bleary-eyed, from the tent flap. He grinned at the young women, rubbing his day-old beard as he did so. He mumbled something about being thirsty and made his way to the wagon's rear where a bucket of water was hung. He poured a ladle of water over his head, rubbed the wetness over his face and eyes, then drank deeply from another ladleful.

At last he turned toward Juliana, Callie, and Matthias, who had joined the young women.

"Sorry," he muttered, seeming embarrassed. "I plumb forgot about your coming. And last night, well—" He winked at Matthias. "—things just got away from me." He stood for a moment as if he didn't know what else to say, then motioned them to follow him into his tent.

Again Juliana caught Callie's eye. She could see Callie take a deep breath before ducking under the flap—as if it could possibly last her until she reached fresh air.

"Now," Zebulon Reed said, after they were seated and introductions had been made. "I understand you have some jewelry you need to sell."

Matthias spoke first. "I told you yesterday that these young women have some valuable pieces. They want to get top dollar—they *must* get top dollar, or there's no deal to be made." He gazed at the trader, his handsome face placid. "It makes no difference to them whether you buy the jewels or not. There are others who are very interested."

Juliana glanced at Matthias, realizing that he was bargaining on their behalf. His look of sincerity seemed so natural that no one could have guessed that it wasn't. Her father would have said a look like that was the sign of a good poker player. He'd also have said it was the sign of a dishonest heart.

She shook the thought from her mind. Matthias was acting

for their benefit. Their trip—their future—depended on this trader's good will. Of course Matthias would try to help them get the highest price for the jewels. He wasn't being dishonest. He was being smart.

Zebulon Reed unfolded a small table and set it in the tent's center. After covering it with a cloth, he lit a lantern and set it on the table. "Let's see what you've got."

Juliana removed the jewelry case from her satchel, wondering briefly if it would be the last time. The diamonds, emeralds, and garnets sparkled under the light.

Callie audibly caught her breath and reached for a dainty ruby ring near her. Juliana caught her hand, holding it in hers. It would be hard enough for Callie as it was. She didn't want her sister to become attached to any of the pieces.

"Mmm," Zebulon hummed as he examined the jewelry. "Very nice. Very nice indeed." He held one piece at a time to the light, turning it, letting its facets cast dozens of reflected rainbows on the canvas walls of the tent.

At last he said, "I think I can offer you a fair price." He scratched his rough beard, squinted his eyes a moment, then quoted an amount.

Juliana gasped. It was more than she had ever hoped—even before the bad news told by the previous day's shopkeepers. "Are you sure—," she began.

"Is that not enough?" Zebulon peered at her intently. "I can only offer you another thousand and not one penny more. I'm sorry, but that's my last offer."

Beside her, Callie squeezed her hand.

"You have yourself a deal, Mr. Reed," Juliana finally managed, with a weak smile. "Your final offer will suit us nicely."

They completed the transaction and shook hands. Juliana placed the cash in her satchel. Matthias urged the young women to meet him by the wagon where they had left the horses, indicating he had further business with Reed. Juliana nodded, and she and Callie left the men together.

❧

"Nice work," Graves said to Reed after Juliana and Callie had left the tent. He counted out the transaction amount plus a nice profit for the trader. He placed it on the table.

Zeb grinned and handed him the jewelry. "I just did like you said. But I don't know why you wanted to put on such a show. Why not just buy the goods outright?"

"Miss St. Clair is too proud to accept that kind of help from me. Just leave it at that." Matthias started for the door, then turned, fixing his eyes on Zebulon. "You understand that this transaction is just between us." He smiled, but his eyes were cold.

Zebulon nodded, rubbing the stubble at his chin. He stared at Graves, then nodded slowly again.

"Good," Graves said, his tone lightening. Then he strode from the tent.

❧

Back in town, Matthias said he would meet the young women in the early afternoon at the livery to begin purchasing the wagon outfit and supplies. He touched Juliana's arm as he said goodbye, smiled at Callie, and took his leave.

On their way back to the hotel, Juliana and Callie stopped by Parker James's office.

Sitting behind his desk, Parker looked up as they opened the door.

89

"Ladies?" His tone was detached. Juliana wondered if he even remembered their earlier meeting.

She moved closer to his desk, and when he stood she introduced Callie. He nodded, his face unreadable. Juliana noticed again the finely chiseled shape of his jaw, the wonderful depth of his eyes, the way his light brown hair fell across his forehead. It was a face that she longed to sketch. She could almost picture the strokes of charcoal on paper capturing the strength so evident in his face, in his bearing.

"Ladies, what can I do for you?"

Juliana felt herself redden, as if he had been reading her mind. For a moment she didn't speak, trying to regain her composure.

"Sir, I've come about a place in your caravan."

He nodded, his expression cool.

"A Mr. Graves visited you on our behalf."

He nodded again.

Juliana suddenly became angry that he was forcing her to lay out their intentions before him, one by one.

"We understand that you have agreed to make room for us."

"I have agreed to *allow* you on my train, Miss St. Clair."

Juliana could feel her cheeks flame. *"Allow,* Mr. James?"

"Yes," he said, with a tight smile. "As I told your—ah, Mr. Graves, I will allow you to join the train as long as he is there to watch out for you, to help you when the terrain gets rough, when the accommodations are not to your liking—"

Juliana interrupted, her voice clipped and controlled. "We will require no special treatment, I can assure you, Mr. James— not from Mr. Graves, you, or anyone else. I told you before— Callie and I will pull our own weight." Callie nodded vigorously beside her.

"I understand your intentions, Miss St. Clair." His tone became condescending. To Juliana, that was worse than his indifference. "But the truth is, you have no idea of the rigors of life on the trail. We're heading into dangerous country. It's not a carriage ride to a Sunday picnic."

"I understand that perfectly well." Juliana could see there was no use pursuing it with him. She took a deep breath, forcing her attention from the man in front of her to the task at hand. "Now," she finally said, "if you can just tell us where we need to sign to be *allowed* in your caravan."

He smiled and pulled the necessary paperwork from his desk.

Later, as they walked to the hotel, Callie drawled, "Arguing with that man is like wrestling a pig. The pig likes it and you just get dirty."

Juliana laughed. "Why do you say that?"

"Didn't you see the way he smiled at you when we left?" Callie asked, with an inward smile of her own.

Shortly after noon, Matthias Graves met Juliana and Callie at the livery. He had inquired about reliable wagon suppliers, and the three of them rode to a farm outside town where a Charles Fitzpatrick operated his place of business. They haggled with him over a used, but heavy and well-built farm wagon. After they agreed on a price, Fitzpatrick also offered them a fair price on a six-yoke team of obviously well-fed, healthy oxen.

"Look 'em over, Cal," Juliana said, joking with her sister. She remembered Callie's worries over buying a scrawny, sickly team.

Callie rubbed the noses of the gentle beasts, looked into their luminous brown eyes, commented on their long eyelashes, and pronounced them fit to carry them to Santa Fe.

Juliana looked skyward. "If only all our decisions could be made on such important attributes." Then she gave Callie a quick hug while they watched the farmer and Matthias harness their team to the new wagon.

Tethering their horses to the wagon's rear, the three drove the rig back into town. Juliana was impressed by Matt's expert handling of the team and told him so. "You'll learn fast," he commented. "But enjoy the ride. Most of the trip to Santa Fe, you and Callie will walk beside the brutes, instead of in the wagon."

Callie looked at Juliana in dismay. "Walk to Santa Fe? I had hoped the book was wrong."

Matthias laughed. "You can't wear out the team just because you want to save those pretty little feet. But you'll get used to it. Once calluses are built up, you won't feel it at all." He laughed again, and Callie looked sick.

Back in town they continued their shopping at the mercantile, purchasing fifty pounds of flour, ten pounds of coffee, twenty pounds of sugar, a barrel of cornmeal, several slabs of bacon, beans, crackers, and some tins of salt and baking powder.

"I want to buy a tent like Zebulon Reed's," Callie announced, as they discussed their supplies. "Only larger. I've read where you can get a sailcloth carpet so that you can keep the whole tent clean." Callie's eyes shone at the prospect. "And let's get two camp beds, sheets, pillows, and counterpanes. Especially counterpanes."

"What are you talking about? We're going to be roughing it." Juliana hotly recalled Parker James's ridiculing words about comfort.

"Just look over here, Jules," Callie interrupted. "Please come look." She led Juliana to the tent display. "I want this one—it's the most luxurious they make. It's from Philadelphia."

"I think your sister's entirely correct." Matthias had joined them. "You have plenty of money to cover your expenses. There's really no reason not to travel in as much comfort as possible."

"With the two of you siding against me—" Juliana shrugged in jest, laughing. "—what can I say? All right, Callie, we'll get the Philadelphia tent." Then she added, "You're in charge of putting it up each night."

Callie groaned but looked triumphant.

They continued to carefully choose their supplies, even the bedding that Callie had asked for. Juliana put her foot down when it came to the sailcloth carpeting. "That's just going too far," she told Callie with a sigh.

It took two more days, and several more trips to the mercantile and other suppliers, to make sure every detail had been covered. The rig was kept at the livery stable while it was fitted with a heavy canvas top, oiled for waterproofing.

Three days later, just before driving the outfit to Shawnee Wells, the caravan's gathering place, Matthias suggested they stop at a farmhouse at the edge of town. There Juliana purchased two crates of live chickens, which Matthias then strapped to the back of the wagon.

At last they were ready.

The sisters stood next to each other beside the oxen.

Juliana grinned, brushed a strand of hair from her face, and pulled her father's old field hat close above her eyes. She raised her whip and popped it above the oxens' bony backs. The beasts hollered and moaned. Then they lumbered forward taking their first steps toward Shawnee Wells with the wagon lurching and rocking behind them. The sounds of squawking and fluttering chickens rose above it all.

Seven

Each day for a week, Shawnee Wells drew greater numbers of Conestogas, farm wagons, dearborns, and carriages. The *remuda* grew in proportion, soon numbering hundreds of cattle, oxen, and horses. This was overseen by eighteen men hired by Captain Parker James.

From the beginning, the Santa Fe traders—the businessmen and their drivers—far outnumbered the other travelers. The muleskinners and bullwhackers at the Shawnee Wells camp, with their peppery language and uncouth ways, kept to themselves. The traders, for their part, camped in tents near their carriages or dearborns. Later they would drive their personal vehicles side by side with their muleskinner-driven Conestogas carrying thousands of dollars worth of goods.

Captain Parker James was the sole owner-operator of twenty-one of the thirty-five trade rigs that would eventually pull out for Santa Fe. James made it clear from the beginning that he was in charge of the Shawnee Wells proceedings and that he alone would be obeyed on the trail. All members of the caravan agreed in writing—before James accepted them into the train—that there would be no challenge to his captaincy.

The captain insisted that all those traveling with unbroken oxen or mules harness their teams to wagon tongues and drive the beasts in and around the grounds, getting them used to yokes and whips. Even the experienced muleskinners were required to join the other wagoneers to practice moving the wagons into a precise circle. This would be a nightly practice, but also a requirement as a measure against Indian attacks.

Captain James called the travelers together daily, usually at the night fire, to speak with them about details of the journey ahead.

"If you haven't already done so," he warned at the first night fire, "get back into town before we leave and buy trinkets and extra food for the Indians. We'll be passing through the lands of the Kansa, the Pawnee, the Comanche, and others. Most of the tribes we'll meet won't be dangerous—if we have something to hand out. They'll follow beside your wagon, sometimes camping right beside you for days on end, waiting to steal you blind if you don't simply give them what they want in the beginning."

Then he paused, looking around the group of travelers. "Since the Santa Fe trade began, fewer than a dozen have been killed. Those killings happened because of stupidity on the part of the travelers. They had lagged behind their party. Stragglers are easy prey, folks. Keep that in mind."

On other occasions he laid out details for their river crossings, telling which rivers would pose the most danger, where they might find quicksand or rapids. He introduced the trail guide and scouts and had them speak to the drivers about the details of moving wagons across a body of water.

One night James spoke of the route in great detail, explaining that they would take the Cimarron Cutoff rather than risk taking the heavy wagons through the safer but more difficult terrain of Raton Pass.

Day after day, Juliana and Callie practiced yoking their oxen and driving them around the flat grassy terrain near Shawnee

Wells. They practiced cracking the whip slightly above the beasts' backsides, popping the air just enough to urge them forward. Sometimes they rode in the wagon to get used to the feel of the swaying, tipping, creaking rig. Other times, they walked beside the lead yoke, urging forward the large gray brutes with calls of *Haw!* and *Hee!*

At night their limbs ached, and they swabbed ointments on their bleeding hands. Never once did either of them complain, though Juliana could see the pain in Callie's tearing eyes when she changed the dressing on her sister's palms.

They practiced pitching their tent. Working together, they timed themselves, trying each day to beat the previous day's time. One evening Captain James warned the entire group of the early morning starts. "We'll be on the trail by sunup," he said. "Those who aren't ready will be left behind." Juliana had the uneasy feeling he was staring at her as he spoke. After that she made Callie work even faster as they practiced dismantling their tent or packing and unpacking their cookware and eating utensils.

Matthias Graves often joined them, offering help if they needed it. His advice was invaluable. He showed Juliana how to make a cookfire with dried buffalo dung, joking with them as Callie wrinkled her nose in disgust.

"You won't find me eating anything cooked over a fire like that," she declared.

Graves replied that this was considered gourmet dining on the prairies—that for generations the Indians had used dung for their fires. He said that it was better than the alternative—burning your wagon piece by piece all the way to Santa Fe, until all that was left was a team pulling the wagon tongue.

While the three of them laughed together, Juliana happened to glance toward the captain's wagon across the night circle and caught him watching them, his face solemn. He turned away when their eyes met.

On the morning of the sixth day, one day before the caravan was scheduled to pull out of Shawnee Wells, Juliana packed her paints, easel, and brushes into her satchel. It was barely light, and most of the wagoneers still slept.

She walked quietly to the *remuda* and whistled for Sir Galahad. He whinnied in reply and trotted to the edge of the herd. She quickly saddled him, mounted, and rode southwest to a grove of golden cottonwoods near a small creek.

As the bright November dawn sent streaks of pale light across the eastern skies, Juliana lost herself in the scene, lightly sketching first the trees, then their reflection in the swiftly flowing creek. She had just begun dabbing cadmium onto the images of autumn leaves when she heard the pounding of horse's hooves behind her.

She turned to see Captain James riding toward her. To her surprise, gladness momentarily lifted her heart.

"Captain?" she said, as he neared.

He nodded his head curtly. "Miss St. Clair." He swung off the Appaloosa, letting the horse drink from the creek. Parker glanced at her painting, then back to Juliana. "Apparently you haven't been listening to my instructions."

"What do you mean, Captain?"

He looked around the area near where they stood, his eyes searching the thick brush and foliage. "I spoke to the entire company yesterday about the dangerous circumstances stragglers can find themselves in."

"I'm sorry, Captain. I don't see the point of this. I'm certainly not a—" she paused, her voice taking on a sarcastic tone— "straggler." She looked at him evenly. "It you mean that I'm taking a chance by being away from the company, then I'm guilty. You'll have to excuse me. I don't believe you made yourself clear when you spoke to the company earlier. You told us of the dangers of being away from the group on the trail—not here at Shawnee Wells."

"We *are* on the trail, Miss St. Clair," he said, his tone matching hers. "The dangers here are just as grave—maybe graver, because we can let our guard down. Protected areas like these"— his eyes scanned the brush again—"are the most dangerous. Families have been massacred in places as 'safe' as this. Use your head, Miss St. Clair. You've got to be on the lookout always."

He swung onto the Appaloosa and looked down at her before riding off. "Don't ride off alone again." He paused. "And maybe you'll make it to Fort La Sal and your waiting festivities."

Waiting festivities? What was he talking about? But Juliana didn't dwell on his final words, only on those that preceded them. As she dismantled the easel and gathered her paints and canvas, she wondered what Captain Parker James had against her. He was right; she hadn't been wise leaving the caravan. She needed to be more careful, and if truth be told, she was glad for the warning.

It was not his words that bothered her. It was how he spoke to her. And it was the way he looked at her when he did. And what an odd remark for him to make about festivities; whatever could he mean?

Mounting Sir Galahad, Juliana thought back to the day she had first met the captain. She had felt something connecting them, a mutual attraction in spite of the dispute over her joining his train. But now? There seemed to be something more. There was a different look in his eyes. Disdain perhaps? Indifference?

She tried to brush Parker James from her mind. But as she headed back to the caravan, Juliana could see his lone figure on the Appaloosa. Try as she might to think other thoughts, he remained in her mind.

Early the same morning, Sun Jones slipped from her sleeping pallet and, without waking Jeremiah, walked a short distance from their tent.

She settled to her knees in a sheltered area near a copse of sugarberry trees and sandbar willows. As was her custom, she began her prayer by opening her heart to God about Jed, her son, the boy she and Jeremiah had just visited in St. Louis. Oh, how she missed their only child! The empty place his going had left inside her caused a sadness she seldom spoke of to anyone but God.

For years Sun and Jeremiah had sought God's leading for their boy. Jed had set his heart on becoming a doctor and returning to Sun's people, the Mandans, to minister to them. Three times the white man had brought a sickness that had taken Mandan lives with the speed of a prairie fire. If it came again, Sun's people might cease to exist.

Jed's dream to save his mother's people was a worthy one, and the young man was working with diligence to see it through. For the next few years he would live with Dr. Noble Jackson Hill in St. Louis. Then the boy hoped to go to Harvard. Dr. Hill had told them with great confidence that the boy's promise would get him there.

Pride in Jed made Sun's heart swell. But her fears for him sometimes caused it to tremble. Each morning she gave her son to God, reminding herself as she did so that God cared for Jed even more than she and Jeremiah did. Her son was secure in his heavenly Father's care—whether sitting near her campfire or in a classroom with Dr. Hill.

After Sun's prayers for Jed, her thoughts settled on their young friend Parker James. Her heart had been troubled for him, and she felt driven to speak to her Lord about him.

When Parker visited them the week before, she had noticed a

change in him, a sadness different from the raw grief that had been there after his Laurie died. This was a darkness that spoke of a deeper loss than even that of his beloved wife. Sun had watched him as he spoke with Jeremiah, noticing his eyes, the set of his jaw, the emptiness in his expression.

Once Parker had spoken openly of the Lord as his friend, talked eagerly with Jeremiah about spiritual matters. He had asked her husband to tell him stories of his friend Jed Smith, a fur trapper who had once tramped the West, exploring, mapping, and speaking through word and deed of the God who walked with him. Parker did not hide his admiration of Smith. And Jeremiah, delighted to do so, had told him more than once how much the young Parker reminded him of the man who had been like a brother to him. But during Parker's last visit, he hadn't once mentioned Jed Smith. He hadn't once mentioned his Lord.

Sun opened her worn Bible to the Psalms, touching its fragile pages reverently, tenderly. The Bible was the same one that had belonged to their friend Jed. It was their most treasured possession. Jeremiah had taught Sun to read with this book, beginning with the first Psalm.

She read the precious verses to herself now, mouthing the words, as she followed along with her finger:

"He shall be like a tree planted by the rivers of water, that bringeth forth his fruit in his season; his leaf also shall not wither..."

She looked up at the sugarberry tree, laden with its sweet, juicy fruit, and thought about the tree's need for water. She knew that the sugarberry only grew near streams that never dried. She reached up and took a small red berry in her hand, turning it and noticing its health.

She remember picking the fruit for her mother when she was

a child. Her mother had shown her how to find the healthiest trees, those planted closest to the streams of water. Once she had made the mistake of picking fruit from a tree farther out in drier land, thinking her mother would not know what she had done. Her mother had spoken sharply, calling her away from her playmates, marching her into the family's tipi. Pouring several berries into her palm, her mother had demanded, her eyes flashing, "Where did you pick these?"

After Sun had told her, she asked how her mother knew. She remembered how her mother took her again into the sunlight and asked her to look closely at the little berries.

Sun had inspected the red fruit, looking with amazement at the tiny plant lice hopping in her hand.

"Berries grow firm and plump on trees nearest water, Sun. Those too far away raise better lice than fruit." And she had sent her daughter back to the river to pick healthy fruit.

Now Sun held the healthy fruit to her lips, savoring its perfume, its sweetness. She thought again of Parker. "My Lord and Father," she began. "You know the life's walk of your child, Parker. Only you can lead him to your streams of living water. We leave tomorrow on a long and difficult journey. But the spiritual journey we face is greater, one in which we need even greater help...." And she prayed on, entreating her Lord on behalf of the wagon captain, on behalf of them all.

The sun was well above the horizon when she rose from her knees and walked back to the tent she shared with her husband.

Jeremiah had already set the morning fire and now, seated beside it, set the coffee to boil in their porcelain pot. He looked up and greeted her. Sun's heart still leapt at his smile. They had been together now eighteen summers; his hair was thinning, his beard sun-whitened, but the light in his dark eyes spoke more clearly than ever of his deep love for her. Whenever she looked into his eyes, Sun thought Heaven must surely be reflected in their depth.

"Miah," she said softly, and touched his ruddy cheek with her fingertips.

He reached up and took her hand, squeezing her fingers tenderly. "You've been praying."

Sun nodded. Sometimes they prayed together at night as the coals died in their night fire. But she knew her husband also liked riding out into the fields or forest alone to speak to his God. And he respected the time she had chosen for herself, the early mornings when the whole world seemed to awaken to the call, the touch, of its Creator.

Jeremiah knew of her joy at the grasslands and forest creatures' sounds, the barking of the squirrel, the soft call of the bobwhite, the roaring hum of life from the honeybees, the dragonflies. They all seemed to leap in animated response to each day's dawning, to each new morning given them by their Creator. Sun rejoiced that she could be there to see it, to feel it.

As he watched her joyful response to dawn's breaking, Jeremiah often said that her father had aptly named her when he chose Morning Sun.

"Miah, I've been thinking of Parker's words about our route," she began.

Jeremiah nodded.

"He said to us all last night we will be taking the Cimarron Cutoff."

Jeremiah didn't look at her, but reached for the coffeepot to pour for them.

"Miah, it brings you much sadness to think about that part of the trail." Sun did not phrase it as a question. She sipped her coffee and waited.

Jeremiah smiled sadly. "You know me too well."

"You have not been on the Cimarron since Jedediah was killed there."

Jeremiah was silent for several minutes. "I can't stay away from the place forever, Sun," he finally said. "It's been fifteen years. Maybe it's time I go."

A time of understanding silence passed between them. Sun knew her husband still felt the pain of his friend's murder.

"Miah." Her voice was soft. "You once vowed to track down the Comanches who killed him—take revenge on them and their families. You searched long for them, but you could not find them. I was frightened by your anger. You swore you would not die until after you saw justice done."

"I'm a different man now, Sun,"

For a moment neither spoke. Then Sun went on. "It is true. But last night I saw a deep burning in your eyes when Parker told us of the route, Miah. Your eyes tell me that there is still pain. That there is still a desire in you to seek justice. You haven't forgotten your friend's death. Even after all these years."

"You know me too well, Sun," he repeated, and taking her hand, he held it tightly between his. They sat together for several minutes in silence. Then the sweet bubbling call of a meadowlark made Sun look heavenward, and she watched the glint of its golden breast catch the sunlight as it flew.

Even the life of a small songbird is in his hand, she thought to herself. *How can I doubt that the lives of Parker James and my Jeremiah are not as precious? I fear for Miah, but I leave him in your hands, Father.* The small bird called out again. Sun watched it light on the topmost branch of a black willow then once again take wing.

She touched her husband's cheek, then rose to begin fixing their breakfast.

 Eight

aptain Parker James rode the surefooted Appaloosa back to Shawnee Wells, disturbed by his encounter with Juliana St. Clair. He wanted to push her from his mind, keep his thoughts on the tasks at hand: getting the wagon train on the trail, pondering the mission that awaited him in Fort La Sal.

But when he had seen Miss St. Clair mount the big gray and ride from the wagon camp toward Whiskey Creek, he knew he had to follow after her. Even if he hadn't felt it was his duty to warn her, he wondered if he could have kept from following.

When he rode up, she had turned with a look of anticipation, as if expecting someone she loved. *As if expecting Matthias Graves,* he thought grimly.

For a moment, as the early morning sun bathed her face, he drank in the sight of her like a man who thirsted after a long desert trek. Then the brief, sweet brightness had shattered when she saw it was him, not her intended. He wondered why she should matter so much. She was betrothed to Matthias Graves. And his heart still belonged to Laurie. He suddenly felt ashamed for the way he allowed Juliana St. Clair to invade his thoughts. As he rode across the morning-damp grasslands toward the wagon camp, he found he couldn't help himself.

As Parker neared the camp, he could see a small company of Conestogas in the distance, heading toward Shawnee Wells on the road from Westport. Lagging behind, a hundred or so head of cattle were being driven by several men in Mexican dress. Parker halted the Appaloosa and for a moment watched the band approach.

A short time later, after he'd entered camp, he dismounted just as Matthias Graves came into sight carrying his saddle.

"Captain," he said in greeting.

"Graves." Parker nodded and looked out toward the Conestogas he'd noticed earlier. "Those yours?" He remembered that Graves had told him he'd have three more wagons joining his party.

Graves grunted an affirmation as he saddled the chestnut. "I've had my men waiting in Westport for the cargo." He laughed amiably, though to Parker it seemed forced. "I was beginning to wonder whether it would arrive in time."

"Steamboat freight?" Parker normally didn't press the traders for information on their cargo, but something about this man and his business increasingly bothered him.

"That's it, Captain," Graves muttered indifferently as he mounted and then reined the mare in the direction of the approaching Conestogas. But he offered no more explanation.

෧෨

By midmorning the Conestoga rigs, with Graves riding beside the lead wagon, pulled into the Shawnee Wells camp. He watched while Graves directed the drivers where to halt their teams.

Parker was still watching when the driver of the lead wagon

unwound his gangly limbs from the wagon bench and jumped to the ground. Parker watched the man intently. There was no mistaking his identity, even from across the wagon camp.

The bullwhacker turned as if he sensed he was being watched. The man caught Parker's look but didn't return even a flicker of recognition. He simply continued a sweeping gaze around the camp, then turned back to the business of unyoking the oxen in his team and turning them out to pasture with the rest of the *remuda*.

Like an expert, Parker thought in amazement. *Bennett Cookingham looks as much at ease as a bullwhacker as he ever has in any other undercover role.* He watched his friend goad one of the stubborn beasts from its yoke.

A muleskinner! From West Point to bullwhacking. He wished he could slap his friend on the back in congratulations. But that would have to come later, when their mission was done.

Bennett stood, leaning against his wagon, talking with Graves and the other drivers. As Parker observed the group, he began to put a few more of the missing pieces together. Could Matthias Graves have designs on the governorship of New Mexico? Was he the one—the heir apparent—that Parker had spoken of to Cookingham? Or was Graves another agent, someone in place ready to help Parker in his mission? Either way it made sense that Cookingham would somehow find a way to join his company.

Across the wagon circle, Parker noticed someone else intently watching the Graves group. It was Juliana St. Clair. She, too, looked puzzled.

❧

Juliana squinted her eyes toward the wagons Matt had ridden out to meet. She saw a long-limbed man jump down from the driver's seat of one wagon. Directly behind him, another driver stretched, looked around, then joined the first.

Callie, wiping her flour-covered hands after another biscuit-making attempt, joined her. "What's wrong?" She looked across the wagon circle.

"Look at the man standing next to Matt."

Callie studied the group. "What about him?"

"I think that's Seth Johnson."

"Who?"

"You remember. Seth Johnson. The man who sat at dinner with us that night on the riverboat. He told us about New Mexico—the U.S. takeover, Governor Bent, everything."

"Of course I remember that man. But that isn't him." Callie's voice sounded certain. "If it's the same man, he would have told us if he was on his way to New Mexico. That can't be him."

"No. Look closer, Callie. I'm sure that's him."

"Why would he be driving a wagon for Matt?"

"Why not? He never told us what line of work he's in. There's really no reason why he couldn't be a driver."

Callie's voice was thoughtful. "Except that he never once told us that he'd ever been on the Santa Fe Trail, or to New Mexico. Everything he knew about it, he said, came from his brother's letters."

Callie was right. "Seems a bit strange, too, that he knows Matt."

"It's just a coincidence, Jules."

"And I suppose it's really none of our concern."

They turned away. But Juliana couldn't shake a nagging feeling that something wasn't right. And she could tell by the look on her face that Callie was thinking the same thing.

The following morning at four-thirty, a bugle sounded. It was followed by the murmurs of voices throughout the wagon camp. Juliana pulled back her tent flap and watched as lanterns were lit inside the camp's tents and covered wagons, casting a warm orange glow that began to dispel the darkness.

Then came the sounds of folks moving about, striking their tents and packing belongings for the first day of travel. In the distance, the cattle moaned and bawled as cattlehands went after stragglers, moving the herd together in preparation for the drive.

Nearby, traders and bullwhackers were lighting breakfast fires, and the smoke curled into the early morning air. The smell of boiling coffee soon followed.

She woke Callie, who grumbled and groaned before tumbling out of her cot to dress in the chill air.

Juliana quickly pulled on her leather breeches and boots and slipped the heavy peasant's shirt over her head. The days were getting chilly. She nearly always wore her woolen cape once her morning's chores were done. But for now, she shivered and pulled on her leather vest, wishing it at least had sleeves. Then she brushed her hair vigorously and fastened it at the back of her neck.

The young women worked quickly, forgoing the breakfast fire and coffee so they wouldn't be delayed in striking camp, harnessing the team, and driving the wagon into line when the bugle again sounded. Juliana was determined to avoid the humiliation of being late. She was glad Callie agreed.

As they loaded the wagon, they munched on Callie's cold biscuits, which Juliana had to admit were getting better, and drank cold coffee from the previous day's supper. By six, the wagon was packed, the oxen yoked to the tongue, and Juliana and Callie, standing beside the team, waited for the bugle to signal that it was time to leave.

Juliana's heart beat heavy in her chest in anticipation, apprehension, and excitement. She took a deep breath and looked at the scene around her. A rose-colored glow backlit the horizon. The tall prairie grasses beyond Shawnee Wells waved gently in the morning breeze, silent sentinels signaling the train's passing.

Thirty-five wagons faced west ready at the signal to fall into their place in line. Impatient teams of oxen and mules hoofed the ground, snorting and bawling. The teamsters spoke in hushed voices, some seated in their wagons, others in place beside their teams. There was a simple majesty to the tall canvas tops, more gray than white in the early dawn. Prairie schooners, they were called. And she could see why. They would soon move through the sea of tall grasses dipping and swaying, their canvases catching the wind like sails

Juliana looked up as a small wagon pulled in beside hers. A smiling Sun and Jeremiah Jones nodded their greeting.

Several wagons behind her, and off to one side, she could see Matt's small armada of Conestogas. Matthias noticed her glance and waved.

Just then the bugle call sounded. It was followed by whoops and shouts and hollers, whips cracking, and beasts braying. A cloud of dust seemed to envelop the train as drivers aggressively fought for the best place in the lineup. Juliana saw how naive she had been to think that the previous night's placement draw would make any difference.

She popped the whip vigorously above her team, shouted at them to move forward. Beside her Callie leaned forward in excitement, hollering at the beasts to go faster.

With quarreling and cursing and mean-spirited comments, the bullwhackers and traders fought their way into the line. Juliana paid no heed and drove her wagon into the thick of the swirling dust and racing Conestogas. Her oxen bawled, jerked, and jumped, skittish at the sudden tumult. But she kept the wagon steady and finally found herself in line about ten wagons from the lead.

As Juliana settled the team into a slow plodding walk, Captain James rode up beside their wagon. He reined the Appaloosa to a steady gait beside them.

He lifted his felt hat, brushing his hair from his forehead with his fingers. "Nice work," he said, as he replaced the hat.

Surprised, Juliana looked at him for a moment, then nodded and laughed. "You didn't tell me that the most dangerous part of the trip would be getting a place in line."

Parker smiled broadly, seeming glad to talk with her. "If you ever find yourself at the end of this stream of beasts and humankind, you'll understand why the rush to be close to the lead."

"Dust?"

He nodded his head slowly. "It's bad enough here. But back there," he gestured to the end of the train, "it gets into your eyes, nose, ears, hair. Stays there until you can soak it out in a long, hot bath at the end of the trail."

He rode next to them in silence for a short distance. "I've seen how the two of you have worked to ready yourselves for this," he began, looking more at Juliana than Callie. "And I want to say, I've been impressed."

Juliana tilted her head. "Why, thank you, Captain."

"I—ah…" He hesitated, looking across the prairie for a moment before continuing. "I also would like to say I'm sorry for some of the things I said to you that first day—about your ability to handle the rigors of the trail."

Juliana didn't speak, but waited for him to continue.

"I had no call to judge you." Parker looked into her face. The sunlight brought out a depth of color in his eyes that Juliana hadn't noticed before. She quickly focused on the oxen, suddenly worrying he might see her look of admiration.

"You had no way of knowing our determination, Captain," she said, still facing forward.

Something had changed in his voice when he spoke again. "At that time I didn't realize your plans either. Plans such as yours require uncommon determination to see them through."

Juliana turned quickly toward him, somehow stung by his tone. But he merely lifted his hat and said, "Ladies," and moved on down the train.

Callie looked at Juliana, raising an eyebrow. "What was that all about?"

Juliana shook her head slowly. "I have no idea."

"How does he know what we face?"

"I don't know that either."

Callie shrugged, sighing dramatically. She popped the whip above the team. "If I were guessing, I would guess the man is smitten by you, Juliana St. Clair."

Juliana tried to ignore the feeling of quick lightness in her heart at Callie's words. "If he is, he has a strange way of showing it." Then she laughed and pulled Callie's hat down over her eyes, taking the reins from her. "But that's nonsense. Utter nonsense."

The first day progressed without mishap. Juliana and Callie marveled to each other that the weather could not have been better, with an early November sky providing a purple canopy over the tall golden autumn grasses.

The stop for "nooning" was welcome. Callie had packed ham and biscuits. And they still had fresh apples from Westport. The cattle and oxen were allowed to graze and drink from a nearby stream, then the teams were once again hitched for the remainder of the day's trek.

In the late afternoon, lazy white clouds billowed to the west. Juliana watched them cautiously, knowing that prairie storms could build suddenly and drop disaster on unwary travelers. But these clouds remained small and harmless.

As they pulled into the night circle, Juliana took pride in the precision with which she drove the team to join the wagon in front of hers. Callie applauded as they closed the circle.

"It's your turn tomorrow, Cal," Juliana said, as they jumped down from the wagon.

Callie grinned. "It'll be easy. We're lead wagon tomorrow."

Juliana squinted at her sister.

Callie laughed. "I drive tomorrow. Just wait till you see where we end up in line."

They unhitched the oxen, drove them to the *remuda*, and checked on Sir Galahad and Darley. Then Juliana sent Callie to pick up dried buffalo chips for the fire.

"You can pick up chips if you want when it's your turn, Jules, but I'm checking for twigs," Callie called over her shoulder as she left camp. "I saw some sandbar willows at a creek not far from here. I'll look over there."

"Callie, be careful," Juliana called after her sister. "Stay with the others." But Callie was out of earshot.

Juliana unpacked the Dutch oven and began fixing a stew of potatoes, onions, and salt pork.

Throughout the camp other cook fires were lit and suppers started. Juliana waited for Callie's return, at first mildly angry that they would be late with their own meal. Then as time wore on, she became worried something had befallen her sister.

Darkness began to fall on the wagon camp. Juliana became even more agitated, finally deciding to saddle Sir Galahad and ride out to the creek.

Juliana kicked the gray to a gallop and followed the direction Callie had earlier pointed out. She hadn't ridden far when she heard the beat of horses' hooves behind her. She turned. It was the mountain man, Jeremiah Jones.

He nodded a greeting. "Miss St. Clair."

Juliana looked at him curiously.

"Sun saw you leave camp. She thought you might need help," he said simply.

Gratitude flooded over her. "Thank you. Sun is right."

"You should not be out here alone."

"I know. But my sister is late getting back to camp. She came out more than an hour ago to look for firewood."

"You should have reported it to the captain." He rubbed his beard, looking thoughtful.

Juliana sighed. He was right. But she didn't want to ask for help—ever—if she could help it. "I know," she said again, hoping her pride had not endangered Callie.

She showed Jeremiah the direction Callie had walked earlier. They rode together toward the creek. A damp, cold dusk had settled. Juliana shivered even beneath her cape.

As they neared the small stream, Juliana called out to her sister. But the only answer was the sound of rushing waters.

"Callie!" she shouted again.

Still no answer.

They rode upstream and Jeremiah joined her in shouting Callie's name. They moved the horses closer to the water, inspecting the areas obscured by brush and water grasses. Still there was no sign of Callie.

With a sinking heart, Juliana suggested they turn downstream. It was nearly dark. Jeremiah said they would look only a short time longer, then they must ride back for lanterns and help—from the captain and others.

"Callie!" Juliana called out again and again, desperately listening between shouts for an answer.

Finally, just after they had reached a steep creek bank near a barren oak, it had become nearly too dark to see. Jeremiah said they must turn back to the wagon camp for help. Juliana nodded, heartsick with worry.

By the time darkness fell, a rescue party of traders, muleskinners, and scouts had organized under the captain's leadership. Some left the wagon camp on horseback, others on foot. Holding lanterns, they fanned out in every direction.

Juliana rode with the captain and Jeremiah Jones.

"We will go downstream," Jeremiah said as they rode away from camp.

"Did you see sign?" Parker asked.

The mountain man nodded slightly but said nothing. Juliana had forgotten until now that Jeremiah Jones had spent decades as a trapper and explorer. For the first time in the nearly two hours since Callie disappeared she felt a faint glimmer of hope.

They reached the barren oak where Juliana and Jeremiah had looked earlier. This time the three dismounted. Parker held the lantern high while Jeremiah inspected the brush.

He fingered a bent twig, then another farther on, and another. He stopped and pointed out dried grasses that had recently been trampled.

"Someone's been here. Callie?" Juliana whispered to herself. Then she cried louder, "Callie!" Then again, "Callie!"

Still there was no answer.

Juliana and Parker followed Jeremiah through a small copse of sandbar willows to the creek bed.

Jeremiah took the lantern from Parker. Holding it a few feet from the ground, he traced recent footprints, a single set. Juliana knew from the size and shape that they had to be Callie's.

She exchanged a glance with Parker. He looked angry. Filled with remorse, she could see why he would blame her. Juliana wished for the thousandth time that she had somehow made clearer to her sister the hazards of going off alone. But she had thought Callie knew. Her sister wasn't a child. At sixteen she was considered nearly a grown woman. She might be impetuous but she wasn't foolish.

Parker joined her in shouting Callie's name as they walked swiftly downstream following the trail Jeremiah had found. Now and then Juliana felt the frigid spray on her face from the racing waters of the creek.

They moved through the underbrush and Juliana tried not to think of the Pawnee or Kansa that might be nearby. Just before they arrived at a small clearing, Jeremiah stopped. He lifted the lantern above his head.

There at the water's edge lay Callie, facedown, her body strangely twisted. She was still as death.

With a small cry, Juliana ran to her sister. Kneeling, she tried to pull her from the water. As Callie's face turned, Juliana could see a wound at her temple, deep and swollen, still oozing blood.

"Don't move her." Parker had stepped closer. "You might hurt her."

He knelt beside Juliana and began to examine Callie, checking for other injuries. He slowly moved her ankles and straightened her legs. He repeated his actions with her arms, straightening them, moving them carefully. Juliana breathed a little easier. At least Callie's limbs seemed unhurt.

Parker handed his handkerchief to Juliana and asked her to dip it in the creek. She handed it back and watched as he carefully swabbed the wound.

"Hold it here—tightly," he commanded, when he was through. "She can't lose any more blood."

Juliana nodded and did as he asked.

Callie stirred, moaning softly.

Parker murmured a few words of comfort to her, then gently lifted her from the water and headed back to the horses. Juliana walked at his side, still holding the cold compress to Callie's temple.

Jeremiah shot his rifle once into the air, a signal to the others that Callie St. Clair had been found.

Nine

❦

Captain James carried the still-unconscious Callie to Juliana's tent and carefully laid her on a cot.

"Get her out of the wet clothes and into something warm. Find every blanket you can to cover her." The captain sounded stern, though not unkind. Then he abruptly left Juliana to do his bidding. He returned a short time later with Jeremiah's wife, Sun, who carried a small stack of clean cloths.

Juliana had placed the last woolen blanket on Callie and knelt beside the narrow cot. The Indian woman touched Juliana's arm, nodded in understanding, then knelt on the opposite side of the cot.

Sun bent over Callie, her long raven-colored braid falling over her shoulder. She gently felt Callie's limbs with her delicate, strong fingers, then focused on the wound, frowning. "Bring me fresh water, Parker," she said without looking up. "And have someone bring warming stones."

He nodded and again left the tent.

Callie's face was pale, almost gray, and her freckles seemed too dark against her skin. Her flame-colored curls, wet and matted, lay against the white pillow. Her wound had turned an angry purple-black. Callie lay silent, seeming to be in a deep sleep, so deep that Juliana could not tell whether she breathed.

"Your sister will tremble when she wakes," Sun said. "The trembling can cause deep sickness." Her strange blue eyes met Juliana's.

Juliana nodded in understanding. She had once seen it happen to a slave who fell from a mare at Stonehaven.

"In a short time we must wake your sister and keep her awake all night."

"Yes." Juliana nodded again, glad for the woman's wisdom.

"We will wait until I have finished here." She gently touched Callie's forehead.

Parker returned with the water. Two traders followed him into the tent with iron buckets filled with stones from the night fire, then left.

Sun began cleaning and binding the wound, her lips moving as she worked. At first Juliana thought she was talking to herself, but as she listened more carefully, it was as if Sun was speaking to a person in the room. Juliana glanced around. But Sun, Juliana, and Parker were alone with Callie.

Callie groaned softly and her eyelids moved, but Juliana was thankful she would not wake until Sun had finished.

Finally Sun directed Parker to wrap the stones and place them on either side of Callie's body. Juliana lifted the blankets while the warm stones were tucked into place.

"Now you need to help me, Juliana."

Juliana had wondered until now if the woman remembered meeting her on the Missouri riverboat. But the warmth with which Sun spoke her name told her otherwise. It comforted Juliana to know that Sun remembered.

"It's time to wake her?"

"Yes. It is time." Sun began patting Callie's wrists and calling her name.

"Cal." Juliana touched her sister's cheek gently, so that she wouldn't move her head. "Callie, wake up."

There was no movement from Callie.

For several minutes, Sun and Juliana spoke to Callie. There was not even a flicker beneath her white eyelids.

Juliana hung her head for a moment in thought, then began to speak of Stonehaven. "Callie," she began, "remember the oak tree where father built you a swing? I remember the sweet smell of springtime, the azaleas in bloom, the bright blue sky—and pushing you in that swing.

"Remember how it felt, Callie? You giggled and laughed as I pushed you higher. Then you'd let the 'cat die down' and jump from the swing, run through the gardens and into the house."

Juliana watched her sister. There was still no indication that she heard her. But Sun gestured for her to go on. Juliana was vaguely aware that Parker watched her intently as she spoke.

"There Father would be waiting. He'd sweep you into his lap and hold you close."

With that, Callie moved her head, nearly imperceptibly, then moaned. Still her eyes remained closed.

Juliana took a deep breath, reaching for pleasant memories that she knew they shared. "Callie, remember the good times at home? The wonderful parties Father held at Stonehaven? Remember the time we decided to decorate with a thousand candles for Christmas?"

She spoke of other special occasions, and some of the ordinary, trying to touch something within Callie—*if* she could hear her—with a story, a memory, anything that would wake her. But nothing seemed to make a difference.

"Callie, wake up; I need you," she finally said, taking her

sister's hand in hers. "Please wake up." When there was no response, Juliana kept her gaze on her sister's small hand, feeling her eyes fill.

"Father, we need your help." Sun's voice was deep, soft, and reverent as she spoke.

Juliana looked up in surprise.

Sun's eyes were closed, but she spoke as if to a friend who knelt beside her at Callie's bedside. Her face held a look of deep love for that friend. "This child has need of your touch," she went on. "We have done all we know how to do, though if there is more to do, give us your wisdom."

Juliana had never heard anyone pray in such a way before. From childhood she had heard ministers pray from pulpits, calling upon the Lord God in intonations of grandeur with words that she couldn't understand.

She was intrigued by this woman who spoke to God in simple words. She turned toward Parker, wondering if he felt as she did. But Captain James had slipped quietly from the tent sometime after Sun had begun to pray.

Juliana turned back to Callie, watching her and listening as Sun spoke her simple words to her unseen Friend. A strange calm settled over Juliana. She wondered if it was her imagination or if she really did feel the presence of Someone with them.

"I know you love Callie, Lord. You love her this moment as if she is the only child, the only one, in your world."

Juliana felt a warmth embrace her at Sun's words. What love could this be? She had never before considered such a personal love from the God of the universe.

"Father, I ask that you touch this lamb with the power that only you have. Please, if it is your will, touch Callie with the same power that raised your Son from the dead."

Juliana's eyes were wide open now. She stared openly at the woman across from her. Love? Power? Resurrection power? Sun's face held a quiet calm and seemed filled with peace. It told Juliana that Sun was in a place she cherished—in the presence of her God and Friend.

Suddenly Juliana, still holding Callie's hand, felt a warmth invade her sister's palm and spread to her fingers. With her other hand she patted Callie's wrist. She watched as her pale face seemed to come alive with color. Callie still did not open her eyes, but her breathing became deeper and more steadily measured.

Several minutes passed. Outside by the night fire, a fiddler began to play. The lonely sounds of a harmonica joined in. Someone sang along for awhile then stopped. Now and then a burst of laughter or the sounds of the teamsters' coarse talk carried across the wagon circle. In the distance the soft bawling of cattle and oxen could be heard as the cowhands settled the *remuda* for the night.

Callie groaned and tried to move her head.

"Don't move, child," whispered Sun. "You must stay still."

"Wh—" Callie's lips moved.

"Don't try to speak, honey. I'm right here." Juliana felt Callie's finger press against her hand. She pressed back.

Callie began to shiver, just as Sun had said.

"We must have more warm stones." Sun looked at Juliana.

Juliana stepped out of the tent into the fresh night air, glad for the cloak she still wore. Carrying the iron bucket, she looked for the captain, knowing she would be unable to lift it herself.

As if he had been watching for her, he appeared by her side.

"How is Callie?" He took the bucket from her hands and walked with her to the fire.

Juliana still expected him to be angry that she and Callie had caused trouble their first night on the trail, but he continued to show only kindness.

"She moved a bit a few minutes ago. But now she's shivering. She's taken quite a chill."

His eyes showed his concern. "It isn't a chill. Her body has had a severe shock. Sometimes that in itself can cause death. You do understand that?"

Juliana did, but she hadn't wanted to think about it. She looked down, her eyes filling with tears, suddenly feeling too weary to take another step. *Callie's death?* The thought was too much to bear. She swayed a bit and without thinking reached toward Parker to steady herself.

Parker put his arm around Juliana, drawing her close until she could regain her balance.

She looked up into his face with both surprise and gratitude. For a moment their eyes met, and she felt weak with the depth of caring, the raw emotion she saw there.

She stepped back, flustered. At the same moment Matthias Graves strode toward them, his face dark with anger.

"What do you think you're doing?" He placed a protective arm around Juliana. In her confusion she didn't protest.

Parker stared at him.

"I told you I would watch out for Miss St. Clair." His unblinking gaze seemed to hold a challenge.

"Then where have you been while—," the captain began.

"It doesn't make any difference. What matters is that I am here now." He looked down at Juliana, his expression changing to one of concern.

This was no time for a confrontation. Juliana put her hand gently on Matt's arm. "What matters is Callie. We need to get more stones from the fire. Will you help me, Matt?" Callie might be dying. She could think of little else. "Please, we must hurry."

Matthias took the iron bucket from Parker, a half-smile on his face. "Captain," he said with a hint of sarcasm, and tipped his hat. Then taking Juliana's arm, he began asking about Callie's condition as they moved together toward the night fire. As Matt scooped the stones into the carrier, Juliana looked back at Parker. He turned away, but not before she caught a glimpse of the anger in his face.

A few minutes later, Matthias walked with Juliana back to her tent. He sat for a while with Juliana at Callie's side, asking questions about the accident and her condition.

After he left, Juliana pulled a chair closer to Callie's cot, her thoughts now on Parker's words about the shock her sister's body had undergone. Death? She lifted Callie's hand to her cheek. No. She refused to think that death would be so cruel. It had been only weeks since their father died. Now Callie? No. Juliana dismissed the thought.

For the first time since they had found Callie sprawled in the frigid creek waters, Juliana began to wonder about the accident. How had it happened? It was obvious that she had hit her head in a fall. But Callie was not one to take chances. As a child she had climbed trees faster and more surefooted than any of the plantation children she played with. Something more than the accident itself nagged at her; it just did not make sense.

She shrugged away the thoughts, wondering in her weariness if her imagination was working overtime. Besides, the most important task at hand was simply seeing to it that Callie got better.

Through the night Juliana sat with Sun at Callie's side, sometimes speaking softly to Callie, sometimes listening to Sun's prayers. The violent shaking had stopped, but Callie still whispered that she was cold.

"You must get some sleep, Juliana." It was near three in the morning. Sun reached across the cot and patted her hand. "You do know that the train will still move on."

Juliana nodded. "But Callie is too sick to move."

"You can't stay here. If you decide not to go with the train, the captain will send you back to Westport. One way or the other, you will have to travel tomorrow."

Juliana looked down at her sister looking so fragile and pale. If they returned to Westport, what would they do until spring when the next caravan formed? Where would they live? Would there be enough money left come spring to get them to New Mexico?

"Could we make a bed in the back of the wagon for Callie? Something comfortable enough so that she won't be in pain?"

"To travel back to Westport?"

"No. To go on to New Mexico."

Sun smiled. "Yes. And I'll ride with you to care for her."

Juliana thought she felt Callie squeeze her hand. "Thank you," she said to Sun.

At Sun's insistence, Juliana turned down the lantern and lay on her cot. She made Sun promise to wake her in an hour so that her gentle friend could also rest.

Before falling asleep, Juliana's thoughts centered on Sun and the intimate way she had spoken to God. She wondered how it would be to have such confidence in God's love and power. She thought about Sun's prayer—"I know you love Callie, Lord. You love her this moment as if she is the only child, the only one, in your world." *What would it be like to be loved by him as if I'm the only one in the world?*

Her drifting thoughts settled on a scene from her childhood, from a time before Callie was born. Someone had given her a Bible storybook with lovely illustrations. One illustration was of Jesus on the day that he blessed the children. He had held the children near him, one little girl sitting in his lap, several others leaning on him the way children often do.

Her father had held her the same way while reading the story. She remembered his laughter, the joy he seemed to take in being with her, reading to her. She closed her eyes and remembered how it felt to have his warm arms around her, hugging her close, loving her as if she were the only little girl to love in the world.

Warm tears stung her eyes at the memory. And she wondered about Jesus. Could it be that he loved her that way? That he could love her as if she were the only person in the world to love?

Across the room she heard Sun's soft voice as she again spoke to her Friend. Juliana's last thought before drifting into a peaceful sleep was that Someone was in the tent with them. She wanted to know him the way Sun did.

⚜

It was late and the wagon camp had quieted for the night when Jeremiah stopped by Parker's tent.

The old explorer looked worried. Parker invited him to sit, offering him a drink.

Jeremiah shook his head, declining, and as was his way got right to the point.

"I went back to the creek—the place where the girl fell."

Parker nodded. "And?"

"I followed her footprints, the marks on the bank, the place she fell. They don't cipher."

"What do you mean?"

"Her footprints move along nice and steady and easy. I could see where she stopped to gather firewood. She was in no hurry." Jeremiah rubbed his sun-bleached beard.

Parker could see the concern in Jeremiah's weathered face. He was not a man who jumped to conclusions. Unwarranted suspicion was not his nature. "Then what happened? You're telling me something changed."

Jeremiah nodded. "It seems that something frightened her. She dropped her bundle of twigs and ran as if for her life."

"There were no animal prints?"

"None."

"How about other prints? Indian?"

"Nothing."

"Then what do you think—"

The older man shrugged. "Maybe she heard something that scared her. Or saw something. I don't know. But I could see where she dropped her wood and tried to scramble up the slope. The spot is mostly mud, wet and slippery. She lost her footing, slipped, and tumbled down the bank."

"And hit her head on the way down."

Jeremiah stared at Parker for a moment, his forehead furrowed. "That's the other strange thing. There are no outcroppings of rock. She fell maybe fifteen feet. But there was no place that I could find where she could have hit her temple." He shook his head slowly.

"Do you think someone else was there? That someone caused the fall?"

"Worse. The grass at the top of the bank was crushed."

"You mean someone had been there waiting for her."

"Yes. And whoever it was struck her with such force—at the place where she's wounded—that she fell down the bank to the water's edge. Her body twisted. She landed facedown near the water and was left to bleed to death or die of exposure."

"You're right. It doesn't make sense. What threat could Callie St. Clair possibly hold? She's barely more than a child."

"She was left to die," Jeremiah concluded solemnly. "Someone wanted her dead."

Neither man spoke for some time, then Parker looked at his friend. "But do we tell Juliana?"

Jeremiah shrugged. "We have no proof." He thought for a moment. "What good would it do to tell her now?"

"I'll wait until the girl can speak. See what she remembers."

The old trapper looked weary and he prepared to take his leave. "One thing we haven't talked about, my friend—"

"What's that?"

"She may still be in danger."

Parker cocked his head. "She heard or saw something she shouldn't have?"

"That's what I'm thinking."

"Someone meant to make sure she would never tell."

The older man nodded again, his eyes looking darker than usual. He stood, brushing off his fringed leggings. "We need to keep a close eye on the girl and her sister. They may both be in danger."

"You'll help me?"

"Of course."

The old trapper slipped into the darkness of the night, and Parker James watched him head toward his wagon. He wondered if he should take anyone else into his confidence. As Juliana's future husband, Matthias Graves was the obvious choice. He had pledged his protection to the young women. But as Parker considered telling him of Jeremiah's suspicions, he knew he didn't trust the man. No. For now he would keep his suspicions to himself. He would make sure Callie and Juliana St. Clair were carefully and constantly watched.

He turned out the lantern and settled into a restless sleep.

Ten

~~~

During the next three days, Sun rode with Callie in the back of Juliana's wagon. She cared for the young woman without tiring, tenderly wiping the dust from Callie's brow, cleaning her wound, and holding a cup of water to her dry lips.

Juliana was touched by the concern of the other travelers. Even some of the old bullwhackers stopped by at the nooning or during the night fire to check on her sister's progress. Parker James looked in on Callie at least twice a day, sometimes riding near them on the Appaloosa, other times dropping by their tent at night. He spoke more to Sun than he did to Juliana, who was unaccountably saddened that he seemed more distant than ever. Matthias was especially attentive, stopping by more often than anyone else to ask after Callie's recovery.

Gradually Callie regained some of her strength, and by the fourth day was spending more time awake than asleep. She complained of head pain and spoke little, preferring to lie with her eyes closed and listen to Sun's voice.

Because the terrain was flat and the oxen still fresh, Juliana spent the first few days of Callie's illness riding on the wagon bench instead of walking beside the team. She enjoyed listening to Callie's murmured questions followed by Sun's soft laughter, a tale from her childhood, or a song that reminded Juliana of the rushing prairie winds.

By supper the third night, Callie sat against propped pillows and ate her first meal. She smiled weakly at Juliana when served her stew. "Not as good as mine," she said, taking a bite of biscuit.

"Certainly not as hard," Juliana joked, relieved to see Callie's spunk returning.

Later that night, Juliana asked if Callie remembered anything from her fall.

Callie looked thoughtful. "No," she finally said, looking puzzled. "Nothing." Then she sighed. "It's strange, I suppose, but even though you've told me I had gone for firewood, I remember nothing of that either. I remember our first day in the wagon—" she grinned, "the way you drove our team to get a better place in line. But I don't remember anything after that. I wish I could."

"It's probably just as well, Cal. Don't worry about it."

As Callie continued to recover, Sun remained with them, sometimes riding in the back of the wagon with Callie, sometimes sitting beside Juliana on the driver's seat.

The weather remained brisk and sunny. Each day the morning sun gleamed on the dried tall grasses of the prairie. By noon the breezes swept across the flat land, rippling the grasses into golden waves. In the evening, when the western sun melted into the horizon, the grasses faded from orange to lavender to pale gray hues. Even when dust covered Juliana's face and the sun glared into her eyes, the look of the changing autumn prairie day after day lifted her weariness.

Juliana thought about her easel and paints packed away in the back of the wagon. So far she had been too busy and too tired to sketch or paint at the day's end. But as she sat behind the oxen for hours on end, popping the whip and calling out commands, she memorized the colors of the prairie, the play of dark and light against the ever-changing skies. She tucked the images away to reproduce on canvas someday.

The train now traveled southwesterly in double lines. Each day Jeremiah pulled his wagon next to Juliana's. She was glad for the company, and Sun must be pleased to have her husband nearby. Juliana gave it no further thought than that.

Within the first week on the trail, the train crossed the tributaries of the Osage River. The banks were shallow and sandy. The wagon had tipped and rattled, lifted in the current, then settled onto sandbars and river rock. But never once did Juliana feel she did not have control of the team or the rig. The crossings had gone much better than she had expected.

A week after leaving Westport, the company camped at Council Grove, then forded the Neosho the following day. A few nights later, while camping at Diamond Spring, the teamsters began to talk of the Cottonwood crossing. Juliana heard someone say it was the most treacherous on the trail. Someone else said that was nonsense, they had seen worse. Juliana decided not to worry about it until she saw it firsthand.

On the morning before they reached the Cottonwood, Sun sat with Juliana on the driver's bench. Each morning since Callie's accident, not only did they ride instead of walking, Juliana also made sure that she maneuvered her rig near the caravan's lead wagon. Here the dust did not rise as thick. She could take a deep breath without coughing. By now the oxen needed little direction from Juliana, so she settled back enjoying the sun on her shoulders and the breeze in her hair.

"Sun," she began, looking across the bench at the woman who had become so dear, "tell me about your childhood. I've heard you tell Callie stories that must have come from your tribe. I'd like to hear more."

Callie moved forward from the wagon bed to join them behind the bench. She leaned against the opening of the wagon's canvas cover. Her face was still drawn from her ordeal. Around the angry gash at her temple the bruise had faded from purple to yellow-brown. But her skin was no longer pale. Now that she felt like sitting, she spent a few hours each day leaning against the canvas cover, looking out at the prairie. Her nose and cheeks had reddened in the sun, something she never would have allowed at home.

The Indian woman turned toward Juliana, her face solemn. "I would like to tell you. But it is not always a pleasant story."

"If you would rather not—," Juliana began.

But Sun reached over and touched her hand. "No. I would like for you to hear." She looked north across the grasslands, her light eyes seeming to mist. For a long time she was silent. Juliana thought she might have changed her mind about the telling.

Then Sun's gaze cleared and she looked back to Juliana. "I am Mandan," she said. "My people were from the headwaters of the Missouri River."

"You said 'were.' " Juliana's voice was gentle.

Sun nodded, her raven-colored braid catching the sun. "Most of my people were killed by a sickness—smallpox—brought by trappers who came to our village by boat. We had no medicines to fight such powerful sickness. Thousands of my people died. Today, in my father's tribe, not even one hundred remain."

"What happened to your family?" Callie asked, leaning closer.

"They are dead."

"I'm sorry." Juliana understood something of what Sun must feel, her family gone, thousands of miles from home.

"Did you get sick?" Callie leaned closer to Sun, looking up at her.

"No. I had left my people by then."

They rode along without speaking for a time, the wagon wheels' metal frames creaking with each turn over the sand and trampled-grass trail. The oxen plodded steadily forward, bawling and snorting from time to time. The sun rose higher in the sky. Behind Juliana's rig dust billowed, nearly obscuring the long parade of Conestogas, farm wagons, and dearborns. In the distance, off to the northwest, the *remuda* could be seen surrounded by cattlehands on horseback. Now and then the muleskinners' cursing or traders' shouting joined the concert of jangling harnesses and popping whips.

Juliana glanced back to Sun. "You left your people to marry Jeremiah."

For the first time since she began speaking of her past, Sun smiled. "Yes. Miah and I left many summers before the sickness took my people."

"Tell me how you met Jeremiah."

Again Sun smiled. "I was a girl of thirteen summers the first time I saw him. He and his friend Jedediah rode into our camp. Many fur trappers visited the Mandan. It was said they appreciated our courtesy and dignity of manner." She looked at Juliana, her light eyes laughing. "But I think it was because of our eyes. Only Mandans have blue eyes. Those who have not seen us before find us curious."

They rode along comfortably for a few minutes.

"Then what happened?" Callie was sounding more like her old self.

"Miah and Jed visited our village many times. Each time I saw Miah I loved him more." She rolled her eyes heavenward. "Oh, what beauty in a man! But I was only thirteen summers, then fourteen, then fifteen. It was a childish love—not that of a woman. Not then.

"Each time Miah came to our village I watched to see if he noticed me. I was the chief's daughter. Oh, how vain I was then! Just for him I dressed in my softest, whitest doeskin dresses, those usually saved only for ceremonies. I brushed my hair until it gleamed. My grandmother fashioned beaded leggings for me to wear over my moccasins. I stood tall before him." She laughed lightly and cut her eyes toward the neighboring wagon where her husband rode with eyes facing forward.

"But he never let on that he noticed. He never spoke to me the words I dreamed he would say. Miah talked to my father and my brothers for hours on end about hunting, fishing, and trapping. During those years he stayed in our village for weeks during the winters, but never once did he do more than just look at me with his dark eyes."

"How could you stand it?" asked Callie. "He must have said *something* to you."

"He did not. I do not think he would have. But something happened to make him think about me."

"Think what?" Callie was caught up in the story. It did Juliana's heart good to hear her sister's voice—and spirit—returning to normal.

"Be patient, little one." Sun turned and patted Callie's cheek. "I am getting there." Then she looked again to Jeremiah.

Juliana could see her deep love for her husband in her face. She remembered when she had first seen the couple on the Missouri riverboat. The first thing she had noticed was their unspoken love for each other, a bond that went beyond words. She had wondered then, and now she thought of it again, would she ever know a love like that of Sun and Jeremiah? Would there ever be someone for her to share such a deep and intimate love? Without bidding, the image of Parker James filled her mind.

Then Sun began to speak again. "By my sixteenth summer,

my father decided it was time for me to marry. I protested. In our village there were many more women than men. So every Mandan brave of marrying age took many wives. My father found a suitable husband for me, a man who already had four wives. He was old and ugly. I told my father I would not marry him."

Callie broke in. "That's what happened to me. My uncle tried to make me marry someone against my will. He was old. And I refused."

Sun turned to her again. "That is why you ran away?"

"How did you know?" Juliana asked, surprised.

"I could tell the first time I spoke with you on the riverboat. I knew—maybe I sensed—that you were running away from something." She was silent a moment. "Perhaps it is because I had been in the same place myself once."

"You ran away?" Callie's voice reflected her astonishment.

Sun nodded. "I did. But I did not get far." She laughed lightly. "I did not use my head. Only my heart. I tried to outsmart the best trackers in the village—my brothers. It did not take them long. They found me. They brought me kicking and yelling back to my father's house."

Callie laughed. "Please tell us more."

Juliana joined in, urging Sun to go on.

"We will have sixty days, and many hours, to tell our stories," Sun said with a smile. "There is no hurry." Her light eyes swept the horizon, then back to Juliana and Callie. "Now it is time for me to hear your story."

As Juliana drove the oxen, and the wagon rattled over rockier terrain, Callie began telling about their life at Stonehaven.

The hours passed pleasantly. Sun told them she had been traveling all of her married life. Finally, though, she and Miah

134

were heading for New Mexico to live in a cabin Jeremiah had built years before. Jeremiah's heart—and hers—was set on settling down in the *Sangre de Cristo* mountains. They planned to spend the rest of their lives in the most beautiful mountain valley they had seen in all their travels.

"*Sangre de Cristo?*" Juliana asked. The name was haunting.

"The blood of Christ," Sun translated. "It is Spanish."

Their conversation turned to practical matters such as cooking and sewing. She freely gave advice to Juliana and Callie as they peppered her with questions from how to prepare for the coming prairie storms to how to find wild onions on the trail.

Just before the nooning, Captain James rode up on the Appaloosa. "Ladies," he said, touching his hat, and reining the horse into step with their wagon.

Juliana noticed the affection in his face as his gaze met Sun's. She glanced at Sun. The same expression filled her eyes.

During the week since Callie's accident, she had seen Parker only from a distance. This was the first time he had spoken directly to her. Except for the brief look he gave Sun, his manner was brusque and businesslike.

"We'll be crossing the Cottonwood in about an hour. We'll wait until we get to the other side before stopping for dinner."

Juliana nodded.

"You've picked the wrong day to race to the head of the train," he continued.

Juliana flushed at his critical tone. "Why do you say that?"

"You'll be one of the first to cross the river."

"I've handled the crossings so far, Captain."

He laughed sarcastically. "Those were mere puddles, Miss St. Clair, compared to what's ahead."

She stared at him without speaking.

"It might be better to let some of the others go first. You can see how they handle their rigs." He paused. "Or better yet, I'll have one of my drivers take your outfit across."

"You'll do no such thing, Captain." Juliana popped the whip at a balky ox, then looked back to Parker. "I am perfectly capable of driving this rig across." She hesitated a moment. "And I'll keep my place in line."

Juliana stared straight ahead at the backends of the beasts, thinking the sight was far better than his angry face.

Parker said nothing more, then turned his horse toward the wagon next in line. Juliana glanced at Sun. "The man's a grizzly," she said.

Sun laughed softly. "That he is. But he can also be a grizzly cub."

"You know him well, don't you?"

"Yes. We have been friends for a long time."

"Tell me about him."

Sun's eyes were soft. "What is it you are asking?"

"Why is he the way he is?"

Sun fixed her eyes on something distant, and for several minutes did not answer. Finally she turned again toward Juliana, her expression kind, "My people had a saying, 'Wise is the man whose discovery comes from within.' Someday when your heart and his are ready, Parker James will tell you himself why he is the way he is. It should come from no one else."

When my heart is ready? What did Sun mean? Juliana cut her eyes to her friend. But Sun said no more. She just kept looking forward as if watching for the crossing.

They rode in silence and Juliana pondered Sun's words, wondering why her pulse quickened at the thought of the man she found so cantankerous.

In a short time, a ribbon of cottonwoods and willows could be seen in the distance, marking the presence of Cottonwood Crossing. As they drew closer, Juliana could see the river at the bottom of a deep ravine. The river was wider than any they had crossed, and it swirled along its course in a kaleidoscope of aquamarine, green, and muddy brown.

The captain halted the train and, standing at the ravine's edge, gave curt instructions. Most of the traders and muleskinners had crossed the Cottonwood before and knew the procedure, but for those who had not he was specific in his directions.

"We'll tie a line onto the back of each wagon," he said, "giving you better braking as you head into the ravine. You will halt at the river's edge. A team of oxen will be in place on the west side of the river—to be tethered to your rig. That will give your team greater strength and stability as you drive them into the water."

He glanced out at the river, then back to the teamsters. "This river's deceptive. It looks tame, but it isn't. There are sandbars in the channel that can create strong backflows—upsetting your team or your wagon if you aren't careful. And as most of you know, this river's known for its quicksand. If an ox doesn't feel the ground beneath it, it'll panic and bolt. Swimming is one thing to oxen, stepping into mud with no bottom is another.

"Some of my men and I will be out on that sandbar." Parker pointed to the river's center. "If you get into trouble, we'll get to you as soon as we can."

As he went on laying out the details of the crossing, Juliana began to wonder if she had spoken too quickly about taking the rig across herself. Then she looked at Parker's face as he continued speaking to the group. She remembered his biting words the first day they met, how he had looked at her palm and declared her too soft for the journey. As she listened to his final instructions, Juliana looked down and examined her hands. Her fingernails were broken and dirty. Calluses, hard as rocks, covered her palms. She smiled to herself, feeling a sense of pride as she looked at them.

No, Juliana decided. She couldn't back down. She had to drive her rig across. She felt the noonday sun beating strong on her shoulders and, lifting her face toward the river, decided nothing would stop her from getting to the other side sitting just where she sat right now.

The driver of the lead wagon moved his outfit into place. As the brake line was fastened to the rear of his wagon, Juliana popped the whip above her team's backs, and moved them into line behind the lead.

She took a deep breath and glanced back at her sister.

Callie, still leaning from the canvas opening at the wagon's bow, grinned at Juliana, her eyes merry with excitement.

Beside her on the wagon bench, Sun gazed at the river in silence. Juliana figured she was praying.

Eleven

The teamsters stood watching at the ravine's edge as Juliana, with Sun Jones at her side and Callie looking through the cover, drove her wagon down the steep, sandy incline. Even with the hold back rope, Juliana felt the team slide and skid as they fought to keep their footing in the loose soil. She shouted to them above the sounds of the creaking wagon, keeping her voice calm as they bellowed and moaned in fright.

She halted the rig at the riverbank, keeping the oxen quiet while her lead yoke was tethered to the eight yoke on the other side of the river. In the back of the wagon, Juliana could hear the racket of squawking chickens whose crates had been unstrapped and moved inside.

Parker, atop the Appaloosa, waited at midstream where the current seemed to ebb and a sandbar arched toward the surface. He had left some of his drivers standing at the east bank to see that the wagons were properly prepared and that the teamsters understood what to do. Two of his men sat astride their horses near him, waiting to ride out and help lead each team across.

Juliana waited for the signal, her heart pounding. She held the whip poised in her hand.

At the signal, she popped the whip and, half-standing, shouted encouragement to the beasts. She felt the spray of the water as the team plunged forward.

She kept her eyes on the backs of the oxen, their gray-white coats now shining wet in the sun. The beasts' stocky legs were beginning to lose the feel of the river bottom, and with snouts in the air, and loud bawls of protest, they swam, nervous and skittish. Underneath, their hooves churned up silt and mud, hiding from view what could be seen of the river bottom. The wagon rocked, the upset animals and the swift power of the current playing with it like a toy.

Juliana shouted again to the oxen, popping and snapping the whip above them. Across the water Parker waited, his gaze fixed on the wagon. The Appaloosa moved nervously in the current, fighting to keep its footing on the sandbar.

The wagon swayed and Juliana could feel it beginning to float. By now the lead oxen were nearly midstream to the sandbar. She had been warned that the feel of footing, then its immediate loss, might confuse the animals, make them even more giddy.

Juliana took a deep breath as she again cracked the whip, urging the oxen through the muddy waters. The current suddenly seemed rougher and the wagon swayed and dipped. Though the tether ropes held, their belongings shifted and slid in back, tipping the wagon even further.

The oxen were mostly over the bar and began to fight the water as they again lost their footing on the other side. The wagon evened out as it crossed the bar, though it still listed dangerously to the downstream side as it began to float again.

Team and rig began to move faster downstream, the sweep of it harder now. The upstream lead ox went under and the one yoked to it fought for an instant then slipped under with its partner. The rest of the oxen snorted and bawled as they felt themselves being sucked into the water.

Parker and his men tried to reach the rig, but it floated and tipped, moving swiftly downstream. Parker shouted to the teamsters on the far bank to goad the tethered team. "Pull the rope tighter—straighten it up!" He shouted. "That's the only way she'll pull out."

But the tether was still too slack.

Juliana stood. She began to whip the beasts, urging them on with shouts and blows to their bony backs. She didn't think about the blood drawn by the whip. She could only think about getting across.

The lead ox found its footing, and with its nose in the air, noisily snorted water and then began to swim. The team calmed. Stunned and worn, they began to move clumsily toward the western bank. Within minutes they had reached the other side.

Juliana popped the whip again. The tired team kept pulling, their feet unsure as they climbed the steep bank with its slippery mud, but the wagon finally pulled out of the water and up to solid, flat grassland.

⌒⌒

Parker turned to watch Juliana drive her rig up the west bank. That he had doubted her courage to get to New Mexico shamed him. He had never seen anything—anyone—quite so magnificent.

He would never forget the look of her as she stood, sun gleaming on her hair, determination in her face, as she whipped the oxen across the river. Even when the wagon tipped, she had not lost control. Her eyes had remained fierce in their purpose. And as she pulled by him, he had also seen in her expression a look of triumph.

He turned back to those still waiting to cross. One by one

they entered the water, and the big Conestogas, the farm wagons, the dearborns, forded the river. It was a colorful sight. The bull-whackers and muleskinners cursed and yelled, shaking their fists at each other and their beasts, charging and splashing through the river, each trying to put on a better show than the last.

The final rigs in line on the river's east side were the three Conestogas belonging to Matthias Graves.

First, Matt drove his rig into the water. The crossing went smoothly, and Juliana nodded pleasantly when Matt looked up and waved as his rig pulled out of the river.

Then followed thin and pale Seth Johnson, seated primly on the bench, never lifting his whip against his team.

The last wagon to plunge into the water was driven by the gangly man known by now throughout the wagon company as Hoss.

Hoss seemed to have control as his team entered the water. Then, as they neared the sandbar where Parker still sat atop the Appaloosa, the wagon tipped, causing a shift in the wagon's cargo. The rig listed precariously to its right.

There was a resounding snap as the tether broke that had been attached to the team on the opposite bank. The oxen struggled briefly to right themselves, but the angle and weight of the sodden yokes threatened to drag them under.

The wagon tipped further, now heading rapidly downstream. It turned, creaking and groaning, into the current.

Parker kicked the Appaloosa into action. He reined the horse toward the rig. At the same time, Hoss dove into the water, coming up near the lead yoke. He reached for the ox nearest him, holding the animal's neck while loosening the yoke.

By now Parker was beside him. Hoss worked with the team, making sure each was loosened from the yoke just enough to get their noses above water.

"Took you long enough to get here," Hoss muttered, his face showing no emotion as he greeted his friend. "A person could drown by the time you decided to mount a rescue."

Parker figured Cookingham had staged the accident to give them time to talk without being overheard. His friend was too smart to let a shift in cargo take his rig under. Parker just hoped no one else would wonder about a bullwhacker who would allow such a thing.

"This was certainly elaborate—are you sure it's worth it?" Parker kept the Appaloosa swimming as he bent down, trying to get hold of the lead yoke. "If you lose this cargo, you'll win no popularity contest with your boss."

"It's ammunition, friend." He didn't look at Parker. Anyone watching would have seen only the concerns of water and beasts on Cookingham's lean face. "The cargo you're saving is ammo."

Parker kept his face expressionless.

"We need to talk," Cookingham went on as he worked. "Tonight."

"There's a stone corral not far from where we'll camp. Meet me there at midnight."

Cookingham nodded slightly, and together they untangled the oxen and led them from the water, pulling the heavy Conestoga behind.

The two men climbed the bank toward the waiting company. Parker noticed that Matthias Graves stared at him intently, his face grim.

&c

At midnight, Parker leaned against a pile of crumbling sandstone at the stone corral. The night was frigid. Even in the pale light of a crescent moon he could see his breath.

143

Hearing the crunch of footsteps on the gravel in a nearby draw, he listened in silence until he saw the unmistakable figure of Cookingham loping toward him.

"Friend!" Cookingham grabbed Parker's shoulder in greeting, a wide grin lighting his face.

Parker nodded. Since Bennett joined the train, the only time they had spoken was in the water at the crossing. It would be good to talk openly.

They spoke for a few minutes about the route and the company. Then Parker peered through the darkness at Cookingham. "Why didn't you tell me you'd be joining on as a bullwhacker?"

"I didn't know it myself when we talked in Westport."

"What happened?"

"Matthias Graves happened." One side of Cookingham's lip curved down.

"What about him?"

"I'm not certain, but I think he's the 'heir apparent.' "

"Somehow I'm not surprised. Where'd you get your information?"

Cookingham's eyes were steady. He seemed to consider his answer. After a moment he said, shrugging slightly, "There's talk."

"Meaning you can't say."

"That's right."

"There must be an informant with the train—or you'd tell me."

Cookingham didn't answer.

Parker sighed and looked out into the darkness.

"You said your cargo's ammunition?"

Bennett nodded. "Two of the wagons are. The other—the one that Graves is driving—has guns."

"Three wagons full of guns and ammo won't win a war."

"They're planning on having more than three by the time we reach La Sal."

Parker raised an eyebrow. "Graves never mentioned others joining us."

"He's thinking that you might balk at his numbers."

"What do you mean?" Parker took a deep breath, worried that he could guess what Bennett was about to tell him.

Cookingham looked at him evenly. "An additional sixteen wagons will meet us along the Cimarron Cutoff."

"Do you know where?"

"No. He hasn't said. I'll let you know as soon as he does." Cookingham paused. "*If* he does."

Parker let a low whistle slide from his lips. "Sixteen wagons that will pull in with ours." He considered Bennett's words for a moment. "Filled with guns and ammo."

"And explosives."

Parker shook his head slowly. "That means he could take over the train. Is that his plan?"

"He hasn't spoken of it."

"What has he spoken of?"

"The Mojada. He has been in communication with them and their leader—Francisco de Oñate in Fort La Sal—since leaving Westport. He speaks of them constantly. He's agitated when he's out of touch with them for any length of time."

"How does he communicate? La Sal's at least six hundred miles from here."

"The messages have been left in prearranged drops; that way the couriers aren't seen by your scouts."

"And he leaves messages for them."

Cookingham nodded. "Sometimes the messages are written, other times the courier speaks to Graves."

"Have you been able to intercept any of the messages?"

"No. He never tells us ahead of time where the meeting place will be or where the courier will leave his message." Cookingham looked thoughtful. "It's important that we find out the details of his plan, and the messages are probably the only way we'll discover the truth."

"The truth." Parker paused, thinking. "Does Graves trust you?"

Cookingham sounded tentative. "I don't know. He's a changeable, volatile man. One minute he's a bloodthirsty madman who will stop at nothing to get his way. The next, he's erudite and charming, generous to a fault, someone you and I would have been friends with at West Point." He shook his head. "You never know what might trigger a change in him."

"But does he trust you?" Parker repeated.

"I don't think he trusts anyone." Cookingham leaned against the sandstone wall, looking up at the stars. Then his gaze once more met Parker's. "You guessed it right that day back at Westport. Our Graves fits your description of the 'heir apparent' to a tee. He's passionate about New Mexico. He's related to the powerful Oñate family, and he's hungry for power—local power. But he doesn't stop there. He wants to be connected to Washington. He's a U.S. citizen and he feels that will give him the backing of our government after the uprising."

"The uprising he's planning by supplying the Mojada with guns and ammunition."

"That's his plan."

Parker had to ask, "Has he said anything about any other plans?"

His friend cocked his head, raising one eyebrow. "What do you mean?"

"He told me he's planning to marry when he gets to La Sal."

Bennett looked skeptical. "I think he'll be a bit busy for that. Tell me more."

Parker recounted the events leading to Juliana St. Clair's joining the train—first the encounter with the young woman in his office, his refusal to allow her to join the train, then the visit from Matthias Graves imploring him to let his "intended" join the caravan.

Cookingham shook his head slowly. "I'm not saying it's unlikely that he's planning a wedding. He may be. But if he is, I would bet it's a cold and calculating move. Do you know who Miss St. Clair's uncle is?"

Parker was puzzled. "No."

"U.S. Senator Caleb Benedict."

Parker let out another low whistle. "He's one of the President's top advisers. She's connected to power in high places." He was quiet a moment. "I had no idea."

"Juliana St. Clair would be quite an asset for a man dead set on seeing his star rise in New Mexico."

Parker nodded slowly. "I wonder if she knows that."

"I don't know. I see them together—they look happy. It wouldn't surprise me if it is a love match, at least on her part." Then Bennett, watching his friend's face, stopped and squinted his eyes at him. "Wait a minute. Why the interest in Juliana St. Clair?"

Parker shrugged.

"You want to steer clear of her, my friend, if she's mixed up in all of this."

"You don't think she could be part of this." Parker's heart

sank. Cookingham surely was reaching too far.

"You asked me a minute ago if Graves trusts me. And I answered that he trusts no one. The same goes for me, my friend. With the exception of you, I trust no one on the train. Especially a woman who spends time in the company of Matthias Graves."

After a few more minutes discussing where they would next meet, Bennett Cookingham left for his tent.

Parker, still leaning against the sandstone wall, stared up into the night sky. He thought about his friend's words about Juliana St. Clair, the woman he knew he was beginning to love. How was she mixed up in this? How could she marry a man like Matthias Graves? Did she know about his plans for New Mexico? Was she, in fact, part of his grand scheme?

He thought about asking her, then quickly dismissed the idea. She might tell Graves of his interest, drawing attention to him and possibly endangering his mission. He decided he would watch. And wait. *And pray,* he thought grimly, *if only he knew Someone was listening. And cared.*

CHAPTER

Twelve

The days passed, fading one into another, as the wagon train wound its way across the prairie. There were more river fordings, but none as treacherous as those they had already passed. The wagons and *remuda* crossed two wide tributaries of the Arkansas without mishap, wagons floating and bobbing, cattle bawling and oxen snorting, bullwhackers shouting. They moved on past Pawnee Rock with its inscriptions by earlier travelers on the trail, and the lower crossing of the Arkansas.

Small, scraggly groups of Indians, mostly Kansa, Shawnee, and Osage, followed the train for days at a time, often camping just outside the caravan's night circle. Sometimes at night, the buffalo-robed braves with their beating drums and dancing chants drowned out the merry sounds of fiddles and harmonicas. But mostly they sat, watching the travelers with luminous dark eyes, the women and children silent and hungry-looking, the hawk-faced braves with their quiet anger.

Captain James had been right, and the teamsters gave the Indians small mirrors, bright beads, and buttons. At mealtime, food was shared. Other times, cornmeal, flour, and tobacco were handed out. But the trinkets and food did not change the hostile looks.

By now most of the teamsters walked beside their oxen, urging them onward with shouts and prods instead of whips. The beasts, heads down and more accepting of the yokes and endless toil, pulled their heavy burdens across the grasslands.

Here the winter-brown grasses were not as tall and the terrain not as flat. Pale sandstone hills appeared, breaking the monotony of the plains. Still there were no trees except the winter-bare cottonwoods and scrub willows marking the icy rivers and springs.

It was December now, and the train had been weeks on the road. More often than not it rained—frigid rain that usually turned to sleet before it was through. The sky hung close and low, the color of ashes. Winds beat against the travelers, incessant, biting winds that caused the skin to sting even through the heaviest clothing.

The trail was now muddy most days. But the teamsters kept moving westward, walking on through the ankle-deep slime, goading their teams as the animals slid and stumbled, bawling in protest.

By now the days held a monotony all their own: wagoneers stopping to grease the axles from tar buckets that swung beneath the wagons, or worse, to fix a broken axle or shoot a lame ox, all the time inching forward in the thin winter sun or freezing rain, one step at a time.

Early on, the wagoneers had driven past herds of buffalo. Now the mammoth animals could be seen in even greater abundance, covering the plains in brown, shifting shadows. The pounding of their hooves against the earth sounded like thunder, rolling, powerful, frightening.

Almost daily, Parker James and his men, the traders and the bullwhackers, hunted the beasts, sometimes for food, but most of the time for sport. It was a sight that would stay with Juliana St. Clair as long as she lived.

Bows and arrows were used because the bullwhackers said only cowards and fools relied on balls and powder.

"One rifle shot," one had explained to Juliana and Callie when they asked, "and them critters'll be halfway to Sunday before you can fire off another shot."

The pattern became the same. The men mounted and came upwind toward the herd, riding slow and easy. The humps of the beasts stuck up toward the gray skies, appearing like great rolling ocean waves to Juliana, who watched with Callie from the back of their wagon.

Though the first time Juliana watched she was quite a distance from the herd, she could hear the snorts of the bulls and almost feel them pawing the earth with their horns bent downward, their big eyes red and wary.

She saw Parker nod to the others as they drew closer to the herd. Then the horses sprang to full speed and moved in to become one with the massive, breathing shadow.

The herd stampeded to a clumsy gallop. The old bulls, seeming at first confused, were the last to move. But within seconds the herd seemed to become one large, angry beast, moving forward, horns low, ready to charge.

Juliana couldn't distinguish one rider from another, though now and then she thought she caught a glimpse of Parker, a flash of blue shirt and leather breeches atop the Appaloosa. She held her breath as she saw him ride side by side with a young cow. It seemed that the two animals moved nearly in tandem, rumps bobbing in rhythm with the nearby sea of cows and bulls and calves. The thundering beat of hooves drowned out all sounds except their own, but Juliana could see Parker's mouth open in a wild and joyous yell. He waved his hat in the air as he rode.

Then he took an arrow from its quiver and notched it to his

bow, pulled back, and let it go. The cow next to him went down. Parker didn't even slow the Appaloosa, but instead, rode wildly on until he'd downed another and another. By the time the hunt was done, three fat cows and four bulls had been killed.

From that night on there was fresh buffalo meat for the company. That first hunt, and the kills to come, would provide enough to last to Santa Fe. The buffaloes were skinned and butchered, and the meat that wasn't eaten was salted and packed away.

Around the night fires, the bullwhackers and traders began to tell tall tales of buffalo hunts, the death-defying feats each had performed to down the fiercest, meanest bulls on the plains.

More often now, Matthias Graves seated himself near Juliana at the night fires. Many nights, as the fiddlers and harmonicas played, Matt pulled her to her feet and danced, his handsome head tipped tenderly toward hers as they moved their feet to the music.

As the weeks wore on and they neared the halfway point of the trail, he became bolder in his intent. One night, as a full moon rose into a bright winter sky, Matthias asked Juliana to walk with him in the moonlight.

Juliana pulled her woolen cloak closer as they walked from the wagon camp up a small rise, then through thick brush toward a nearby spring. She shivered at the sounds of distant wolves howling and crying. Somewhere closer, perhaps in the topmost boughs of a barren black willow, the mournful sounds of a screech owl carried toward them on a biting breeze.

As they drew farther away from the camp, the sounds of the fiddle and someone singing *Way Down in Mexico* carried toward the couple.

Matthias took Juliana's hand as they walked, tucking it with his into the pocket of his greatcoat.

"Do you know the song they're singing?" he asked, looking down at her, his eyes warm.

"No, I haven't heard it before."

He explained that it was the marching song of General Kearny, who had taken New Mexico for the United States. "The last verse goes, 'Then we'll march back by and by, Yeo-ho, Yeo-ho. And kiss the gals we left to home, And never more we'll go and roam, 'way down in Mexico.'"

Matt laughed softly at the words. He touched Juliana's hair, then brushed a stray lock from her face. It was a tender gesture, somehow comforting, and Juliana smiled up at him.

Then he touched her face, gently lifted her chin, and bent to kiss her on the lips.

Juliana stepped back. "No, Matt. Please."

He cocked his head. The briefest shadow crossed his face, then his smile returned. Juliana wondered if she imagined his look of displeasure.

"I'm sorry." His apology sounded genuine. "It's just that here in the moonlight...you look so beautiful. Irresistible, I'm afraid." He shook his head slowly. "I'm sorry if I offended you. Please forgive me?"

Confused, Juliana didn't speak. This man had been a good friend throughout the trip. In recent weeks, Parker James had barely spoken to her. Sometimes she still caught him watching her. She had also noticed the troubled expression on his face. She had wondered if she was the cause, but quickly dismissed the thought. How could she be of any importance one way or the other? After all, they seldom spoke. And though her own heart beat wildly whenever he came near, she had no illusions that his might do the same.

But Matt, on the other hand, had been a perfect gentleman, helpful, attentive, always close at hand. Though he had never caused her heart to pound, she had grown to care for him.

Juliana took his hand. "I forgive you." She laughed softly. "I treasure your friendship, Matt." She paused. "I'm not ready for anything beyond that."

He was silent a moment. "Friendship? Juliana, I don't consider our relationship a casual friendship."

Juliana tilted her head, surprised at his sharp tone.

He went on. "I thought you were aware of my intentions from the beginning."

She shook her head. "What do you mean?"

He took a deep breath. "Don't you know how I feel about you?"

Juliana gazed at the handsome man in front of her. A look of affection had returned to his face.

Matt reached for her hand. His voice was husky as he again began to speak. "Juliana, I love you. I have loved you from the moment I stepped onto that Mississippi riverboat and saw you watching me." He sighed deeply. "I haven't wanted to speak too soon, but—" His voice broke and he looked away, swallowing, as if he were having a difficult time expressing himself, then looked back into her eyes. "Juliana, I want to marry you."

Juliana caught her breath. But before she could answer he brought her hand to his lips, gently kissed her fingertips, his dark eyes filled with warmth. "Don't give me an answer yet, darling," he said. "I know this comes as a shock. But please, promise me you'll think about it."

Her mind in turmoil, Juliana nodded.

Then, with her hand still tucked in his, they began to walk along the creek bed. Matt told her about the place he was born, Fort La Sal, and the large family—mother, father, aunts, uncles, and cousins—awaiting his return. In great detail, he described his home where she would live as his bride. It was staffed with servants. She would want for nothing, he said with pride. She would be surprised at her status in the local community.

He smiled and spoke with a deep and confident voice as they walked. "Juliana, I wish I had the words to express how I feel about you." He sighed and looked up at the stars, looking nearly overcome with emotion. "I wish I could let you see into the future—into my future. There's a world that is waiting for us. For *us*, Juliana. I can't tell you any more now—but there is change coming to New Mexico. And together, you and I can be at the forefront of that change. We will serve our country. For generations people will remember us for what we've done."

Juliana tried to follow his rush of words, his rush of emotion. "Matt, I don't understand —"

He laughed quietly, shushing her. "Oh, my darling, there will be all the time in the world for you to understand—someday soon. But for now just consider saying yes. Just think about joining me—in marriage—to build a future that will live on beyond our years."

Juliana laughed lightly. His excitement was almost contagious. "I promise I'll think about it, Matt." She withdrew her hand from his, and he took her arm as they headed back to camp.

That night as she shivered on her cot under a pile of blankets, Juliana thought about Matt Graves.

Matt's proposal could take much of the uncertainty from her future. He offered her the security of a home in the place of her childhood dreams, New Mexico. She and Callie would not have to worry about what they would do, where they would live, once they arrived at their destination.

A large adobe house filled with servants. She thought of Stonehaven and how she missed it. It would be nice to have the comforts of a beautiful and spacious home again, to be part of the local society, not to have to worry about buying her own land, building a small house for herself and Callie, and farming the land. She sighed, smiling to herself as she shivered under her blankets. The adobe Matt described sounded warm and pleasant; she would never be cold again.

She thought about his talk of the future. What could he have meant? The political climate in New Mexico, she thought, was calm. The U.S. takeover had been peaceful.

What could he possibly mean, "build a future that will live beyond our years," or "for generations people will remember us for what we will have done"? The words puzzled her. What *will* he—or we—have done?

Was it connected somehow to the U.S. takeover in New Mexico? Maybe Matt was traveling there as an emissary for the president. Again she smiled to herself, this time at the irony. When she left Stonehaven and Uncle Caleb she had thought she would never again be part of the political world. And here she was, about to get into the thick of it—that is, if she said yes.

If she said yes. She dwelt on that thought. Juliana knew that she did not love Matt. At least not in the way she thought she would love the man she married. But she cared about him, and he treated her with affection and respect. Maybe their love would grow into the heart-pounding love she had always dreamed of.

Yes, that's probably how it happens, she decided, before drifting into a dreamless sleep.

༒

Later, not far from where Juliana and Matt had taken their moonlight walk, three men stood talking. The men—Matthias Graves, Seth Johnson, and the bullwhacker known as Hoss—

kept a lookout for the lone rider who would join them.

The men spoke in hushed tones, discussing the coming wagons. For the first time Matthias gave out details about the "armada." The drivers were military men, he said, as were the cattlehands that would be along to handle the group's *remuda.* "It will happen on the Cimarron Cutoff," he said, looking south-west.

"We're nearly there," Hoss commented, keeping his voice indifferent. "How much longer do you figure it will be?" He looked directly at Matthias Graves.

"That is what we're waiting to hear. As soon as the courier gets here." Graves stared back, his eyes glinting in the moonlight. "Any special reason you want to know?"

"Seems like an obvious question to me," said the pale Seth Johnson.

Graves laughed, lightening the mood. "I guess you boys want to know what you face in the days to come. Nothing wrong with that."

He leaned against a sandstone rock, crossing one boot over the other. "When the armada joins us," he said, "we will take control of the caravan. We will do it quietly. Believe me. I've waited for this moment, carefully planning every move. We do not want to alarm anyone—least of all James. So after my men join us, the day-to-day activities will continue just as they are. No one will be aware of anything different."

He looked thoughtful. "We will *allow,*" he smirked at the word, "the captain to operate in the same manner as always. He will be kept unaware that anything has changed."

"Does he know you've got other wagons joining up?" Hoss asked the obvious question.

"Not unless you've told him." Graves laughed at his joke, but his eyes remained hard, fixed on Hoss.

157

Hoss didn't speak.

"Shouldn't you tell him ahead of time?" Seth Johnson peered at Graves through the darkness. "I mean—the captain may feel threatened, put up his guard, if you don't."

Graves was silent as if considering his words. "There's no need. I think it will do him good to be caught off guard." His mouth twisted into a smile.

The sound of distant hooves carried through the quiet night.

Graves looked toward the sound. "This should be our man." He sighed and whispered, mostly to himself, "And now, *mis compadres*, we learn when our performance is to begin."

The man, dressed in black, moved swiftly and quietly toward them. He slid from his horse, greeted Matthias, and looked pointedly at the other two men.

"It is all right," Graves said. "They know why we are here."

The man acknowledged Johnson and Hoss, then went on to tell Graves the latest from the armada, which was being led by a man named Enrique. "They're twenty miles out," he said, "About a day's hard drive. You tell us where and when—and we'll be there, any time from tomorrow on."

Matthias considered the courier's words before answering. "Tell Enrique to follow us out of sight at least three full day's travel between the caravan and the armada. Under no circumstances is he to come closer." He paused. "The timing must be perfect. Not a moment too soon. Or too late."

"You'll leave word?" pressed the courier.

Matthias nodded and told him where.

Hoss, keeping a disinterested look on his face, listened attentively as Graves gave directions to the place. It was the first time that Graves had told the location before a message drop.

He knew he would have to plan his timing even more closely

than Matthias Graves planned his. He would need to get to the message after Graves delivered it and before the courier picked it up.

He would have to let Parker know what Graves had planned. The more detail Parker had, the less peril for him and the whole company. Hoss listened as Graves continued his conversation with the courier. After a few more minutes, the man mounted and rode to the northeast.

The winter moon was high when the men left to return to camp. As they walked, Graves fell in beside Hoss, matching his stride. He threw an arm across the thin man's shoulders.

"Something tells me you have great interest in the affairs of New Mexico."

Hoss didn't speak.

"You look half asleep, *mi compañero,* when we speak of things to come. But I see great intelligence in your eyes." Graves heartily patted Hoss's back. "A person's soul shows through the eyes, and I have an inordinate ability to read that soul." His voice held its usual arrogance as he spoke.

"I don't know what you mean." Hoss forced his voice into a dull monotone.

Graves stopped and turned toward Hoss. "I think you know perfectly well what I mean, friend." His lip curled up on one side. He slapped Hoss's back once more before disappearing into his tent.

Cookingham stood for a moment in the moonlight. A sudden chill caused him to shudder. He let out a deep breath and entered his own tent, closing the flap behind him.

Thirteen

The following morning, Juliana walked beside her team, calling out to the oxen and urging them with the goad from time to time. Sun Jones fell in beside her and Callie rested on her cot in the wagon. Though her wound had healed, Callie still tired easily and spent much of her time under the protection of the rig's canvas canopy.

The day had dawned clear, but it carried a heavy, windless feel.

"A storm is coming," Sun said, looking off to the northwest.

Juliana squinted in the same direction. "I don't see any clouds building."

Sun smiled. "We do not always see the clouds."

Usually Jeremiah Jones followed Juliana, but today Matthias Graves had pulled his wagon into line directly behind her. She was conscious of his watchful gaze, which she felt rather than saw.

"Sun," she finally said, "last night Matt asked me to marry him. She kept her voice low, not wanting to be overheard by Callie and Matt, especially by Matt.

Sun turned toward her, her light eyes piercing Juliana's. But she did not speak.

They continued to walk. The only sound was the jangling of the yoke chains and the occasional bellow or snort from an ox. Finally, Sun said, "Do you love him, Juliana?"

"I don't know. He says he loves me. He has told me about his home in Fort La Sal. He has family there. He makes the life we would have together sound full. Exciting."

"But do you love him?"

Juliana considered her friend's words. Without realizing it, she had been asking herself the same question. She shook her head slowly. "There's a lot about him that I am fond of—his charm, his intelligence, his concern for me—and for Callie." She smiled, remembering how often he had come to their rescue. "Maybe we have the kind of love that will grow with time. Many people do, you know."

Sun looked thoughtful, but said nothing.

Juliana continued. "I know this is sudden. Unplanned. But it would solve a lot of problems—" She popped the whip over the oxen's backs.

"And perhaps cause many more."

"Because I don't know him well?"

"Because of many other things, Juliana."

"Such as?"

Sun looked off to the north again, seeming to consider the sky and what it was bringing. She turned again to Juliana. "Have you asked God to guide you in this?"

Juliana was surprised. Many times she listened to Sun and Jeremiah talk to God about guiding them. They spoke to him simply and directly, as if he was a fellow traveler, someone whose judgment they trusted.

Though Juliana understood and even envied the couple's faith, it had never once occurred to her to seek God's will in *her* life.

"I've never thought that God cared much one way or the other about my decisions." She studied Sun's ageless face as the older woman replied.

"Ah. There you are wrong. He does care." Sun gazed at Juliana, her blue eyes unblinking. "He has only the most tender thoughts toward you."

"How do you know that?" Juliana sighed. "How can you be sure?"

"He says to us in his Word, the Bible, that he has loved us with an everlasting love. He says, 'I have called you by name, and you are mine.'" Sun's eyes filled with joy. "Can you imagine that?" She paused, then whispered, "Morning Sun." Again she looked toward the horizon and the quickly rising sun. "When I was a baby my father looked out at the awakening sun. He lifted me heavenward and declared that my name from that day on would be Morning Sun. My heavenly Father knew my name also. Juliana, he had known my name from time's beginning."

"Those are beautiful thoughts, Sun. But how do you know they're true?"

"The Bible is God's Word," she said simply. "God does not lie. And he never changes. What he said many summers ago is the same today."

She paused, and a change came over her face. "But there is no way for *me* to convince you that the words of our heavenly Father are true. That you must discover on your own."

They walked on without speaking. The sun, now higher in the winter sky, seemed warmer than usual, the air still. It had not rained for a week and the dust kicked high around the caravan. Juliana pushed a strand of hair from her eyes and looked northwest. Behind a distant cluster of sandstone hills, low storm clouds had begun to gather. The oxen bawled and she goaded them with her whip handle.

The wagons, now strung out in a single line, headed into rougher terrain. The yoke chains jangled as the beasts pulled their loads through the ruts and over rocky hills.

As they walked along, Juliana thought about Sun's words. "Tell me about your courtship with Jeremiah," she finally said. She wanted to know how God had been a part of their relationship.

Sun laughed and looked briefly skyward. "Ah, my story. Yes. I will tell you more of my story."

By now, Callie had clambered from the wagon and walked beside them. Juliana took her sister's hand, squeezing it briefly. Callie smiled. Juliana knew that she relished Sun's stories.

"Now, where did we leave off—?"

Callie jumped in. "You told us about how you ran away. Your brothers—the best trackers in the village—brought you back to your father's home."

Sun laughed softly at the memory. "Oh, yes. That was quite a time. My mother cut her hair. She said I had shamed my father's lodge. She said that no young woman in the village had ever dared to leave as I did. It simply was not done. It was not even thought of.

"You have to understand, in a Mandan village everything is done in a certain way. Natural order is the way of life. When children enter a lodge, they move around the inside in one direction only, circling the fire as if they are moons to the earth. They sit only when told to sit. They eat the food that is given to them whether or not it tastes good, whether or not they are hungry.

"Every ceremony has meaning—whether celebrating the harvest of maize and squash or the hunting and dressing of buffalo.

In my father's village, the marriage ceremony was the celebration of coming life. Ceremonies are sacred and, if followed correctly, bring great blessings to the village.

"Not to do so was thought to bring hunger or starvation, weakness and defeat to our braves.

"So for me to run away was a dangerous action—not just for me but, as everyone knew, for the entire village. When I returned, I was rejected by those who had been my friends. Even my brothers and sisters did not speak to me. I was made to stay in my father's lodge all winter while he decided what to do with me. Even the man who had bargained with my father for me turned his back, afraid for the disaster that might strike him if I were to live in his lodge."

Callie matched Sun's stride and fell in beside her. "Jeremiah must have come back to your village. But how did he get in to see you?"

"What I had done caused many tongues to wag. Even tongues outside my village. Word got to Jeremiah and his friend Jed where they were trapping beaver. They left their winter camp and walked with their horses through many valleys to my father's village.

"They arrived in a sudden and terrible snowstorm." Sun's eyes were merry. "Of course, that meant they could not leave until the snow melted. They had time to speak to my father about many things."

"Including you," Callie added.

"Yes. They spoke of me. Miah told my father that he wished to marry me."

"What did your father say?"

"At first he said no. But Jeremiah is not one to give in easily. He knew that some things speak with greater power than words. First he offered my father some of his finest beaver pelts. My

164

father was unbending. So Miah offered him the choicest pelt—that from a white beaver. My father considered Miah's proposal more carefully, but still he said no."

"What changed his mind?" Callie still walked beside Sun. Juliana had lagged a few steps behind to goad a stubborn ox into line.

"Miah offered him twenty-five of the finest ponies in the big valley. He described them to my father. They were tall and strong, their coats the color of fire, their eyes holding the flash of lightning. They were unlike any ponies belonging to other tribes, Mandan or not."

Sun glanced at the wagon in front of them. Jeremiah seemed to sense her gaze. His eyes met Sun's. He nodded slightly and smiled.

Sun laughed softly. "My father said he would give me in marriage to Jeremiah Jones for such a gift. It seemed to him I had brought great blessing to our village after all."

"Why do you laugh?" Callie had noticed the exchange.

"Because he had no such horses."

Juliana laughed with her. "So, in the dead of winter Jeremiah had to go out into the valley and find these glorious horses?"

Sun nodded. "Yes. That is what he had to do."

Callie shook her head slowly, not seeing the humor. "But what did you do then? Did you know that any of this...bargaining, was going on?"

"Oh, yes. It was the talk of the village. By then my father was allowing others to visit me in his lodge—and now they wanted to come. My cousins told me about Miah's offer. No other bride had ever brought such a price. I was becoming someone of, how shall I say it...importance?"

Juliana prodded the oxen. "You never knew Jeremiah loved you until then?"

165

"No. I had never dared to hope he loved me as I did him."

A soft wind had begun to blow. It lifted Juliana's hair from her face. "When did you know that you loved him?

"I loved him from the first time I saw him. But I did not know it until later. Until later when I looked back. Then I knew that I had loved him from the first day he came to our village."

"How did Jeremiah find the horses?" Callie was persistent.

"As soon as my father agreed to the wedding gift, Miah left with Jed Smith to round up the horses. They were gone for all of the winter. People in the village began to whisper among themselves that Jeremiah Jones would never come back for me. I died a thousand deaths that winter, hoping above all other hope that Miah would return to me."

"And he did," Callie said.

"Oh, yes. He did. It was on a fine morning eighteen summers ago." Sun again looked northward across the dried prairie grasses toward the place where the Mandan once lived. "He and Jed rode to my father's lodge and halted the horses—not twenty-five, but twenty-seven beautiful ponies—at our door. In a flurry of activity, the villagers gathered close by, waiting to see whether my father would accept them."

"And he did," Callie said again.

Sun nodded. "He could not seem too pleased, you understand. He looked in the animal's mouths, patted them and grunted to himself, muttering from time to time that they were not the magnificent animals that Miah had promised. The whole village waited to see what would happen." Her eyes were soft with the memory. "At last he looked at Jeremiah Jones and nodded, his face solemn. Then he looked at me and smiled. It was the only time I remember my father smiling."

Then Sun went on to describe the wedding ceremony held in her village. It was a great celebration, she told them. Her father had gained great wealth and status. The wedding feast lasted a week.

"Then Miah and I left with Jed Smith. We traveled into the mountains of the West, hunting buffalo and trapping beaver. It was a peaceful time."

"You asked me about seeking God's will. You didn't know God then, did you?" The lead oxen balked as they headed into a ravine. Now walking slightly ahead of Sun and Callie, Juliana pulled hard on the lead. The animal bawled and snorted then followed the lead to the left.

Sun caught up with Juliana and walked beside her. "You are right, I did not know God then. But there was something in Jedediah Smith that was different. He was never without a small brown book that he read as soon as it was light in the mornings—sometimes while riding on his horse. And he always read it the last thing at night by the firelight before falling asleep. Miah was used to it, but I watched with curiosity as Jed Smith looked to the heavens with his eyes wide open and spoke to Someone we could not see.

"Sometimes by the night cookfire, Miah and I would ask Jed about his God. Sometimes we talked through the dark hours. He told us of God's love. I had never heard of such a god. The Mandan worshipped many gods, but none of them represented such a thing as love. At first I thought Jedediah's God was just one that the Mandans had left out or did not know about. Then one day Jed told us how his God sent his only Son to earth as a sacrifice for all the people on earth—the white man, the Mandan, the Sioux, the Comanche.

"He told how this Son, Jesus, had his hands and feet pierced and fastened to pieces of wood. Then the wood was hammered into the ground until it stood like a tree. Jesus hung there until he died.

"I wept when I heard the story. How could Someone love

anyone else that much? To give the life of your child to save another. To send your child to suffer and die. Jedediah said that God would have done such a thing if only to save one person. I kept thinking, What if I was that one person? How could God love me enough to let his Son be killed for me?

"I found it amazing that God knew me. But Jedediah said that God knew me even before I was born. That he had seen my face and knew my name when he gave his Son as a sacrifice for me.

"Jedediah stayed with Miah and me for many months. Even after he left us, we spent hours speaking of Jed's God and Jesus, his Son."

For several minutes no one spoke. To the northwest, storm clouds had begun to build, just as Sun had said they would. The breeze was kicking into a brisk, cool wind.

"I've heard you speak to God as your friend," Juliana said. "How did that happen?"

Sun did not answer right away but squinted her eyes straight ahead as if thinking. "At first, Miah and I were not ready to give our lives to God. Neither one of us doubted this God's existence—we had seen him in the life of our friend, Jedediah Smith. We knew God was real. But for both of us—though we arrived at our conclusion separately—the idea of sacrifice was unthinkable.

"God sacrificed his Son. If he required a similar sacrifice from me, could I do it? What if he asked me to sacrifice the one I loved, could I do it? I did not think so. And I did not want to find out. I could not risk it."

"But what changed your mind?" Juliana persisted. Suddenly this was terribly important to her.

"Jed Smith's death."

"Oh, no." Callie's voice caught. "Your friend died?"

"It was three years later. He was on the Cimarron Cutoff, going after water for his friends, when he was ambushed by the Comanche."

"And killed," Callie whispered.

"Yes. Killed."

"Didn't that make you angry with God?" asked Juliana. "Your friend had been killed. How could a loving God let that happen?"

"At first it did. Especially for Miah. He was angry. He swore he would take revenge on the Comanche in his friend's name. He fell into a deep and long sadness. I, too, felt that just as I was beginning to find my way to a God of love, I had instead found a God who did not care about his child."

"But something made you change your mind." Callie had caught up with them and now walked between Juliana and Sun.

"The trappers traveling with Jed later found his Holy Bible, that same brown book, being traded by the Mojadas in Santa Fe. They had traded some Comanche for it somewhere on the Cimmaron. In it was a letter with instructions that the Bible and the letter were to be brought to us if anything happened to him.

"One of the trappers found us at the Bear Lake rendezvous the next year. We, of course, had already heard about Jed's death. We had also heard that his body was never found. We figured his Bible and journals would also never be found."

Sun went on to tell of the comfort she had felt holding Jed's Bible and journals in her hands. "I did not know how to read then, but Miah read Jedediah's words to me. It was as if our friend had come back from the dead to speak to us. Long after the rendezvous at Bear Lake, we read from his journals and his Holy Bible by the light of our night fire.

"Something began to change in me. One night Miah read words of the Resurrection. And I began to consider something I had not understood before. Jesus died a painful and suffering death on the cross. He was buried. His friends mourned—just as Miah and I mourned for Jed. But three days later, this Jesus, this Son of God, came alive again.

"Think of it—," Sun turned to look at Juliana. "—death had no power over this man, this God.

"Then I began to listen to what Jedediah wrote about paradise. He was looking forward to someday being with the Savior he loved. There was no fear of giving up his life. I realized that death itself did not need to be feared. That if I surrendered my life to him, this same resurrection power would raise me from the dead to be with Jesus in paradise forever. Just as it had for Jedediah."

Callie looked thoughtful. "You said that you couldn't give your life to God because you were afraid of sacrifices. Did you still worry about them?"

"Jed wrote in his journal of worrying about the same things. He said that he finally realized that all he had to do was surrender. God would do the rest. If sacrifice was required, God's resurrection power would give him the strength. He also wrote that God will not give us anything beyond what we can bear." She smiled. "After Miah taught me to read, I found that verse in Jed's Bible."

"So you gave your life to God."

Sun's face took on a light that seemed to come from her soul. She smiled. "I gave my life to him as a living sacrifice. It could be no other way."

"You had to do it? Because of Jeremiah?"

Sun laughed. "Oh, no. Jeremiah had nothing to do with it." She paused. "I just knew that an inner voice from someplace deep inside, a whisper that I knew came from God, was calling me to come to him.

"It was the voice of Someone I felt I had known a long time, but only just found that I recognized. Early one morning I got up to gather wood for our fire. Watching the rising sun, I felt its warmth on my face. Suddenly, almost without realizing I was going to, I knelt—the way I had seen Jedediah do so many times—and talked to God. I told him simply that I had heard his voice and I wanted to belong to him."

"It was that simple?" Callie asked.

Sun nodded. "Yes. But my life changed forever."

"But what about Jeremiah? Did he know any of this had happened to you?" Juliana asked.

"Miah was fighting a different battle with God. He carried much anger because of Jedediah's death. The men had been close. They had trapped together for many summers. It was different for Miah." She paused. "His story should be saved for another time. It would be best for him to tell you himself."

The women walked on without speaking. The howl of the distant wind was rising, growing louder now than the hoofbeats and jangling chains of the teams.

Soon the sky was overcast. They traveled a few more miles and the wind picked up, howling even louder through the rocky passes. Stinging dust blew into the traveler's faces. Bandanas were pulled over noses and mouths and hats were yanked close to eyes. The oxen kicked and snorted, startling easily.

Parker rode up on the Appaloosa, halting as he reached Juliana's wagon. He tipped his hat. The horse danced sideways, skittish in the wind.

"We'll be stopping for the nooning a bit early," he said, looking off to the northwest, then back to the women. "Depending on how severe the storm is, we may put in for the night. Be prepared to circle the wagons when we stop." The wind blew his hair away from his face.

Juliana nodded. For a moment their eyes met. Then he set his mouth in a line and looked away, moving to the next wagon in line.

As they walked on toward the nooning, she yanked the lead on the stubborn oxen, flicking the whip over their backs from time to time. She considered Sun's words about God. They were beautiful thoughts. How wonderful it would be to belong to a personal God. Someone who cared.

But that could come later. There was really no need to dwell on such things now. She was young, she had a whole lifetime ahead. And hadn't she done all right up until now? Why did she think she needed God? She was strong. She had proven that to herself.

And now she had the offer of a romantic life in New Mexico. A life filled with wealth, political intrigue, and, of course, a man who adored her.

She had left Stonehaven with a dream. Now that dream would be fulfilled in greater portions than she could have imagined.

She smiled to herself. Without realizing it she had just made the decision that she would tell Matthias Graves that yes, she would become his wife. *Mrs. Matthias Graves.*

Her mind filled with daydreams, the adobe in Fort La Sal, a wedding in the land of the renaissance light, the soirées the dashing *Señor* and *Señora* Matthias Graves would hold...when Parker James suddenly rode up beside her again, interrupting her thoughts.

"Miss St. Clair," he said, his voice nearly lost in the wind. "I need to speak with you privately."

She raised her eyebrows and nodded. "Yes?" She waited for him to go on.

"Sometime before the night fire—if you can arrange it. It is of utmost importance." He sounded businesslike.

Juliana tilted her head, wondering what he could possibly want. "Of course. Just let me know when."

He nodded and rode to the lead.

Juliana glanced back at Matthias driving the wagon behind her. His handsome face looked dark. He obviously had not missed the exchange.

Fourteen

By the time the wagons had circled for the nooning, the sky had turned an angry gray and an icy rain hit the teamsters at a slant. The temperature had dropped to near freezing.

Captain James gave the order that the company would remain at the campsite for the night, possibly longer. He warned the travelers to place extra supplies of food and bedding in their tents and to drive the teams out to pasture with the *remuda*.

As the teamsters began to pitch tents, they found it nearly impossible to keep them stable against the increasing winds. Even the fastened-down wagon covers flapped and blew open.

Juliana and Callie fought to hammer the tent stakes into the ground. Juliana's cape blew wildly behind her as she worked and her hands and face grew numb in the slicing sleet.

Finally the two young women carried from the wagon their camp cots, bedding, and food supplies, fastened the flap, and settled in for the storm. Before long the howling wind died to a whisper and the beating of the sleet dropped to silence.

Juliana lifted the flap and peered out. "It's snowing, Callie. Come look. It's beautiful."

Callie joined her. They watched in awe as the dollar-sized flakes floated from the nearly black sky.

Within an hour the gentle flakes had turned to smaller, faster-falling flakes. Even the dark clouds had disappeared behind a blanket of falling snow. Now only stark white was visible: the white of the flakes falling faster and closer together deepening the snow on the ground.

"It's turned into a blizzard, Jules," Callie whispered, the next time she looked out the flap. "I can't even see Sun and Jeremiah's tent from here."

"Or Matt's." Juliana peered over her sister's shoulder. She shivered. "Close the flap, Cal."

Juliana decided to use the time to sketch, something she had almost given up during the rigors of life on the trail. She was glad she had thought to bring in her art supplies before the storm hit full force. Callie pulled out her journal. They spent the afternoon working in the light of their lantern, laughing and talking.

"What kind of an adobe will we have built?" Callie asked as their conversation turned to New Mexico. "I want it to be on a hill near a meadow." And she went on to tell of the place she had in mind.

Juliana smiled. So much of what Callie described was straight from the mouth of Maurice Dupree. As Callie talked, Juliana was reminded of her dream. The renaissance light of the mountain meadows, the bright sounds of the birds, the vivid color of the wild flowers, piñon pines, and juniper.

Callie's voice was merry as she talked about how the two of them had braved the elements to take this trip. "And we're almost there!" she declared. "Juliana, think of it. We're pioneers. Did you know that only one other woman has traveled the Santa Fe Trail before us? I've been told that someone named Susan Magoffin left for Santa Fe—and Chihuahua—less than six months ago. She's only seventeen, a newlywed traveling with her husband."

Juliana cocked her head. "Where did you hear about this?" It always surprised her that Callie found out details of people and places before she did.

"Parker James mentioned it at the night fire a few nights ago—I think you were out walking with Matt." Callie excitedly went on with her tale. "Susan's husband runs his own trading company. I think that's how Parker knows them. He couldn't get away from his business, so right after they were married they left on a trading trip to Mexico."

Juliana thought briefly about what it would be like to be married to someone like Parker James. Always on the move. It would be much the same as Sun and Jeremiah's marriage. How would it be to have the sky as your roof? The trees as a canopy over your bed, the prairie grasses as your carpet? The thought seemed somehow liberating.

She shook her head slightly. No. It could not be considered. A person needed a home. A solid and spacious adobe home. With warmth. And comfort.

Life on the trail wasn't for her. Or was it? She had never been happier. She loved looking out at the stars at night, taking comfort in the way they seemed to cover her like a blanket. Or the smell of the cookfire first thing in the morning as she sat nearby, sipping coffee and watching for the first pale rose light of dawn. Or looking out across the swaying tall grasslands, the golden autumn grasses as tall as Sir Galahad's eye.

And she had learned that the strength of her own hands could accomplish things servants had always done for her before. Saddling a horse. Driving a wagon. Pitching a tent. Cooking and baking.

She would never forget the thrill of driving those stubborn

oxen across the Cottonwood Crossing. The wagon had swayed and threatened to tip, but she had urged the beasts across, whipping them, driving them. She looked down at her callused, tanned hands.

Would they ever be smooth and white again? Did she want them to be?

Callie chattered on, and Juliana's attention focused again on her sister's words. "Think of it, Jules. We're pioneers. We're doing so much more than I ever thought we could. We don't even need to hire someone to build our adobe. I think we ought to build it ourselves. We can find out how to make our own adobe bricks. We can design it just the way we want it. And I want a garden. We can grow our own corn. And raise horses and cattle.

"And I was thinking, why don't we plan to build our place near Sun and Jeremiah? In the *Sangre de Cristo* mountains. I bet we could find the meadow we're looking for there." Suddenly Callie stopped and looked hard at her sister. "Jules, you aren't answering me." Her freckled face looked worried. "Is something wrong?"

Juliana took a deep breath. "Callie, I have something I need to tell you."

Her sister cocked her head. Juliana could tell by the look on her face that she expected something serious. She sighed again. Callie was going to be disappointed with her news.

"Last night Matt asked me to marry him."

There was a stunned silence—no sounds from outside where the snow continued to blanket the land, no sounds from inside the tent where Callie sat staring at her.

"You told him no, of course," she finally stammered.

"He asked me to think about it."

"But you are going to tell him no...aren't you, Jules?" There was a quaver in her voice.

"He is offering us a wonderful life, Callie."

"*Us?*"

Juliana nodded. Though Matt had not specifically mentioned Callie in their plans, family was obviously important to him. Of course he understood that wherever Juliana lived, Callie, as her responsibility, must live also. She was sure that the newlyweds' spacious adobe would also be Callie's home.

"He has wealth and prestige in New Mexico. He has told me about his people, his family." She could see the shocked look on her sister's face and hurried on to assure her that all would be well. "Callie, think about how kind he has been to us. He is a man of honor. He has protected us and offered us only the best advice. He has been a good friend."

"You don't have to marry your friends." Callie's lips formed a straight line as she muttered the words.

For a moment neither one spoke.

Then Callie locked her clear green eyes on Juliana's. "Do you love him, Juliana?"

It was the same question Sun had asked earlier. Did neither woman think she knew her own mind?

"There are different kinds of love, Callie. Often compatibility and friendship lead to a more enduring love." Even as Juliana spoke, her own words sounded leaden, recited.

"Have you told him yet? I mean, have you actually said yes?"

Juliana shook her head. "No. But I intend to."

"I will never do that."

"Do what, Cal?"

"I will never marry someone I don't love."

"I never said I don't love him." Juliana's voice had taken on a harsher tone. She reached over to touch Callie's hand. But Callie pulled hers away and went back to writing in her journal.

The blizzard continued through the evening. Just before nightfall, Matthias stopped by to check on the young women, kissed Juliana on the cheek, spoke briefly, then left again. A short time later, as they were setting out their cold supper on the small camp table, Jeremiah brought a johnny cake that Sun had baked the night before.

After supper another voice called to them from outside the tent.

Juliana opened the flap.

Parker James stood a few steps back, a light snow dusting his shoulders and hat. He nodded his greeting.

"Captain?" Juliana said softly, wondering at the warmth she felt someplace deep inside just looking at him.

"I was wondering if we could speak privately."

She glanced at Callie.

"If you wouldn't mind—could you come with me to my tent?"

It was the place he regularly conducted business. To Juliana it was the same as going to his office. "No, I don't mind." She grabbed her cape and hat and with a glance at Callie's knowing look, she hurried out into the snow.

In one hand Parker held a lantern in front of them to light the way. With the other he reached back to take Juliana's hand. The simple gesture touched her. His hand felt strong and warm in hers.

They walked through the deserted camp. It seemed the cold had caused folks to turn in for the night.

When they reached his tent, the captain hung the lantern on a hook at the center pole. He nodded toward a chair near his table, then sat opposite her. It struck her that it was obviously a businesslike arrangement. Almost as if he had taken care to see that nothing personal could be construed from their meeting.

She looked at him expectantly, waiting for him to begin. He brushed the melting flakes of snow from the light brown hair that seemed always to fall across his forehead.

"Miss St. Clair," he began, his eyes never leaving hers. "I have some important questions to ask you. You may think I am getting personal. But before I begin, I must point out that my questions are directly related to the well-being of this wagon train."

Juliana stared at him, wondering what she could possibly know that had to do with the safety of the caravan. "Go on," she said.

"Please don't take offense at what I am about to ask you."

Juliana thought she caught a shadow of sadness in his face. When she answered, though, her voice sounded harsher than she intended. The truth was, he *had* offended her several times with his words. Why would this time be any different? "I can't promise you that I won't until I hear what you have to say."

"I'll get right to it then. I understand you are betrothed to be married."

She caught her breath. "How could you possibly know that about me?"

"Your intended told me." He paused a moment. "Is it true?"

She refused to answer. Instead she asked a question of her own. "What could my betrothal possibly have to do with the train's well-being?"

"It's not your upcoming marriage I'm concerned about, Juliana."

It was the first time he had used her given name. His voice sounded almost tender as he said it. "Then what is it?"

"It's the man you are planning to marry." He stared hard at her. "How well do you know Matthias Graves?"

"That *is* personal, Captain. Not to mention slanderous on Matt's account."

Parker sighed, looking undecided about saying more. "We have reason to believe that Graves is planning a takeover of the wagon train."

"That's foolish." Juliana felt like laughing. The captain had gone too far. "Why would he want to?"

"That's what I hoped you might tell me."

"Even if I knew anything—which I don't—what makes you think I would be disloyal to the man I plan to marry?"

Parker frowned, still holding her gaze with his. "Honor, Miss St. Clair. Because of honor."

She tilted her head. "Honor?"

"I have watched you since you joined this train. I believe you are an honest and honorable woman. That's the only reason I came to you."

"Why do you think this about Matt?" she finally said.

"We understand that he has an armada of wagons waiting for a signal to join us—perhaps ambush the train. Has he said anything to you about them?"

"No." She felt that Parker was not purposely lying to her. But she wondered why someone would tell him such a thing about Matt. Was the captain afraid of him?

"We understand the wagons are filled with guns and ammunition."

"Captain, I don't know who is giving you your information. Whoever he is, he's a bold-faced liar. Matt is a man of fine standing in New Mexico. He would have no reason to—"

James interrupted, his stern voice leaving no room for question. "My sources are reliable."

She had heard enough. Juliana pushed back her chair. The meeting was over. But Parker held out his hand to stop her. "Please, I need to tell you more. Please, stay."

She wondered what was coming next.

"Graves plans to overtake the train at a place called Devil's Gate on the Cimarron Cutoff."

He sounded certain.

"How do you know this?" she asked.

"We've intercepted his courier."

"Where is this courier?"

"He's being held a distance from here. In an old trapper's shack through a draw this side of Devil's Gate."

Juliana sighed. "You know this as a certainty? I mean, Matthias's plans for the train?"

Parker nodded without speaking.

"Why would he do this? It doesn't make sense, Captain. Why would he plan such a thing?"

Parker shook his head slowly. His expression was inscrutable. "I don't know." He pulled out a pocket watch. Its thin, round case was gold with his initials engraved on top. "It's late," he said. "I'll see you back to your tent." He snapped the cover closed.

"Captain," Juliana said, looking into his eyes, as she stood. "Why did you tell me about your suspicions?"

He helped her pull her cape over her shoulders. A warmth flooded over Juliana as he straightened her collar. His face bent close to hers. In his eyes she saw the same raw emotion she had noticed the night Callie had been hurt. She felt the urge to reach out and touch his face with her fingers, then caught herself and stepped back.

"You didn't answer me," she finally said. "Why did you want me to know this about Matthias?"

"As I said, it was on behalf of the entire caravan. I thought perhaps you knew something that would help."

He opened the tent flap and they stepped out into the night. Again he held the lantern before them as they stepped through the snow. She reached to take his hand.

The night was quiet. Some of the tents held the glow of lanterns inside them, but most were dark. The only sound was the crunching of Parker's and Juliana's footsteps in the snow.

When they reached her tent, he turned toward her, still holding her hand. "Juliana, will you tell me if you find out anything more?"

She nodded, suddenly not wanting him to leave. They stood gazing at each other for what seemed like forever.

He set the lantern on the ground. Around them the snow continued to float downward in the lantern's soft glow. The night was still, so quiet that Juliana thought he must surely be able to hear the wild beating of her heart.

Parker smiled, and with his fingertips brushed a flake of snow from her cheek. Almost without realizing it, she moved toward him. At the same time, Parker tilted her face toward his and kissed her softly on the lips.

Then he turned abruptly, and without a word he picked up the lantern and walked into the night. Juliana stood for a long time looking after him, watching the soft glow disappear into the still-falling snow.

⤙⤚

Parker walked back to his tent, his thoughts and emotions in a turmoil. There was no doubt in his mind that he loved Juliana St. Clair. Just whispering her name fed his spirit, brought life to that place inside that had known years of soul-famine. For the first time since Laurie's death he felt alive.

That awakening to life had begun the first time he set eyes on her. He thought of her now, the way her steady gaze had met his earlier as they talked, her eyes as clear as a pure mountain pond. And her hair. How he longed to run his fingers through its auburn thickness, lift it to his face and drink in its fragrance. Hadn't Sun Jones called it the hue of a western sunset? He smiled. Sun was right. Just as she was about so many things.

Parker stopped at his tent to stamp the snow from his boots before entering. As he reached to open the flap he stopped, sensing that someone was inside.

He turned down the lantern and set it quietly aside, felt for his gun, and pulled it from the holster.

"Hey, old man, don't get any wild ideas."

Parker laughed and entered the tent, jamming his gun back into its holster. He would know Cookingham's voice anywhere.

"You sit around in a man's tent in the dark, you're likely to get yourself shot." Parker grabbed the lantern from outside but didn't relight it. He knew Cookingham shouldn't be seen if anyone happened by.

Cookingham laughed softly. "If you hadn't been out gallivanting with a certain young woman, you'd have been here to receive your guest."

Parker was suddenly serious. "What did you see?"

"I saw you walking with Juliana St. Clair back to her tent." Cookingham paused. "I hope for your sake that Graves didn't see the same thing."

"I tried to find out what she knows, Bennett. And I think we've been wrong in assuming she's in on the plans for Fort La Sal. I'm fairly certain that she knows nothing of what Graves has planned."

"You surely didn't tell her what we know." Cookingham's voice was harsh. "I can't believe you would jeopardize our mission—"

"Relax, friend. You know me better than that. I told her some partial truths. Led her to believe we're worried that Graves is planning to take over the train—bring in his armada of ammunition-filled wagons."

"What was her reaction?"

"She didn't believe it. At least, at first she didn't."

"But you convinced her. How?"

"I told her that we've caught the courier—know the time and place of the armada intercept."

"But that's not true—" Cookingham began, then added, his voice that of a matter-of-fact agent, "You did it to set her up."

"To set up Matthias Graves."

"You sound sorry."

Parker was always being surprised by Bennett's ability to read his mind. "You know me too well. I *am* sorry. I was finally winning her trust—but still, I had to deceive her."

"What else did you tell her?"

"The time and place of a fictitious ambush. And where we're holding the courier."

"That's good, even though none of it's true."

Parker sighed. "I figured that she'll tell Graves our suspicions. That way he's forced to leave a message for the next courier—for you to intercept, just as we had planned."

"Only now we've got the upper hand," Cookingham added, the doubts gone from his voice. "We know when he'll send the message—"

Parker interrupted. "Tomorrow. At least, that's my guess. With this storm settling in, we'll be here another few days. I would think Juliana will go to him with her suspicions tomorrow. He'll leave a message—which you, of course, will find and then put back for the messenger."

185

"What about the courier you said we're holding in the trappers' shack? What if Graves goes there? Finds it empty?"

"My plan is that he will."

"What good will that do?"

"I plan to meet with him there away from the train where we can speak privately."

Cookingham sounded skeptical. "You don't plan to tell him we know what he's up to in La Sal." It was more a statement than a question.

"Of course not. I plan to play it out—just as I told Miss St. Clair—as if he's planning a takeover of the train. Nothing more. I'll play the role of the conscientious captain. A captain worried about insurrection among the trading troops."

"How do you know when he'll go there?"

"My guess is, as soon as he hears about the messenger we are supposedly holding—right after he leaves a message for the real courier."

"The one I will intercept."

"That's the one," Parker laughed lightly. "It sounds like we're going to be busy tomorrow."

Cookingham sighed. "And it all begins first thing in the morning—if Miss St. Clair tells him what she knows."

The men talked on into the night, detailing their plans. Before Cookingham left, Parker bent forward earnestly. "Above all else, we've got to keep Graves's wagons from joining us. The best way to do that is to make sure the messenger is caught on his way to the armada. That way Graves doesn't know the man didn't make it. And the armada stays put, waiting for word to move."

"And I'm the one who has to do it." There was no question in Cookingham's voice.

"If we're going to save Governor Bent, we've got to keep Graves from taking control."

"I know, my friend. I know." And Bennett Cookingham walked out into the snow.

A few minutes later, Parker relit the lantern and again pulled the watch from his pocket. For a long time he gazed at the miniature painting of Laurie he still kept in its cover. He still loved her. And he knew he would until he died.

He studied her features. How different she was from Juliana St. Clair. Laurie had been soft, with ivory skin and raven hair. She had been quiet-spoken and gentle-natured.

He tried to picture Laurie driving a team, cracking the whip over oxen backs, standing in the wagon the way Juliana had done at the Cottonwood, whipping and shouting the beasts onward through the treacherous river.

Somehow, quiet, gentle Laurie didn't fit into the same picture. And it wasn't fair of him to compare the women.

His thoughts turned to the woman who had sat across from him tonight with her flashing eyes and high-spirited look. There was something about her...a strength of spirit that seemed to speak to him without words, a sense of knowing things about her he had never been told—as if they had been acquainted for years.

He was being drawn to Juliana St. Clair and felt powerless to do anything about it. He thought about his future, how it had seemed so bleak just a few short weeks ago. And now?

He sighed. Now? Now he knew only this. He loved Juliana St. Clair.

God help him, he loved her. He wanted this woman, this stubborn, beautiful woman in his life. Forever.

Immediately after breakfast the following day, Juliana made her way through the snow to Matt's tent, asking to speak privately with him. Standing at the tent's opening, he told her he was meeting with Hoss and Seth Johnson but would come by to talk with her later. She nodded wordlessly and returned to her tent to wait.

By now more than a foot of snow lay on the ground, and a light snow was still falling. Juliana and Callie talked about how difficult it would be for the oxen—and the teamsters—to keep their footing once the train began moving again.

"The trail's not visible. I'm glad Captain James has good scouts along." Callie sounded excited about getting started again.

Juliana nodded, a feeling of warmth again settling within her at the mention of Parker's name.

A few minutes later Matthias called to Juliana from outside the tent.

She opened the flap. There Matt stood, tall, handsome, and refined. He smiled warmly into her eyes. This man was her friend. How could she have doubted him? The captain must have been mistaken.

"The snow is letting up. Would you like to walk? Perhaps get rid of any cabin fever that may be threatening?"

Juliana laughed. As always he was thinking of her well-being. She grabbed her cape, pulling it close with a flash of remembrance. Parker had pulled it around her shoulders and looked into her eyes just the night before. But no, she shook the image from her mind. She had other matters to attend to.

"You're frowning, darling." Matthias took her hand as she stepped from the tent.

"It's nothing," she said, noticing how different her hand felt in his. Different from the way it had felt in Parker's.

They walked toward the *remuda*, a distance from the wagon circle. "I figured we needed to check on the horses," he said in explanation.

Again she felt grateful for his concern. She had worried during the night about Sir Galahad and Darley.

They were nearly there when Juliana brought up her conversation with Parker James.

Graves stopped, turning abruptly to face her.

"He asked you *what?*"

"He asked if you had ever told me about a planned takeover of the train." She suddenly laughed, realizing how foolish the idea was in the light of day—now that she had mentioned it to Matt.

But Matthias didn't laugh. "What else did he say?" His voice was brittle.

Juliana took him through the details of the conversation. She told him about everything except their walk back to her tent in the snow.

For a while Matt didn't speak. They picked their way through the snow drifts in silence. She could see his jaw working in quiet anger.

A few minutes later Juliana found Sir Galahad and Darley, made sure they had plenty of feed, then turned to rejoin Matt. He took her hand and they headed back to the camp. It was difficult walking, and he pulled her close to help her keep her balance.

Finally he spoke of the armada.

"Juliana," he said, his arm encircled tightly around her shoulders. "I have much to tell you. I don't know where to begin. I have not wanted to worry you. So I've said nothing. But I can see now that I should have taken you into my confidence."

He looked out into the falling snow as if looking for the right words to tell her.

"Captain James is trying to discredit me."

"Why would he want to do that?"

Again, several moments of silence passed. Finally Matt sighed. "Captain Parker James is heading to New Mexico province to lead a revolt against the government of the United States."

Juliana gasped. "That can't be."

Graves looked at her sharply.

"I—I just can't believe he—"

He nodded, as if understanding. "Of course the captain seems to be anything other than who and what he really is. I was surprised—to say the least—when I found out." He smiled down at Juliana. "After all, I recommended his commerce company to you."

"And your wagons?"

"He's right about that—I do have a number of wagons that will join up with us at a given point. I do not know how he discovered the information, though I have my suspicions." He stopped walking and, still holding her close, gave her a serious look. "Juliana, darling, it is apparent he will do anything, even

190

deceive you or others, to keep my armada from joining this train. He has obviously found out I have been sent to stop him from leading the revolt."

He fixed his gaze somewhere in the falling snow. "If stopping a bloody massacre of my people requires my taking over the caravan, then yes, I am guilty as charged." His dark eyes seemed to take on a passionate light.

"This man," he went on, "this man James, masquerades as a simple trader, but our government knows what he has planned. And I will stop him." He turned to her abruptly. "Tell me again everything he said last night."

Juliana again related the details of her conversation with Parker.

"You are sure he said he had captured my courier?"

"Yes."

"Would you like to ride with me to the place?" His expression turned hard. "We will see then how the captain has tricked you—purposely deceived you to lay a trap for me. Because, Juliana, I do not believe my courier has been captured. This trappers' cabin—if it truly does exist—will be empty."

Juliana considered his offer. Yes. She had to go. If it was true, if Parker James had deceived her, she wanted to know. Matt's words were convincing, but she must see for herself.

But a deep, cold sadness blanketed her heart, just as the snow blanketed the ground around her. She sensed that Matt was right. Why else would Parker have told her where he was holding the courier? He had been specific—"In an old trappers' shack through a draw this side of Devil's Gate," Parker had said, practically giving her the directions to the place. He had said nothing of keeping them to herself. He had wanted her to tell Matt. It was a trap. Matt was right.

She nodded slowly, and they turned back to the *remuda* for

the horses. A short time later, after leading the horses back to camp, she saddled Sir Galahad, and he, the chestnut. Before leaving camp, Matt rode to Seth Johnson's tent, spoke with him and the man called Hoss, then nudged the chestnut to where she waited atop the gray.

They rode slowly from the wagon circle toward Devil's Gate and the trappers' shack, the horses gingerly picking their way through the drifting snow. By now the snow had stopped falling, but the sky remained a deep, ashen gray. A brisk wind howled from the northwest.

Nearly a half-hour later, Juliana spotted the shack. It was just as Parker had described, in a draw at the mouth of a canyon of jagged, red snow-covered buttes. Devil's Gate, he had called it.

As they drew closer, they could see a single horse tethered to an outside post. It was Parker's Appaloosa.

They tied their horses nearby and made their way through the snow to the weathered cabin door.

Juliana dreaded what she would find. She hoped that the courier would be there— disproving all that Matt had told her. She didn't want to see Parker's face and find out that he had lied to her. Had used her.

She remembered the feel of his lips on hers, the tenderness in his eyes as he gazed into her own. Had he planned it all to mislead her? She shivered. How could any man be so callous?

Matt pushed open the door, his pistol in hand. He nodded for Juliana to follow him.

At first Juliana thought the one-room shack was empty. It was dark and had a dank and musty smell. Then her eyes adjusted, and she saw Parker James sitting in a straight-backed chair across the room. He faced the doorway. A rifle lay across his lap. The expression on his face was impenetrable, cold, hard, like chiseled granite.

Juliana glanced around the sparsely furnished room. He was alone.

The two men stared at each other. For a moment neither spoke.

Finally Graves broke the silence. "I figured you had set this up."

James said nothing.

"The question is, why? Why did you have Miss St. Clair lead me out here?"

"To warn you."

Graves laughed. The sound was brittle. "Warn me, *compadre?* Warn me about what?"

"I know your plan—I know all about your advancing wagons." The corner of the captain's mouth curled in a hard, half-smile. "If you make a move against this caravan, I'll meet your challenge head-on. There will be no takeover."

Graves laughed again, this time softly. "You——and the rest of the train—will not have a chance, Captain, if I decide to move against you. You have no idea what you are up against."

"I will stop at nothing to block any move you make. I am in command here. You challenge that command and your life will be worth—," he paused, emphasizing the word, "—*nothing.* Nothing at all." He stared hard at Graves, his eyes unwavering. "I will protect this train at any cost. Even at the cost of your life— or the lives of others who are in this with you." Parker's words were clipped, hard and angry.

"That's quite a threat, Captain." Matt's voice took on a sarcastic tone. "But somehow you don't scare me." He caught Juliana's eye and gave her a half-smile, as if to reassure her that he was in control.

Then he looked back to Parker James. "Captain," he said softly. "I know who you are and what you have planned in Fort La Sal."

Though his expression didn't change, Juliana saw a flicker of fear in Parker's eyes. It lasted just an instant, then disappeared. But in that instant, her heart felt as if it would explode. For what she saw in his eyes told her that everything Matt had spoken of earlier must be true. For the mention of Fort La Sal to elicit that response, it had to be true.

She quelled the impulse to go to Parker, fall on her knees before him, begging him to tell her that Matt was mistaken, that he wasn't involved in an uprising in La Sal. She looked at his hard face, unable to stop the anger and disappointment that flooded through her.

She swore to herself that she would do everything in her power to stop him. She would help Matt. She would do anything he asked of her. She whirled abruptly and stormed from the room. Matthias Graves followed her.

Soon they had mounted the horses and were riding through the draw back toward camp. The sky had turned a deeper gray, and a heavy snow had begun to fall.

༄

Parker stood in the doorway of the trappers' shack, his greatcoat pulled close against the chill, his felt hat slung low over his forehead, watching the two figures disappear into the snowy landscape.

He hadn't expected Juliana to accompany Graves to the cabin. When she walked through the door he would have given anything to erase her look of shocked surprise, the look of one who knew she had been betrayed. Already he was haunted by the expression that crept into her eyes as she gazed at him, as she listened to the accusations hurled between himself and Graves.

There was no doubt. He had used Juliana. Now as he thought of the look on her face, he tried to excuse himself for doing it. The reasons had seemed so clear-cut at the time. He had to get Graves away from camp so that Cookingham would have time to intercept the courier's note—the letter they both knew Graves would leave at the drop-off point. The letter from Graves to the armada captain would tell when the wagons would come. Deceiving Juliana was necessary to ensure that this happened.

And the truth was, he had wanted to test her, to find out if she had known of Graves's activities. Last night he had been sure that she didn't.

But something had happened a few minutes ago in the cabin. He had seen her expression change, harden toward him. Her eyes had flashed with anger. He didn't blame her for being angry with him for his deception. But the look on her face held deeper emotion than that. And it had happened at the instant Graves had said he knew what Parker had planned in Fort La Sal.

What was it that Graves thought he knew? He couldn't know about the mission to save Charles Bent. Only one other person knew of the mission. His friend, Cookingham.

Graves could not know their plan. No. His accusation had to do with something else. But what?

Still pondering the question, Parker mounted the Appaloosa, nudged his flanks with his heels, and headed back to camp.

∼≈∽

At midnight, Parker heard the crunch of footsteps in the snow outside his tent. He grabbed his pistol and silently rolled from his bed, pointing the gun in the direction of the footsteps.

"Hey, it's me," whispered a voice.

"I swear, one of these days you're going to get yourself shot, my friend. You almost got it last night. Tonight I came even closer—"

195

Cookingham entered and folded his lank body into a chair at Parker's table. Parker pulled up the opposite chair. He didn't light the lantern. "What did you find out?" He could barely see his friend in the darkness.

"You guessed right. Before Graves left for Devil's Gate, he left a message for the courier. I watched the drop. It's in a pile of stones east of camp. A place near Sand Creek."

"You read it?"

"Yes."

"Well, what did it say, old man?"

Cookingham's voice held a tone of admiration. "You should never have left the Army. You're too good. You guessed his next move right on the money." Bennett chuckled. "He's going to send that courier hightailing it back to Enrique at the armada, calling for immediate departure. He wants them to take the Raton Pass route to Apache Canyon. The armada is to intersect our path at the old Spanish Fort."

"That's a departure from his original plan."

"Yes. It seems he's worried that we're onto him. He plans an ambush."

"I knew we could force him to act. Only this way we'll be ready."

"This also means I've got to watch for the messenger and go after him."

"You always did get the exciting jobs," Parker said, tongue in cheek.

"Exciting? Standing watch over a pile of rocks? Then following some lowlife across the prairie? It's just going to be cold and miserable. Whose idea was this assignment, anyway?"

"Yours, my friend. Remember?"

Cookingham grumbled something incoherent, then became serious again. "There is a flaw in our plan, you know."

"I know. I was wondering when you'd bring it up."

"He's going to reckon that someone's feeding you information. He's an intelligent man. He may already suspect it's me."

"I understand that."

"There's nothing we can do about it, though. Right?"

"I'm sorry."

Cookingham sighed. "Easy for you to be sorry. You're not the one running around out there unprotected."

"I thought about that, too. You can't come back after you've got him."

"I'd already figured that."

"And?"

Cookingham grinned. "We'll surprise our friend at Apache Canyon. He'll be expecting an armada—instead he'll find us waiting to arrest him. If I can convince this courier to testify, we've got our man. I'll take him back to Fort Leavenworth."

"I would bet that won't make a difference at La Sal."

"You're right. The Oñate family will act without him."

Parker nodded. "I know the Mojada well. Bent is still in danger. Once incited, the Mojada won't care whether Graves is there to step into place as governor or not. They'll be out for blood. It's probably already too late to stop them."

"That means you've still got to get him out."

"I'm well aware of that, my friend." Parker was silent for a moment. "You haven't mentioned Seth Johnson. How far is he willing to go to protect Graves?"

"My guess is that Seth's a weak link. He'd never do anything on his own. But I'd keep an eye on him. Don't trust him."

"One thing I do know. I've got to get the caravan moving again. Tomorrow. The way I see it, you and I had better plan to meet at the old fort on Christmas Eve. You with the courier in tow, and me ready to hand over Matthias Graves on a silver platter."

"What a way to celebrate." Cookingham's voice was solemn. "That's a little over three weeks from now."

"There's one more thing, Bennett."

"I know what you're thinking—what if I don't get my man? If anything happens to me, you won't know until the train reaches Apache Canyon. Graves's armada could be waiting instead of me."

Parker nodded. "It's crossed my mind."

Their conversation drifted to old times, their years at West Point, some of the tight spots they were in together in the Army. It struck Parker that it was almost as if they were saying goodbye. Suddenly he feared for his friend. Though they had been in more dangerous circumstances than this in the past, something told him this was different. Graves was unusual. More than double-faced, he seemed to be two different people. That made it hard to read him, harder to anticipate what he might do. And that ability to anticipate, Parker knew, could make the difference between life and death.

Cookingham uncoiled his thin body and stood to leave.

"Take care, old man." Parker walked with him to the tent flap.

Bennett nodded. "You're in the middle of a bear's den yourself." He slapped Parker's back affectionately. "Graves knows you're onto something. He's not sure what. But something tells me he's meaner than a wounded grizzly when he's riled. Watch yourself, *amigo*, while I'm gone." He smiled, pausing for a moment, then patted Parker's back again. "Until Christmas Eve then, my friend."

Then Bennett Cookingham turned and was gone, disappearing through the flap and into the night.

$\mathscr{S}ixteen$

The next morning, the bugle sounded at four-thirty. The skies had cleared and a freeze had set in during the night.

Tents were struck and belongings quickly packed into the wagons. To stand still was to invite the cold to settle through to the bones Juliana told Callie, as they hurriedly loaded the wagon.

The bullwhackers swore at the cold, causing Callie to roll her eyes and Juliana to look down in embarrassment. Other travelers simply mumbled complaints as they swilled cold coffee and bit into hard biscuits.

Holding a lantern, Callie drove the team from the *remuda;* then Juliana helped her hitch the beasts to the wagon tongue.

The snow had thawed some before nightfall the previous day, then frozen solid when the temperature dropped. Now it held a crust as slick and sharp as glass. One step into it, and an ox or a person would sink into the soft snow and get nasty cuts in the bargain. Once the train started moving, and dawn brought visibility, the snow was spotted with blood from wounded oxen.

The caravan moved slowly, single file, toward Devil's Gate. As usual, Sun and Jeremiah had pulled their wagon close to Juliana's and now held their place behind her.

Juliana and Callie walked alongside the lead oxen, coaxing the balky team through the snow with prods and popping whips. The beasts' breath steamed in the frigid air. Juliana's rig was halfway back from the caravan lead and she planned to get no closer. Captain James rode mostly at the lead, and she had no desire to see him or talk with him. She had noticed he was keeping his distance from her as well.

It took two days to move through the valley of Devil's Gate. Finally the caravan pulled out of the valley to the sand hills beyond. By the third day, the skies had cleared to a brilliant purple-blue and the winter sun cast a thin heat on the rocky, uneven terrain.

Hard-packed snow turned first to dirty slush, then mud. Now the oxen slipped, hollering and bawling, as they fell, stood, then fell again. Some of them went lame and had to be shot. Others limped pitifully along, moaning in protest.

After a few more days, the ground hardened, and the train moved forward fifteen miles one day, then seventeen, then finally twenty. The weather held and the terrain again smoothed out. Each day they moved closer to the Cimarron Cutoff.

The train crept along the north bank of the Arkansas River, and the travelers could see the wide ribbon of it in the ravine below, its might evident even from a distance. Swollen with the recent storm, it swirled, raging and dark between its banks. The caravan would need to cross it before heading on to the Cimarron.

Juliana and Matt had hardly spoken since the day they met Parker at the trappers' cabin. Though always the gentleman, lately Matt seemed preoccupied, watchful. She attributed it to thoughts about the uprising he had accused Parker James of planning.

One night they took a walk in the moonlight. It was a warmer evening than usual, and the merry voices of folks glad to be out of their tents carried across the barren landscape. As they walked from the night circle, Juliana and Matt could hear the sounds of banjo playing and fiddlers, and from time to time, the mournful wail of a harmonica. Someone told a story in a deep guttural voice. It was punctuated with hoots of laughter.

Juliana had grown used to the sounds of the train, especially the sounds of singing and dancing and storytelling around the night fire. It was a time of boisterous camaraderie, a time to tell a better story than the last, using more shocking and colorful language than the last, a time to muse on the day's events and tell tall tales of travels to come.

As they walked, Juliana mentioned the uprising, asking if he knew any more about it.

At first Matt looked at her, his eyes sharp, as if watching for something in her face. Then he relaxed and his expression softened, his dark face suddenly looking tired.

He took her hand. "You are concerned about my country."

"I thought it was *our* country," she said, her tone soft in jest.

He did not return her smile. "Of course," he said. "That is what I meant."

"Tell me what's going on, Matt. I can see that you're worried."

He shook his head. "There is much I would like to tell you, darling. I do not know, though, if it's time."

She wanted to know how he planned to thwart the uprising that Parker James planned. The man had to be stopped. If she could, she would help. "It's time, Matt. I want to know everything."

"Do you mean that?" He looked into her eyes expectantly.

Juliana kept her hand in his. "Yes. I do."

Matt looked thoughtful. He studied her face as if deciding what he wanted to say. "Juliana, I have been in contact with the U.S. government officials in La Sal."

She tilted her head, nodding slightly.

"They have asked me to become Governor of the province."

Juliana was stunned. "Matt, that's wonderful."

He smiled. "Yes. It is."

"But, how—," she began, "—what about Charles Bent? I thought he—"

Matt touched his fingers to her lips. "I don't know how, darling. All I know is that there is a man on this train who wants to stop me."

"Parker James."

"Yes." He took a deep breath. "But that is for me to worry about." He smiled warmly. "Right now I have something else I want to ask you."

She looked up at him, waiting, yet somehow knowing what he was about to ask.

"Darling, I asked you a few weeks ago to become my wife. But I wasn't entirely honest with you." He lifted her fingers to his lips and kissed them. "By becoming my wife, you will become the wife of the New Mexico Provincial Governor." His dark eyes searched hers. When she didn't speak, he went on. "I knew from the first moment I saw you, Juliana, that you would be perfect as my wife." He looked away from her, his voice taking on the fiery passion she had heard before when he spoke of New Mexico. "You will stand by my side in the governor's palace. We will serve my people together." He turned back to her. "You do understand, Juliana? You understand the importance of this? The honor of it?"

Honor. Parker James had said he saw honor in her. She quickly brushed the thoughts of him from her mind.

"I do," she said to the man in front of her. "I do understand."

"Will you become my wife, Juliana?"

"Yes, Matt. I will marry you."

Matt took her into his arms. His lips found hers. It wasn't a tender kiss, a touching kiss like the only other she had known, that sweet kiss of Parker's. No. This was different. There seemed to be no love in it. Only some deep, animal hunger. It frightened her. Matt kept his lips on hers, holding her in a tight grasp. She couldn't breathe. She couldn't move.

In confusion, Juliana pushed against him, laughing lightly in embarrassment. "Please, Matt, don't."

His face looked dark. He cocked his head. "Don't?" Then his expression changed. He pulled her gently closer, reached to hold her face in his hands. "I am sorry. I have waited so long." Now he seemed embarrassed. "My emotions carried me away." He kissed her on the forehead, then smiled into her eyes. "I have something for you, darling."

She waited while he pulled a satin box from the pocket of his woolen greatcoat.

Matt led her to a clearing where a spot of moonlight lit the area. "Please, sit down." He held her hand and helped her take a seat on a sandstone rock. Then he knelt beside her.

"In my country," he began, "it is tradition to give your betrothed a gift of great value. Irreplaceable value." He paused, watching her face. "It seals the man and woman together."

"But I have nothing for you."

"You have given me yourself. There is no greater gift."

Juliana suddenly shivered. Could she really give herself to this man? There had been no mention of love. Did he love her? She knew that she didn't love him. But what had she told Callie?

Sometimes love grew out of respect and friendship. Love would come. It had to. She looked at Matt kneeling beside her. What if it didn't? Could she live with a man she didn't love for the rest of her life? Would all he was offering her be enough?

"You look sad." Matt placed his hand beneath her chin and tilted her face toward him. "This is not a time for sadness," he said. "This is a time for great celebration."

She nodded. He was right.

Then he took hold of her hands and gently turned them palms up as they rested in her lap. Smiling into her eyes, he placed the satin box in her grasp.

She removed the lid and gasped.

"Are you surprised, darling?"

Juliana couldn't speak. She couldn't move. She just looked at the open box in her hands.

Matt reached into the box and picked out an emerald ring. It sparkled in the moonlight. He lifted her hand and placed it on her finger.

"It's all there," he said, looking down at the jewelry in her lap. "Every piece."

"But, how—," she finally managed. "I thought they were sold."

"They were."

"How did you get them back?"

"It was I who bought them." He sounded triumphant. "I bought your mother's jewels so that I could present them to you later."

Juliana remembered how he had bartered with the trader for a good price on their behalf. His face had been so sincere. At the time, Matt's false candor reminded her of the gambler her father had often mentioned when teaching her about honor. A man like that, he had said, was good at poker, but probably carried within him a dishonest heart.

As she looked at him now, she knew that it wasn't the act that bothered her. It had been a generous act. No. It troubled her that he could look sincere even when he wasn't. It also troubled her that he looked that way most of the time. And she couldn't tell the difference.

In the distance the wail of the harmonica drifted from the night circle. Someone joined in with singing. Soon the voices of traders and bullwhackers and cattlehands joined in, their rough voices somehow blending together in a haunting and sad melody.

Matt took Juliana's hand and helped her to her feet. He put his arm around her and they walked back to the night circle.

It's going to be all right, she told herself as they walked. *Everyone has jitters when they decide to marry. I'll get over it.* She looked up at the handsome man walking beside her.

Provincial Governor, she thought with pride. *And I will be his first lady.* She smiled to herself. *Yes, I'll get over the trouble in my spirit. Matt was right when he said we have something to celebrate. Our future is bright. This is a time for great celebration!*

She took his arm as they entered the circle. As they did, a man seated next to the fire turned to look. His gaze held hers for an instant. Juliana caught her breath. It was Parker James. And no matter what he had done, there was something about him…she didn't allow herself to finish the thought. Instead, she turned away, lifting her chin, and tilting her face away from him.

A few minutes later, after they had been seated near the fire, Matt stood and spoke to the fiddle player. Then he turned to the rest of the company.

"I have an announcement to make," he said, his voice filled with pride. "I want you all to know that Juliana St. Clair has agreed to become my wife." He smiled her direction. She stood and joined him, taking his hand. The crowd clapped and whistled and stomped.

Matt went on. "We will be married as soon as we can get this caravan to Santa Fe."

"Let's get it on its way!" someone shouted. There was more laughter. "What're we waitin' fer?"

Matt held his hand up to quiet them. "I've asked the fiddler to play a song in honor of this beautiful woman who has consented to be my wife." Then he nodded at the fiddle player.

A sweet tune began and Matt swept Juliana into his arms, whirling her around the camp fire. Some of the others grabbed partners, bullwhackers and traders, some dancing together, some dancing alone. The music was too soft. Too sad. Juliana was glad when it ended.

Then someone yelled. "Hey, we wanta dance with the bride. Let us have a turn."

Matt raised an eyebrow in Juliana's direction. She nodded. It was a time of celebration. They meant no harm. Let them celebrate together the coming wedding.

Then someone else yelled. "I say, let the captain go first." There was laughter and shoving. Someone pushed Parker toward her.

He hesitated for a moment, his eyes searching hers. Then he moved forward and took her in his arms. The musicians began to play—the concertina, the fiddle, the banjo, the harmonica, blending together in sweet harmony.

His gaze didn't leave hers as they whirled around the circle. Her heart ached, and she didn't know why. Was it her disappointment in him? The hurt he had caused her? She gazed into his clear eyes and thought about honor and goodness and honesty. How could she have been so fooled?

Someone once said that eyes were a window of the soul—if that was true, then the captain's seemed to be reaching out for her. And she felt something inside herself respond to Parker. It frightened her.

She halted abruptly, though the music hadn't stopped. She turned away from him, though his arm still held her. She couldn't look for one more moment into his eyes. What she saw there sliced her to the core. She felt hot tears threaten to spill.

She looked to Matt and he wound his way through the dancers toward her.

"Captain," he said curtly. Then taking her arm, Matt led her away from the circle. She did not turn to see if Parker's eyes were still on her.

‿

Callie stood by Sun Jones at the edge of the night circle, watching Juliana as she danced first with Matthias Graves, then with the captain. She felt no joy for her sister, then immediately felt ashamed that she didn't.

She wondered if it might be simple jealousy. Juliana had found herself a handsome and prosperous man. He was from the land her sister had dreamed of since childhood. The land of the golden dreams.

Then Callie's gaze locked on Matt's face as he watched her sister dance with Parker James. His expression changed from that of a pleasant, sophisticated gentleman to something almost sinister. Dark and brooding.

Callie watched the transformation, realizing that it was somehow familiar. As if she had seen it, or something like it, somewhere before. It frightened her. She felt like crying. Like running.

But she didn't. She reached for Sun's hand and clung to it as if she were a child again. Sun's tough, warm hand squeezed hers in return, almost as if in understanding.

Then Callie let go of Sun's grasp and followed Juliana and Matt as they walked to the St. Clair tent. She stood in the shadows until they had said their goodbyes and Matt strode to his own tent a distance away.

"Juliana, why didn't you tell me you'd decided?" Callie confronted her sister as soon as she entered the tent.

Juliana looked up in surprise. "You sound angry."

"I'm your sister. You should have told me first."

Juliana laughed lightly and put her hand out to take Callie's. But Callie backed away. "Callie, I just decided tonight. I'm sorry. I would have told you first thing." She hesitated, her voice dropping. "I really didn't know that Matt was going to announce it to the company. I should have stopped him. But it happened so fast—"

Juliana seated herself on the cot and Callie dropped to her own cot across from her. "Jules, it's not that I don't want to be happy for you. I do. I really do." She paused. "I'm just surprised, that's all."

"I told you weeks ago that he had asked me."

Callie nodded, choosing her words carefully as she went on. "I guess I was hoping you'd decided your answer would be no."

"Hoping?"

She nodded again. "Something is wrong about it, Jules. I can't put my finger on it. It's just that—" Callie's voice broke off.

Juliana waited.

Callie finally spoke in a rush, wanting to be honest, but not wanting to offend her sister. "Maybe it's just that I don't think you love him."

Juliana's eyes pierced hers. "How would you know that, Callie?"

She sighed. "I thought it would be different for you. I know you so well. I thought when you fell in love..." Callie stopped, then added lamely, "I thought you would look different."

Juliana suddenly laughed. "*Look* different?"

When Callie spoke again, her voice had dropped to a whisper. "Jules, you look sad. You don't look like someone in love."

Her sister tilted her head as if Callie had struck some truth she hadn't considered. And her look was pensive. Callie could see a sadness had settled into some place deep inside.

"That's ridiculous, Callie. Of course I'm happy. I just have a lot to consider. Our lives are going to change. You have no idea what's ahead." Then Juliana described all that Matt had told her about the political events about to take place in New Mexico. "We will live in the Governor's Palace," she concluded. "Callie, our lives will be more than we ever dreamed they could be. Wonderful times are ahead of us. These are big changes. I admit I'm preoccupied with everything that has happened. With all that is to come."

Callie reached for her sister's hand. "But what about love, Jules? You've never once told me you love Matthias Graves."

Juliana stared at her for a moment. "That will come with time." Then she smiled, stood, and picked up the satin box Matt had given her earlier. She handed it to Callie.

"This is Matt's betrothal gift to me, Callie. Open it."

Callie lifted the lid. Before her sparkled the necklaces, rings, bracelets, rubies, diamonds, emeralds, and pearls that had once belonged to their mother. "He bought them for you," she whispered in awe.

Juliana nodded. "Matt cares a great deal," she said.

Callie stared at the precious stones. But suddenly instead of the sparkling jewels, the image of Matt's face appeared in her mind. It was dark, sinister. A sneer grew at the corner of his mouth, appearing like an open wound.

She shivered, feeling frightened and cold. Tears rushed to her eyes. A searing pain struck behind them. But all she could see was darkness, and that wound of a mouth, half-laughing, half-jeering.

Callie shook her head slightly, trying to clear the image from her mind. She looked back to her sister. Juliana watched her, a quizzical expression on her face.

"Callie, what's wrong?"

But Callie could only cry. The image finally disappeared.

$\mathscr{S}$*eventeen*

B y sunup the next morning, the wagons stood waiting in single file at the upper crossing of the Arkansas River. The *remuda* crossed first, downstream from the wagon crossing, and the hands drove the animals south along the *Jornada*, the Cimarron Cutoff.

One wagon at a time the teamsters headed their teams down the incline and into the treacherous waters. Sinkholes were a danger, and the oxen stumbled and bellowed in protest as they moved from sandbar to sandbar.

Captain James rode the Appaloosa to the far bank, then turned to watch the wagons cross, ready to ride back across if needed. As dawn broke, and a pale light spread from the east, he looked up at the winding line of wagons heading toward him.

By now the teamsters had an easier time crossing. He thought back to earlier fordings, the near losses of wagons and cargo. The Cottonwood stood out in his mind, and he remembered the look of Juliana St. Clair as she drove her team across.

Parker's eyes sought her now. First he spotted Sun and Jeremiah Jones. He knew Juliana's wagon would be near theirs. Jeremiah had lived up to his promise from the night that Callie was injured. Not a day had passed that Jeremiah had not pulled his wagon next to the St. Clairs. Parker doubted that Juliana or Callie even realized it, but Jeremiah's watchful presence was there to protect Callie, if she needed it. The mystery of her accident had never been solved, though now Parker had his suspicions.

He spotted Juliana. She was several wagons back, seated calmly on the wagon bench, Callie at her side, her team standing quiet as she waited to drive them into the water. With the day still early, she was bareheaded. Even from where he sat, he could see her auburn hair hanging past her shoulders, struck into red-gold flame by the early morning sun.

When Juliana's turn came, she drove the team into the water with her usual determination. For the briefest moment, her eyes met his as she neared the sandbar where the Appaloosa stood. Then she turned her focus to the opposite bank, cracked the whip above the oxen, called out to them, and plunged forward through the waters.

The rest of the wagons crossed without mishap. On the south bank, the wagoneers filled barrels with water. They couldn't count on rain, and it would be three days until they struck another creek or stream.

A short time later, the caravan had again headed out. This time, because of the dangers of the Cimarron, the teamsters pulled their wagons into four parallel lines, narrow at the lead, fanning out toward the last. That way the wagons were in place to more quickly form a circle in the event of a Comanche attack. The *remuda* traveled slightly behind with the cattle hands ready to drive the animals into the safety of the circle.

Parker nudged the Appaloosa forward to take his place at the train's lead. A quiet watchfulness settled over the travelers. Comanche country was deceptive, peaceful-looking, almost majestic with its low sandstone rock formations rising to meet a vivid sky. Traders familiar with the route knew better than to let down their guard. Their eyes constantly darted from sandstone rise to dry creekbed, watching, waiting.

Not many travelers had been killed during the years since trade with Mexico had opened and the Santa Fe had become a regular trail. But the Cimarron Cutoff had been the place of many raids, even the place of Jed Smith's death at the hand of the Comanche back in '31.

This was going to be a difficult route for Jeremiah and Sun. Jeremiah had told him it was the first time he had traveled it since his friend Jed's death.

Parker took his place at the lead, his eyes constantly searching for Indian sign. By now the sun was high, the sky clear, the terrain mostly smooth with sparse vegetation. The place seemed peaceful enough and he slung his hat low over his forehead and leaned back into the saddle, deep in thought.

As usual, his mind turned to Juliana, though now it seemed that she was never far from his thoughts. The distasteful memory of Graves's announcement at the night fire was quickly replaced by the memory of holding her in his arms, dancing, whirling around the night fire. The way the firelight danced in her eyes and caused her cheeks to flush. The way she looked up at him, making him wonder if she was affected by him the way he was by her.

The ache deep within him had only grown worse since last night. How could she think of marrying Graves? He had to warn her. But he knew he couldn't. The risk was still too great. Besides she probably wouldn't believe him anyway. If she told Graves Parker's suspicions, the mission, his friend Cookingham, and Charles Bent would be in jeopardy, perhaps leading to fatal consequences for them all.

She had a transparency about her—that part of her honorable nature he had seen from the beginning. That could be her undoing. If Juliana believed what he told her, Graves might notice a difference in her. Her own life would then be in danger as well. No, he concluded. He must remain silent.

He couldn't tell her that the man she was pledged to marry craved power. That he was a traitor and opportunist, bent on treachery and murder to get his way. How could he tell her that the only reason Graves wanted her at his side was to use the stature of her uncle, U.S. Senator Caleb Benedict? The man wanted the endorsement of the U.S. government when he took over as governor. Graves believed that marrying Juliana ensured that endorsement. How could Parker tell her that?

The caravan moved on across the dry, flat land. In the distance, sand hills and rocky mounds broke the monotony. Scrub grass, mostly brown, grew in tufts along the trail. A steady wind blew out of the west, kicking up dust and dried grass.

Parker left his place at the lead, riding for a while among the travelers to let them know when they would stop for the nooning. He greeted Sun and Jeremiah, spoke briefly to Callie and Juliana, then rode on back to the last in line, the Conestogas that strung out far behind the rest, those belonging to Matthias Graves.

Graves tipped his head in Parker's direction as he approached. "Captain," he said, his voice a monotone.

Parker nodded in return. "I notice your wagons are lagging behind. Any reason for that?"

Graves kept his eyes on the wagon ahead of him, instead of on Parker. "I've got my reasons," he said with a shrug.

Parker figured he was feeling penned in. It had been more than a week since Graves had left the message for his courier. He was probably wondering why he had heard nothing in return. And the man Graves knew as Hoss had disappeared with no trace.

Parker knew he must be wondering about the turn of events. So far, though, he hadn't sent Seth Johnson to investigate. The small, pale man still sat driving the wagon behind Graves, as silent and sullen as usual.

"This is Comanche country, you know."

Graves smiled, one side of his lips curling upward. "I'm well aware of that, Captain." Still he kept his eyes facing forward.

"Just make sure you keep up with the train, Graves."

Graves didn't answer.

Parker reined the Appaloosa around and headed back to the lead.

After the nooning, the train moved on. It was mid-December and they had two weeks to get to Apache Canyon. Parker planned to move them forward at a pace of twenty miles a day—more if the terrain and weather permitted. That meant they would ride until sunset each day. It would be tiring, both for teams and teamsters, but he couldn't let up. There could be no delay in meeting Cookingham at the old fort.

Besides, as time went on, Cookingham's parting words comparing Graves to a wounded grizzly settled into his gut, causing a nervous churning. Parker kept a wary eye out for any changes in the man's behavior or conduct. And he realized he was worried more by Graves than by the Comanche.

Parker now made regular patrols of the night camp after most folks had turned in. Guards were posted around the night circle and *remuda*, on the lookout for Indian activity. But by necessity he had not taken any of them into his confidence about Graves.

At night, since Cookingham's departure, the captain had made a habit of posting himself near Graves's tent, watching, waiting for the man to make a move. Sometimes he stayed near Johnson's sleeping quarters, but he never went far from Matthias Graves.

215

The first night on the Cimarron Cutoff, Parker took his usual place across from Graves's tent. He had just settled back into the shadows when Juliana St. Clair lifted the flap of her nearby tent, and holding her cape tightly around her, stepped out into the darkness.

She walked without sound, picking her way around tents and wagons, until she found an opening in the circle. Then she nodded to one of the cattle hands who guarded the camp and headed toward an outcropping of sandstone a short distance away.

Parker fell in beside her as she walked.

She looked up in surprise at the sound of his footsteps, her face barely visible in the darkness.

"Captain," she said, her voice low. "You startled me."

"I've warned you before about leaving camp like this," he said.

"I'm not going far."

"Anyplace outside the circle is too far, Miss St. Clair."

Her clear eyes studied his. She didn't answer him.

"You must return to camp."

Juliana made no move to turn back, just looked at him with those clear, unblinking eyes, and a stubborn set to her chin. He sighed. She was strong-willed, even in something like this. For a moment, neither spoke. He pictured himself lifting her in his arms and carrying her back to camp. That was probably the only way she would go. But of course he couldn't do that. Besides, he would rather be out here on the prairie with Juliana St. Clair than anywhere else he could think of.

He sighed again. "I'll accompany you, if you like. You really shouldn't be out here alone."

"Suit yourself, Captain." The stubborn tilt of her chin remained.

Then she fell silent as they walked. In the distance an owl hooted, followed by the mournful cry of a wolf. They walked on toward the mound of stones. The wolf sang again. Farther away the yips of coyotes carried toward them on the night breeze.

"Why'd you come out here?" Parker finally asked. "You surely know it's not safe."

"I just needed to think, Captain. That's all." Juliana didn't look at him. "I hadn't planned to go beyond shouting distance." She paused. "Besides I know you've got guards posted beyond the circle. I wouldn't have chanced it otherwise."

They reached the sandstone mound and climbed to its crest. Juliana sat on a tall flat stone, pulling her cape close against the night chill. Parker sat near her, watching her profile as she gazed into the night sky.

"Juliana—" he began, feeling an urgency to tell her of his feelings for her, though knowing that he couldn't.

She turned toward him, her expression holding something akin to sadness, perhaps anger. "Your term is too familiar, Captain."

"I'm sorry, Miss St. Clair." The moment passed.

She studied his face, as if fighting her own battle of words and emotions. Finally she said, "I once trusted and respected you."

Parker felt that he had been hit in the stomach. "What?—" he began.

She went on. "I know that we didn't hit it off—that day in your office when you refused to allow me on your train. I hated what you stood for. I hated that you were the barrier between me and my getting to New Mexico. You were the only winter train, and you knew it, yet you refused to let us join you.

"That, Captain, was understandable. You didn't know me. You didn't know that I had what you call grit. Your attitude, high and mighty and distasteful as it was, at least was excusable."

Her voice lowered in anger. "Though I disliked you, I did respect you. I trusted your judgment." She paused, staring out at the canopy of stars. A wolf cried from somewhere far beyond the sandstone mound, echoing through the darkness.

Parker didn't speak.

"But now, Captain—" She turned to face him. "What you have done—are planning to do—is despicable. You once spoke to me about honor, the honor you saw in me, when you your-self—" Her voice broke. She bit her lip and turned away.

"—lied to you," he finished for her.

She nodded. "Yes." Her tone was hard. "You deceived me."

"Juliana—Miss St. Clair." Parker took her hand. "There are things going on that you know nothing about. And I can't tell you. There were reasons for—"

She interrupted. "I know all about your reasons, Captain. Believe me, I know." Now her voice was low, sad.

"What is it that you think you know? You must tell me."

As she answered, her eyes spoke of her grief, even in the night darkness. She took a deep breath. "I know that you masquerade as someone very different than who you really are. You pretend to be noble, honest, and just. When in reality, you plan murder and treachery."

Parker shook his head. "What are you talking about?"

"You know very well, sir, what I am referring to." Her tone was cold.

"Is this what Graves has said about me?"

She didn't answer.

He laughed, though the sound of it, he knew, was brittle. "If you only knew what he has planned." Parker spoke more to him-self than to Juliana.

218

"I do know his plans."

He looked sharply at her. "You do?"

"Of course. And I will do my best to help him when we get to Fort La Sal. He *will* become Governor, regardless of your pathetic efforts to stop him."

Parker stood, suddenly angry. Waves of disbelief flooded over him. How could he have been so foolish? She *did* know. He felt sick. Juliana St. Clair was wrapped up in the heart of the planned uprising—just as Cookingham had suspected in the beginning. How could he have been so blind?

He looked down at the woman. She faced away from him, as if having dismissed him from her presence. The wind lifted her hair, riffling the folds of her cape. She looked west, and there was a regal slant to her head.

Regal. Majestic. Of course. As he watched her a feeling of sickness began to spread from deep in his soul through his entire being. He put the pieces together. By marrying Graves and helping him plan and execute the La Sal uprising, she would become the wife of the Governor, the first lady of New Mexico.

All the nobility and honor he thought he had seen in her before had been a sham. She had deceived him.

He stared at her. "You must return to camp. Now."

Juliana turned to him, lifting an eyebrow at his cold tone. Then she nodded, rose, and walked ahead of him back to the wagon circle.

Eighteen

The caravan moved along the Cimarron Cutoff. To the east, herds of buffalo, numbering in the tens of thousands, colored the land in sweeping, rolling tones of brown. Their pounding hooves sounded so much like thunder that many times the travelers looked to the skies, thinking a storm was on its way. Some of the old-timers explained that the beasts gathered along the southern plains in greater numbers in the fall and winter months. The train did not stop to hunt for sport. But the scouts took down enough of the giant beasts to provide plenty of fresh meat for the travelers.

Small bands of Comanche followed the train, usually seen only by the scouts. When they did come closer, it was to beg, not raid. Sometimes the braves rode silently beside the wagons for miles at a time, looking hawkish and proud, black hair gleaming in the sun, bronze skin draped with buffalo robes.

The train made good time, keeping to the twenty miles a day the captain had planned. The weather, though cold, held steady until the caravan was two days out of Apache Canyon.

Early the morning of December 22, just after dawn, a light snow began to fall. Though the snow remained light and barely dusted the ground, the terrain grew rougher as the day wore on.

Rocky soil and deep ravines slowed the train. A Conestoga and three of the farm wagons lost wheels and the caravan halted early for the nooning to make repairs.

Callie found a nearby tree for shelter and told Juliana she wanted to spend some time alone, writing in her journal. Juliana knew that her sister was still having a difficult time with the upcoming marriage. And though she seldom spoke of it, Callie still grieved for Stonehaven and their father. Writing was her way of coming to grips with her feelings. Juliana nodded, her smile gentle. "Go ahead," she said. "I want to spend some time with Sun and Jeremiah."

For many days, Juliana had purposely avoided her friend. Though Sun had never said so, Juliana felt that she disapproved of Matthias Graves, that she was disappointed in Juliana's decision.

But lately, Juliana missed Sun's companionship, her good sense, her stories, her warmth. It was time to close the distance Juliana had put between them. She wanted to remain Sun's friend.

She found Sun near her wagon, setting out corn cakes and cold meat under the shelter of the wagon cover.

Sun looked up and smiled when she saw Juliana. "It is good to see you," she said. "Will you join us?"

"Thank you. Yes, I would like that." Juliana hesitated. "But I really came to talk to you, Sun. I've missed you."

"I have been waiting." Sun set out another tin plate. "I am glad you came. Miah is hunting rabbit for tonight. We can talk together while he is gone."

They spoke for a few minutes about the day's travel, the snow, the short distance to Apache Canyon. Then Sun's light eyes met Juliana's. "We will be in Santa Fe soon. Is that where you will be married?"

"No. Fort La Sal."

Sun nodded slowly.

"After I meet his family."

"The Oñate family."

Juliana was surprised. "Have you heard of them?"

Sun sliced the buffalo meat and set out three servings. For a moment she didn't speak. "Everyone in New Mexico knows the Oñate family."

"They're his mother's people. Tell me about them, Sun."

Sun's broad face wore a look of wariness that Juliana hadn't seen there before. "You will have to make your own decision about them, Juliana. Once I told you there are things you must discover on your own that no one can tell you. This is one of those things."

"When you told me that before—you spoke of Parker James."

"Yes."

"Since then I have discovered things about him—things you didn't tell me. But things that aren't good, Sun. Things that I don't think you know."

Surprise registered on Sun's face. "Did you discover these things yourself?"

"He deceived me. That I discovered—saw with my own eyes. Because of his deception, the rest fell into place. What I was told fits the man."

Sun's eyes penetrated her own. "What you were told? Who told you these 'things' about Parker James."

"Matt did."

Sun turned to her dinner preparations. There was silence between them. Juliana wondered if she had offended her friend by speaking against Parker. But they obviously didn't know the

Captain as well as they thought they did.

Sun turned to her. "I heard you talking with Parker James. It was the night that the wolves cried."

Juliana looked at her in surprise. "I thought we were alone. I didn't know that you or anyone else could have been near."

"I had left the camp to walk alone and pray. I stopped in a shelter of stones, not far from where you spoke with Parker."

Juliana waited.

"I have seen the figures that you draw. The eagles soar in the heavens. The ravens tear their carrion. And people. I have seen you draw both the good and the mean in spirit. Your lines are honest. The shadows, the light, speak the truth about what you see." She paused. "But you do not see the light in Parker James. You do not see the shadow in Matthias Graves."

Still Juliana didn't speak. She had never heard Sun speak in such a way. Her voice was low with passion.

"You are wrong about Parker James, Juliana. Jeremiah and I know him well. He is a good man. But you will have to discover that yourself."

The set of her mouth told Juliana that Sun would say no more on the subject. Soon Jeremiah returned with two rabbits for supper. After they were skinned and placed in the salt barrel, the three of them ate their noon meal. They spoke only about the train and the journey ahead.

The Captain soon sounded the call for the afternoon march. Juliana left for her own wagon.

⚜

As Sun readied the wagon for leaving, Jeremiah watched his wife. "Your eyes are sad," he said, as he helped her pack the plates.

"I have much to talk to our Lord about."

He touched her hand. "You are worried about Juliana?"

She nodded. "I feel I should have warned her."

"About Graves?"

"Yes."

"But what could you tell her that she would believe? That the Oñate family is powerful? That her intended's uncle is playing the rebels like our fiddler plays his fiddle? That the family she's marrying into has been involved in murders and political schemes for generations?"

"You are wise, husband. She has the head of a mule—just as my father used to say about me." She laughed softly. "I do not know that this young woman will believe anyone. Matthias Graves has shown only one side to her. She has seen only the light—the warped light—in him. He has hidden the shadows. No one can tell her what she needs to know. She must find out the truth on her own."

Sun looked out at the falling snow, shielding her face from the flakes as the couple headed their team into place. "But my prayer, Miah? My prayer is that her discovery will not come too late."

Jeremiah cracked the whip over the oxen. The two of them strode together near the lead yoke as the caravan began moving closer to Apache Canyon.

&⊷⊙

On Christmas Eve of 1846, the wagon train reached Apache Canyon. The day dawned clear. The storm of the previous days had moved east, leaving a thin blanket of white on the jagged walls and cliffs of Apache Canyon. Parker had left the wagon camp before dawn, telling the teamsters they would camp at the canyon's mouth for two days in honor of Christmas.

The ruins of Spanish Fort lay hidden from view about three miles up the canyon. Riding in the dried mud of an old creek bed where the horse's footing was sure, Parker nudged the Appaloosa's flanks, urging him into a gallop.

He reined the horse around the last bend before approaching the fort. It was a simple adobe building. Three of the walls had long before crumbled. The one remaining stood, a pitiful bulwark, protecting the rundown adobe behind it. A crude wooden door hung half off its hinges. It swung, creaking eerily in the wind as Parker approached.

Rounding the wall, Parker breathed a sigh of relief. Cookingham's horse grazed peacefully in a nearby clump of dry grass. Not far from it, another horse raised its head and neighed softly.

As Parker dismounted, Cookingham called out. "Hey, old man. I thought you'd never get here." He bounded from the adobe, his long legs taking the distance in a few strides. Grinning, he pounded Parker on the back. "All's well?"

"All's quiet so far. You're the one I've been worried about. Tell me how it went."

They stood outside for a few minutes, Bennett filling him in on the details. He had the courier tied up inside. It hadn't been easy, he said, but he had convinced the man to tell him the details of the uprising, including Matthias Graves's part in it.

"Graves is definitely our man, my friend," Cookingham concluded, scratching his red hair. "Francisco de Oñate is the leader in La Sal—but he's following Graves's instructions to the letter. Graves has big plans, and a peaceful takeover isn't one of them." Bennett looked pale. His big eyes blinked. "This uprising—if we can't stop it—is going to be bloody. Worse that anything we've seen so far. Graves wants it that way. Wants to teach the locals a lesson in loyalty they'll not soon forget. "Graves will stop at nothing, and from what I gather, he uses brutality—even revels in it—as a means of control. To him, power is everything. And it doesn't matter how he gets it or uses it.

"The man inside—a half-breed named José—has seen Graves in action. Says there's a side of him worse than any savage on the plains. Says he once saw him scalp a white man. Slick and clean as any Indian could. Said it looked like he'd had practice."

Parker let out a whistle. "I'm surprised the man will talk."

"I told him he didn't have a choice. He's going to Fort Leavenworth as my prisoner anyway. If he tells us what he knows, he'll get off easy. That way someday he'll be free to go back to New Mexico."

Cookingham grunted a laugh. "I finally convinced him. But it took several hundred miles and a few missed meals."

Parker slapped his friend's back as they headed into the adobe. "You've done well, old man. Couldn't have handled it better myself. Let's see just what else this José can tell us about La Sal."

&⟶

"Jules, it's a beautiful day!" Callie looked outside the tent. "And it's Christmas Eve." She turned back to Juliana. "We've got the entire day ahead of us to do what we want—no trudging through the snow and mud. No cracking whips at stubborn oxen. No stepping in cow patties. No spreading bear grease on the wheel hubs." She stretched luxuriously. "The day belongs to us."

Juliana laughed as she brushed her hair until it shone, then fastened it with a green ribbon at the base of her neck. "We've not only got the day—there's a party at the night fire. Christmas carols. Sun's going to tell the Christmas story." She turned from her looking glass and met Callie's eyes. "Who would have thought last year—when we watched the servants decorate the Christmas tree at Stonehaven—that this year we'd be on the Santa Fe Trail bound for New Mexico? Celebrating in a tent." She glanced at their simple cots, their old clothing hanging on hooks. "And about to sing carols at a camp fire in a wagon circle."

Callie grinned. "Somehow I like it better."

"I do, too, Cal."

Callie's eyes began to sparkle. "Jules. I've got a great idea. Let's take Sir Galahad and Darley out for a ride, and. . ." She paused dramatically.

"And?"

"Cut a Christmas tree for the party tonight."

"That's a great idea, Cal." Juliana hesitated, hating to disappoint her sister. "There's one problem."

Callie lifted an eyebrow.

"There are no pine trees around. At least I haven't seen any."

"Ah, but you are wrong, *ma cherie*. There are the finest pines around, the majestic, though small, piñon pine. I am told they abound upon the cliffs of Apache Canyon." She dropped the fake French accent, and looked serious for a moment. "Please say yes. It'll be fun. I promise."

"What are we waiting for? Let's go." She grabbed Callie by the waist and the two of them headed out to the *remuda*.

She stopped abruptly at the wagon circle. "Callie, we can't go alone. We're still in Comanche country. It would be foolish."

Callie's face fell.

"Let's ask Matt to go with us. Come on." She started to move toward his tent. "Come on, Callie. This will be the first Christmas we'll have with the three of us." Callie looked reluctant. Juliana reached for her hand. "This is a wonderful way to start our celebration."

Minutes later, the three rode off across the plains. Matt carried a plains rifle slung across the saddle in its scabbard, balls and powder in pouches at his side. A hatchet was tied to the saddle. The three reined the horses around the canyon walls, heading them into the higher country above the canyon.

The morning sun hit on a slant and the snow dazzled and shone in its light. As they rode higher up the cliffs, a sharp breeze stung their faces. Juliana looked back at the wagon camp several hundred feet below. Again she was reminded that the tall canvas-covered Conestogas looked more like ships than wagons—clean, shining ships in full sail on a snow-covered sea. From this distance there was no evidence of the soil and grime from their weeks on the trail. No evidence that the canvas tops were ragged and patched or that the snow had turned to muddy slush. She could only see the illusion of white ships sailing on a sparkling sea.

She remembered Sun's words about light and shadow. What had her friend said about Matthias? The words settled hard in her mind. *The shadows, the light, speak the truth about what you see. But you do not see the light in Parker James. You do not see the shadow in Matthias Graves.*

She glanced at Matt riding beside her. He turned toward her, his handsome face beaming. He smiled. She searched his dark eyes, but there was no depth, no soul shining through. It was as if they only reflected something of herself, something that she wanted to see. The *light* she wanted to see. Maybe he guarded the shadows, she thought, allowing her to see only what pleased her.

Juliana shivered, even in the sun's warmth, and turned away. Matt's dark eyes with their flecks of reflected light and the wagon covers' false gleaming seemed too similar. As the horses climbed, and she considered it, pondered it, Juliana knew that she had made a mistake. She had missed the shadows.

Before long they reached the top of the mesa. Callie was

right. Groves of piñon and spruce grew thick across the flat terrain. She shouted in delight and kicked Darley into the forest to search for just the right tree. After a few minutes, another triumphant shout carried through the trees. "It's here! I found it. Hurry!"

Juliana and Matt rode to the spot. Matt toppled the tree and tied it like a sled behind Callie's horse. "It's your tree. You get the honors of pulling it back," he said with a laugh.

They started working their way down the cliffs. The sun now hung high, casting a hard light on a south-to-north slant. The sky had turned a vivid blue, nearly causing Juliana's eyes to ache. The dripping sound of melting snow was all around them. And the horses slid and slipped as the slush-covered mud gave way underfoot.

They had reached the mouth of the canyon. To the east was the wagon camp. To the west, deeper in the canyon mouth, lay the ruins of the old Spanish Fort.

"I want to see the fort," Callie announced as they rested at the bottom of the sandstone cliffs. "It's from the time of the Spanish *conquistadors.*"

"You're always picking up information that I never hear," teased Juliana, shaking her head. She knew Callie wanted to explore, but she simply wanted to return to camp. She knew she had some hard decisions to make about Matthias. She needed time to think, to plan what she would say to him.

"Let's go in and find it."

"I really would rather not—," Juliana began.

Matt interrupted. "I don't think it's far. It wouldn't take long."

"Please, Julie?" Callie looked at her, imploring.

Juliana sighed then nodded. Something didn't feel right about it. Maybe it was just that her nagging thoughts about Matt weighed heavily on her. Made her want to retreat from the world of people—even Callie—and be alone.

They rode deeper into the canyon. Its red walls had darkened with the wet of the melting snow. Now they stood like jagged vermilion sentinels against the purple sky.

The Christmas tree Callie dragged behind her horse had begun to pick up mud in its branches. Juliana looked at it, surprised. The deep green boughs carried bits of red clay, an eerie decoration, looking at a distance like holly berries, but on closer inspection, startlingly like blood.

The canyon, with its cliffs jutting skyward, brought early shadows to the floor below. Now the sun had crept past high noon, and the shadows lay crossways, darkening the place where they rode.

Callie rode lead as the canyon narrowed and the horses fell into single file. She loved the adventure of it, the thought of visiting ruins hundreds of years old. Maybe they would find an artifact, a conquistador's helmet or something. She had heard of that before. She smiled, gazing at the red-soiled canyon floor with its patches of rock and snow.

"Hey, look up ahead!" She turned to make sure Juliana and Matt were looking. "There it is!" She kicked the bay with her heels, galloping ahead toward the crumbling fort wall.

Callie slowed Darley to a walk, reining the horse around the wall. She stopped in surprise. The captain's Appaloosa lifted its head from a tuft of grass. Two other horses stood beyond him.

At the same moment, Parker James came out of the adobe.

Callie stayed atop the bay, stunned.

"What are you doing here?" the captain demanded. "Who else is with you?"

Confused, Callie glanced behind to where Juliana and Matt

had been moments before. They were not in sight. She looked back at the captain. The bay danced sideways, its ears back, nervous. "My sister," Callie said, confused. "And Matt. Matt Graves. They were right behind me."

"Get down, Callie." Parker's voice was low, strangely calm.

She cocked her head.

"Now." His voice was still low, though now it held a quiet anger. "I said, 'get down.' You're in danger. Come with me. Now."

Callie didn't like the look on his face, but she obeyed and slid down from Darley's saddle. Parker grabbed Callie's arm and moved her quickly to the adobe.

They had just reached the doorway when a shot rang out.

"Let the girl go, James."

Callie recognized Matt's voice. He and Juliana must have taken cover on the other side of the wall.

Parker pushed her through the doorway. He crossed at once to the room's only window. Standing to one side, he shouted in the direction of the voice. "Come out where I can see you, Graves. Then we'll talk about the girl."

The sound of Matt's laughter was the only reply.

Callie fell where the captain had pushed her. Her eyes adjusted to the dim light. She saw movement. A man, she thought his name was Hoss, moved to the other side of the window where the captain stood. Both of them held rifles.

She tried to stand.

"Stay down," the captain hissed.

She dropped and crawled to the corner. Another movement nearby caught her eye. She turned to look.

The small adobe room whirled. Callie felt herself falling. And there was pain. Oh, the pain! She touched her head, felt the scar, and began to cry. She thought she heard someone screaming. Then she realized it was her voice. Screaming for Juliana. Screaming for help. Only no sound came out of her mouth.

She looked into the face of the man in the corner. Those eyes had looked at her that night by the creek. She felt him chasing her. Her breath came in gulps, just as it had that night. Her legs were weak. She had run until they nearly gave way beneath her.

Then she had stumbled. She looked at him now and remembered how it felt to pick herself up, then stumble again. She remembered the feel of his fetid breath on her neck. He grabbed for her, this man who sat in the corner. As he did, she crawled up the riverbank.

She had pulled away. She had panted and crawled. He grabbed her foot. But still she fought. She had kicked again. This time he howled, doubling over in pain.

Callie looked now at his face and remembered how he had looked as he clutched his groin and rolled into a ball at the creek's edge.

Callie had won. She remembered now the feel of triumph. Danger had passed. So she stood, brushed herself off. Turned to make her way up the creek bank.

But someone else had been waiting. He had waited in the shadows of the black willows. Pistol in hand. But she didn't see the glint of its pearl handle until too late.

His dark handsome face had smiled at her. She thought he'd come to help. She remembered how she had smiled at him. Held out her hand so he could help her up the bank.

There had been someone else there too. In the shadows. The pale man, Seth Johnson, had watched. He hadn't helped her. He had only watched, his face white as Matthias Graves lifted his pistol to strike her.

Matt, their friend, their champion, smiling, taking her hand in his, drawing her toward him at the creek bank, the pearl pistol handle glinting white against the shadows.

Then all had gone black.

Callie looked frantically toward the door of the adobe. She had to warn Juliana.

Nineteen

Juliana and Matt had dismounted and taken cover behind the old fort wall as soon as they heard Callie speaking to Parker James.

"Matt, what's going on?" Juliana moved closer to Matthias.

He put his fingers to his lips, shaking his head slightly.

"But why would Parker James be out here?" she whispered. "Why would he take Callie like that?"

Matt's face was dark. "I don't know." He hesitated. "Something's gone wrong."

"What do you mean?" Juliana looked at him sharply. His face remained inscrutable.

Matt pulled his plains rifle from its scabbard and grabbed the balls and powder. For a few moments neither spoke as he readied the rifle.

"You can't shoot," Juliana whispered. "Callie's in there."

"This is just to make sure we get out alive."

"I'm not leaving with you, Matt. I told you, I can't leave Callie."

He stared at her, his gaze without emotion. Juliana remembered the first time she saw him, how his eyes seemed to glint a gun metal gray. She had noticed the color, but how could she not have noticed the rest—the darkness, the cruelty they held?

Several minutes passed. Juliana could feel her heart pounding in fear for Callie. For herself. What were they mixed up in? Then Parker James called out to Matthias.

"Graves," he said, "you might as well give up. We've got your courier. He's told us everything."

Matt sidled over to the corner of the wall, his rifle at his side. There was a hard look on his face. He cut his eyes to Juliana. His menacing look told her to say nothing.

James went on. "You're expecting your wagons to ambush us in the pass. You're expecting them to back you up right now.

"But I've got news for you, Graves. They're not here. They're not even close. We had your man send them on a wild buffalo chase."

Juliana could see a flicker of anger on Matt's face. His lips were set in a straight line. He didn't answer Parker.

"It's over, Graves. Your game is over."

Matt laughed, a bitter, mocking sound. "You may think it's over, James. But you have no idea what you are up against. The wagons are nothing compared to what awaits me in New Mexico."

"You'll never make it there. You might as well give up now. The courts will be lenient if you give up now."

Matthias laughed again. "By whose authority do you speak? As captain of a wagon train? Do you take me for a fool?"

A different voice called out from the adobe. "You are speaking to agents of the U.S. government. I would suggest you come out now with your hands in the air."

Matt cocked his head, surprise registering on his face. "Is that you, Hoss?"

"It is."

Juliana let out a breath, looking in confusion to Matt. "I thought—" she began.

He shot her a dark look and she didn't finish. She stared at him, realizing at that moment that he had lied to her. He had lied about Parker James. He had lied about himself.

"It's *you,*" she whispered hoarsely. "You're the one who's planning the uprising in New Mexico. It's been you all along, hasn't it, Matt? You lied to me. It's you, not Parker James."

"Shut up."

Juliana tried to move away from him. In her mind, she measured her chances. She had to get around the wall then run to the doorway before he could squeeze off a shot. He wouldn't have time to reload. She guessed that he would save the shot for his own getaway. If she ran now she might make it.

Graves anticipated her thoughts and grabbed her arm. Squeezed it until it ached. "Do not think of leaving." His lip curled. "You will stay with me." He let go and cocked the rifle. With the other hand he pulled the pearl-handled pistol from its holster. With a sinking feeling, she realized he had two shots. One for her. One to save himself.

"When I give the signal," he said, "we will run for the horses."

"I told you, I'm not leaving here."

"You will do as I say." His eyes were bright as he looked at her. Too bright. "If you want to live, you will come with me."

She knew that he meant it.

Inside the adobe, Parker and Bennett Cookingham spoke in low tones.

"He's going to make a run for it." Parker loaded his Hawken with a ball and powder. Cookingham had done the same earlier.

"I'll try to make it to the wall, see if I can get around to the other side, get a shot off as he leaves." Cookingham squinted as if measuring the distance with his eyes. "What about the St. Clair woman? She's with him."

"She'll probably make a run for it with him. You were right about her. She's known about the plan from the beginning."

"No!" Callie had overheard their conversation. "You're wrong. Juliana doesn't know about him."

The men turned toward her. The girl was crying. "We've got to warn her. You've got to help me get to her. She must get away from him." Callie's face was white with fear. "She had no idea—you've got to believe me."

Parker exchanged a look with Cookingham. The girl was distraught, frightened. Of course Callie would say anything to save her sister. "We'll do our best," he said, to placate her, and then turned back to the window.

"Cover me, friend," Bennett said a moment later. He moved to the doorway. The weathered door creaked on its hinges. He stopped, waiting for a sign of movement outside.

Parker nodded, signaling that it was clear from his vantage point. Cookingham ran for the wall, loaded rifle in hand.

"You can't let her go." Callie moved closer to the window. Her eyes were wild and red-rimmed.

"Get down," he muttered fiercely. "You'll be hurt if there's gunfire."

"You don't understand." The girl's voice bordered on hysteria. "That man—the one in the corner. He was there the night I got hurt."

Parker looked at her sharply. "We'll talk about this later." He forced a gentler tone into his voice. "Please, Callie. Sit down. Be calm. I promise, we'll try to save your sister."

Callie stayed near him. It seemed she hadn't heard him. Her

voice took on a monotone. "I was gathering wood. I came upon three men. At first they didn't see me. But I heard them talking. Something about more wagons coming. Something about plans they had in Fort La Sal."

Parker didn't take his gaze from Cookingham, who moved silently toward the far end of the wall. But he heard every word that Callie said. He didn't stop her from talking.

She gulped and took a shaky breath. "I stepped on a twig. It snapped. They turned to see me. I saw their faces. Matthias Graves. Seth Johnson. And a man I didn't know. The man sitting in the corner over there. He's the one who chased me. I tried to get away. I ran. I ran until I couldn't run any more."

Her voice took on a singsong tone. Parker could feel her unblinking eyes on him. As he watched Bennett creep along the wall, she continued. She related how she had finally kicked the man and managed to get away.

When she told how Matt had struck her with the butt of his pistol, he looked at her and finally saw her despair. Saw that there was much more to Matthias Graves's deception than he knew. Maybe he was wrong about Juliana and her involvement.

He drew the girl close. With one arm holding the rifle, he placed the other around her as she began to cry.

"When I saw the man in the corner I remembered everything. I knew all about Matt. I knew that everything about him is a lie. But Juliana—Juliana doesn't know." She looked up at him, imploring. "I've got to tell her, Captain. I've got to—" But Callie didn't finish. She suddenly bolted for the door.

On the other side of the wall, Matthias nodded toward the horses. "Let's go," he said simply.

"No."

He pointed the pistol toward her.

She nodded, realizing he would shoot before she could get

away. She reluctantly turned to walk toward Sir Galahad.

Juliana had taken just a few steps when Callie bounded around the wall.

"Julie!" she screamed. "Stop—"

Matt spun, pistol in hand. It was pointed at Callie. A shot rang out. At the same instant, Juliana lunged at him. The gun flew from his hand and his shot missed its target.

He swore and grabbed for Juliana. But she had scrambled toward Callie, out of his reach. His dark eyes darted from her to the chestnut, as if assessing the worth of fighting to take her along. Then he swore again and made a run for the horse.

Cookingham rounded the wall and fired. But the chestnut had already taken Graves out of range.

Parker James joined him at the front of the fort. "I'll follow him," Cookingham muttered.

Parker nodded in agreement as his friend saddled one of the waiting horses, then turned toward him. "Keep an eye on our prisoner. We don't have a case against Graves without him."

"If I don't see you before, we'll meet in Santa Fe." Parker raised a hand in farewell. "Good luck, my friend."

Bennett mounted up, then paused for a moment in the saddle. "You take care, old man. I have a feeling you've got a lot on your mind right now." He glanced at Juliana, who was heading into the adobe with Callie. Then he gave Parker a knowing smile. He pulled his hat low and, giving a half-salute with his rifle, reined the horse around to head out of Apache Canyon on the trail of the chestnut.

❧

Much later—back in their tent after riding back to camp with the Captain, his prisoner, and Callie's Christmas tree

239

trailing behind—Juliana and Callie talked for hours about what had taken place.

Callie told Juliana everything she could remember leading up to her accident. They tried to piece together the things Matthias Graves had told Juliana about his role in New Mexico politics.

Finally Juliana said, "I see now what he tried to do—convince me that he was the rightful governor of New Mexico. He lied about the U.S. government backing him. He twisted things so it appeared that Captain James was readying troops to lead a rebellion or an Indian uprising again him." Juliana frowned. "What I don't understand is why he wanted me to marry him."

"Maybe falling in love with you wasn't part of his plan. It just happened."

"No. He's not in love with me. If you could have seen the look in his eyes when I told him I wouldn't go with him, that I wouldn't leave you, Callie—" She shuddered. "I'll never forget his anger. It was in his eyes. There was something evil there, seething deep in his eyes." She was quiet a moment. "No. He could never have loved me and then looked at me that way."

Tears suddenly filled Juliana's eyes. "How could I have been so blind? He hurt you. He meant for you to die in the creek, then pretended he cared. Do you remember how he came around to check on you? He was so attentive."

"When I survived, he probably wanted to know if I had any memory of what happened."

Juliana nodded slowly. "I should have suspected—"

Callie took her hand. "Don't blame yourself, Julie. There was no way you could have known. I didn't even know."

"And Parker James," Juliana went on. "I said some terrible things to him. I accused him—," her voice faltered. "I actually thought he was the one—" Again her eyes teared. "I've got to

240

talk with him, Callie. I need to ask his forgiveness."

"He needs to ask yours, Julie. He hasn't been exactly open with you."

They talked on a few minutes longer. Then Callie suddenly smiled, the color and softness returning to her face. "It's Christmas Eve. Can we forget all about this for tonight." She sighed, the old Callie returning. "I do so need a party, Juliana. Let's wash off the tree, get someone to help us put it up near the night fire. After supper we'll get everyone to join in and help us trim it." She giggled. "I want to see those old muleskinners string popcorn."

Juliana laughed, wiping her tears. They left the tent and headed off hand in hand to find Jeremiah and Sun to help with the tree.

Juliana left Callie laughing and talking and fixing the tree with Sun and Jeremiah. She smiled, thinking of Callie's words: She too needed a party. She needed to forget Matthias Graves. He was gone. And, she hoped, out of her life forever.

She took a deep breath and realized she had carried a heaviness inside for weeks. Since she had told Matt she would marry him. Now it was gone. Even with the fresh knowledge of his treachery, the sadness was gone.

It was time to look to the future. She and Callie had almost accomplished what they had set out to do: They had almost reached New Mexico. It was time to celebrate, and celebrate she would!

In her tent, Juliana grabbed soap and a towel, then headed to a nearby creek, upstream where she hoped no passersby would happen along. She stepped out of her clothes and into the creek. The waters were icy, but she held her breath, shivering as she scrubbed her skin pink. Then she plunged her head underwater, sputtering when she came up for air. She rubbed her hair with the soap until bubbles foamed, then plunged under the icy waters again.

Juliana toweled off and quickly dressed, then headed back to camp.

By now it was nearly dark, the early darkness of late December. She sat on her cot, brushing her hair dry, feeling its waves in her fingers, watching it gleam in the lantern light. Then she pulled the green velvet dress—the only frock she had brought—from her one large satchel. With the damp towel she rubbed out its wrinkles until the folds fell softly downward.

A few minutes later, Juliana had just pulled the dress over her head when Callie returned in time to fasten the tiny buttons that lined the back.

Callie helped her adjust the folds of velvet at the neckline. Her neck was bare to her shoulders, where the velvet formed a full sleeve to the elbow, then narrowed to her wrist.

Tilting her head, Callie stood back and let out a whistle. "You're beautiful, Jules. That shade of green with your hair and your eyes. It's perfect." She smiled. "There's one more thing." She pulled a cameo and pearl choker from a satin drawstring bag and started to fasten it around Juliana's neck.

Juliana shook her head. "I don't think so, Callie. I don't even want to look at mother's jewelry. It reminds me too much of Matthias."

Callie smiled impishly. "I have a confession to make." Her eyes danced. "Matthias never had this piece."

Juliana tilted her head. "He didn't?"

"I hid this cameo for you and some ear bobs for me before you sold the jewelry to the trader."

Juliana smiled slowly. "You did?"

Callie nodded. "I did." She fastened the cameo choker around her sister's neck, then gave Juliana a quick squeeze.

A few minutes later, the young women pulled back the tent flap and headed for the night fire.

Smells of mesquite and roasting buffalo wafted toward them. Already the fiddle and harmonica had begun their playing. Soon the concertina joined in. The triumphant sounds of *Hark! The Herald Angels Sing* had never seemed so beautiful.

Juliana reached for Callie's arm. Her sister looked up at her, eyes bright with excitement.

As they stepped into the clearing near the fire, Juliana sensed that someone was watching her. She turned.

There stood Parker James. His eyes sought hers.

Twenty

❧

When Parker James saw Juliana enter the clearing near the night fire, he caught his breath. It was the first time he had seen her wearing anything but leather breeches and a shirt. Yet here she was, standing before him in a soft, deep-colored gown. Her auburn hair was swept up and tied with a dark ribbon, emphasizing her long, delicate neck.

As she stood there gazing at him, he was reminded of the first day he saw her. She had stood in his office in a patch of streaming sunlight, her hair a golden halo in the sun. Now, in the firelight, her hair held the sheen of the dancing light it reflected.

Parker moved toward her, wanting to speak to her, to ask her forgiveness. He knew he must talk with her. It couldn't wait. There was too much to be said. He made his way through the crowd of bullwhackers and traders, hearing snatches of laughter and music. Some of the men called out to him. Others stopped him to slap him on the back with holiday greetings. He nodded and returned their good cheer, then tried to wind his way toward Juliana.

He had almost reached her when she turned away from him, her attention caught by others in the crowd.

A few minutes later, supper was served. Parker spotted Juliana sitting with Callie, Sun, and Jeremiah. He filled his plate with roasted sausage *boudies* stuffed with buffalo and wild sage and onions, then sat near them.

The conversation turned to Christmas memories. Callie regaled them with tales of plantation Christmases. Jeremiah told about his and Sun's first Christmas together. It had been spent in the Divides, trapped in a one-room cabin under fifteen feet of snow. Jed Smith had been with them, he said, and told them the story of the first Christmas, about the birth of Jesus, the Christ.

Sun's eyes were soft with the memory. She picked up the narration. "In those days it was just a story. A beautiful story, but nothing more. It was not until later that I understood what it meant." Her eyes found those of her husband, and he nodded slightly. But she said no more.

As the group spoke of other memories, Parker grew quiet, thinking about Laurie, the one Christmas they had celebrated together.

He stood, excused himself, and left their company. As he walked away, he noticed Juliana's quizzical look.

After supper, Callie got her way, and the Christmas tree was trimmed amid singing and laughter. Popcorn popped over the cookfire, and a few of the revelers clumsily set to the task. The attempts didn't last long, and Callie and Sun did most of the stringing.

Someone had brought candles and they were fastened to the tree, though someone else suggested they wait until midnight to light them. Jeremiah said he would read the Christmas story from his Bible at the lighting. And Parker suggested that Sun also say a few words.

Until then, the storytelling, singing, and dancing would continue. The winter sky was alive with stars. The fiddler began to play some dancing songs. Soon a concertina, a couple of banjos, and some harmonicas joined in. Someone blew on a jug in time to the music, and one old trapper tapped on his washtub.

With whoops and hollers, the Virginia reel began. It was followed by circle dancing. Then someone shouted out that it was time for couples.

"But there's barely no women," someone else called out.

"Doesn't matter," came the answer. "Dance with yerself."

Callie, Sun, and Juliana took turns dancing with the bullwhackers and traders. The men straightened their shoulders, attempting to dance like gentlemen.

Juliana exchanged a glance with Callie over stepped-on toes. Around the night circle they whirled, the merry music, the singing, the laughter blending together in a harmony that Juliana knew she would remember for the rest of her life.

At the end of another reel, Juliana felt someone tap her shoulder. She turned.

"May I have this dance?" Parker's eyes seemed to bore right through her.

She nodded, and he swept her into his arms. She felt the strength of them holding her, the warmth of him near her.

They danced without speaking. The music played on, but Parker suddenly stopped. "I really need to speak with you, Juliana." His voice was husky.

"I know," she whispered.

"Do you mind—can we go someplace where we can talk?"

He took her hand and led her through the dancers toward the wagons. He helped her step across a wagon tongue, and they walked into the night. A creek, rushing with its winter fill, flowed nearby. They walked along its bank for several moments without speaking.

Finally they stopped at a small rise above the creek. Parker put his hands on Juliana's shoulders and gently turned her to face him.

"I have so wrongly judged you—" he began.

Juliana reached up and touched his lips with her fingertips. "There is no need to apologize. If you only knew what I suspected of you! It is I who should be asking your forgiveness."

He placed her hands in his, holding them as he looked into her eyes. "Juliana, I want—No. I have to tell you I'm sorry. I thought you were in on Graves's plans. That night we talked. You said you knew all about him—that you knew what he had planned. You said you intended to help him—" His voice broke. "I never gave you a chance to tell exactly what it was you *thought* you knew. My training at West Point taught me better than that." He shook his head slowly. "I should have realized he would do anything to get his way."

"The night we first spoke—when you told me about capturing the courier, that you knew about Matt's plans for a wagon ambush—I believed you, Parker." Juliana looked down, suddenly not wanting to look in his eyes. "When Matt took me to that trappers' cabin the next day and I saw you there—I knew you had lied to me. Everything he told me from that time on pointed to your deception."

Parker tried to speak, but Juliana shook her head. "No. Please. Let me finish."

She looked out at the night sky, the feel of tears behind her eyes. "He told me that he was going to be Governor of New Mexico. He said he had the backing of our government."

Her eyes again met Parker's. "He told me that you were going to lead the uprising against him. His armada of wagons were to keep that from happening."

Parker squeezed her hand. "If I hadn't lied to you in the beginning, none of this would have happened. There was too much at stake. I knew I had to set him up—get him to make a move so Cookingham and I could act. I never thought about it backfiring." His voice dropped. "I never thought that I would risk losing the woman I love."

She swallowed. "Love?" she whispered.

He nodded and cupped her face in his hands, tilting it toward him. "I fell in love with you the first time I saw you." Parker gazed at her, his adoration clear. "The day you walked into my office"—he paused, laughing softly at the memory—"and announced you needed a place in my caravan."

"And you said no."

"I don't think I meant it."

She raised an eyebrow. "But finally you said we could join you. What changed your mind, Captain?"

He stepped back from her, a new thought suddenly hitting him. "You probably never knew."

"Knew what?"

"When Graves paid me a visit on your behalf, he said you were his betrothed. As soon as you reached New Mexico and met his family, you were to be married."

"He told you that?" She was silent for a moment.

Parker nodded.

"That was a bold-faced lie. He hadn't even asked me." She paused, trying to sort it out. "It wasn't until just a few weeks ago that he first mentioned it."

"And you said yes."

Juliana sighed. As painful as it was, her betrothal to Matt was something she needed to talk about with Parker. "Yes. I said I would marry him."

"Did—do—you love him?" There was a look on his face, half-expectant, half-fearful.

She gazed at the man standing so close to her. She studied his face, the cut of his jaw, the shock of hair falling across his forehead, the light in his eyes. She reached up and traced his face with her fingertips.

"Sun once told me that she cared deeply for Jeremiah the first time she saw him, but she didn't know it until much later." Juliana's voice softened with the memory, with the knowledge that it was the same for her. "Once she knew for a fact that she loved Jeremiah, she thought back. She realized that there wasn't a time when she had not cared."

Parker cocked his head, waiting.

"That's what I am just beginning to realize about you. Something caught hold of my soul the first time I saw you. Though when you turned my palm over"—she held her hand out now, studying it in the moonlight—"and told me I was too soft to make it on the trail, I was sure I hated you." She laughed. "But even as I walked away from you, I remember that I felt I had known you forever. There was something familiar, something so very dear—" She stopped, not finding the words to finish.

Parker took her hand and gently rubbed her calluses with his thumb. Then, lifting her hand to his lips, he kissed them.

"You haven't answered my question about Graves," he said. "Why did you say yes?"

Juliana frowned. "I got caught up in his passion for New Mexico." She explained to Parker about the old artist, Maurice Dupree, how he had instilled in her a dream to go to New Mexico, belong to the land, find that perfect renaissance light for painting. "Matt told me about his family in La Sal, the adobe where we would live, that I would be the governor's wife—" She paused, suddenly feeling ashamed that such a title could have impressed her. "I told him yes for all the wrong reasons."

She gazed steadily at Parker. "I told myself that I could learn to love him. He had done so much for Callie and me. Right from the first. He even stepped in to save us from harm on the Mississippi riverboat. Time after time he came to our rescue. He gained our trust. I thought I respected him—" Juliana felt she couldn't go on.

"I think we've wasted enough time talking about Matthias Graves," Parker said gently.

Juliana nodded, grateful for his understanding. For a moment, neither spoke. Juliana listened to the sounds of the night. The usual plaintive cries of wolves, coyotes, and owls carried from distant mesas and canyons, but they no longer struck such lonely chords.

Above the sounds of the plains rose the voices from the wagon camp, now singing Christmas hymns. *Silent Night,* sung in the guttural tones of the bullwhackers and traders, drifted to the place where Juliana and Parker stood.

Juliana gazed into Parker's eyes. She thought about the light and shadows that she and Sun had talked about. How could she have missed the light in this man's eyes? Here they stood in the darkness, with only starlight above them, and she felt she could see through to the depths of his soul.

She touched his face. "I love you," she whispered. Then she repeated the words, feeling her soul leap inside as she did. "I love you, Parker James."

"Oh, my beloved," he whispered huskily. Cupping her face in his hands, he kissed her forehead, her cheeks, her chin. He drew back slightly, again gazing at her with adoration. "I love you, Juliana."

Parker pulled her closer. Juliana slipped her arms around him, feeling his warmth, feeling the pounding of his heart.

He bent toward her, lifting her face toward his. His mouth

covered hers. Juliana felt the softness, the tenderness, of his lips. She looked up at him. The caring in his eyes shone even brighter. He caressed her face, then touched her hair. It seemed to Juliana that he almost trembled as he brushed it with his fingers.

"My precious Juliana," he breathed. Then he drew away from her. "Marry me, Juliana," he whispered. "Please say you'll marry me."

Standing on tiptoe, Juliana touched the side of his forehead, his cheek, his jaw. He closed his eyes and she pulled him closer, kissing his eyelids, the cleft in his chin.

He opened his eyes, and she smiled into them. "I thought you'd never ask," she said, laughing softly. She took a deep breath, again feeling the sting of tears, this time joyous tears, behind her eyes. "I *will* marry you, Parker." Her voice was husky with emotion. "I will. Oh, yes, my dearest, I will!"

He pulled her again into his arms. For a long time they stood holding each other. Above them the stars blazed, and around them swirled the sometimes merry, sometimes plaintive music of Christmas.

Parker kissed Juliana softly again, then the two of them walked arm in arm back to the wagon circle and the night fire.

Near the creek, not far from the rise where Juliana and Parker had stood, there was a movement in the brush. Seth Johnson, who had sat silent and undetected only yards from the couple as they spoke, crept downstream, keeping a lookout for any other revelers who might have left camp.

He had been nervous since Graves hadn't returned from his outing with the St. Clair women earlier that day. Something had gone wrong. Graves had told him what to do if anything like this happened. He was to comb the environs for a courier in the hopes that instructions would tell him his next move.

If no one came for him, he was to hightail it to Fort La Sal.

Contact Francisco de Oñate. Get instructions from him. He sighed. He'd gone out to scour the landscape for word from Graves. But he'd found nothing. No messenger. No message. Nothing. He spat in disgust.

That was just like Graves to take off without telling him what to do. Well, he'd show Graves. He'd show the Oñate family he could act on his own. He had information that Graves would kill for. He laughed to himself, wondering how he could use it to his best advantage.

What he'd heard straight from the lips of that St. Clair woman and the Captain would put him in fine stead with Graves. Graves could use something like this, use it well. Graves would be grateful that Johnson had come up with a plan like this on his own. After his boss became governor, he would reward those who had served him well. He wondered what position he'd be given.

He grinned, laying out in his mind the details of his plan. Before he left for Fort La Sal, he had one more stop to make. He slipped closer to camp and mingled among the dancers until he saw the captain whirling around the campfire with the woman. No one paid Johnson any heed as he backed into the darkness, then turned and crept into Captain James's tent.

Twenty-One

Near midnight, the musicians stopped playing at the captain's signal. He stood, and the rest of the travelers stopped their dancing and looked in his direction. With Juliana at his side, Parker nodded toward Jeremiah, who stood with his Bible in hand. The old trapper moved closer to the night fire, a thoughtful expression on his weathered face.

He looked at the ground a moment, seeming shy in front of the large group, rubbed his beard, then cleared his throat. He nodded at a few of the bullwhackers seated by the fire, then smiled slowly and began to talk.

"Some of you knew my friend Jedediah Smith," he began. "Most of you have heard of him. One of the finest mountain men who ever lived. First man to find a route for wagons to get through the Divides, first white man to go on foot to California.

"I count it one of the finest times of my life to have known this man as my friend. We trapped together. We lived together with the Mandan—," he smiled at Sun, "—the Pawnee, the Cheyenne.

"Jed Smith had a reputation for loving God. Carried this here Holy Bible in his saddle bag." Jeremiah held up the Bible in his hand, then let it drop to his side. "Some of the others, well, they gave him a hard time about that." There was a splattering of knowing laughter among the crowd.

"But they soon found out, being religious didn't mean a person was weak." Jeremiah grinned. "They never made that mistake twice." He paused a moment, looking out at the stars. "Most folks learned that Jed lived what he preached. He loved his God. And he loved his fellow man. He'd give his friend—or his enemy—the coat off his back on a winter night.

"Jed's God was more than some Being that existed way out there somewhere—" he gestured toward the sky. "Nosiree. Jed's God was his friend." Jeremiah thumped his chest. "His God lived inside him."

He stopped for a moment, seeming to gather his thoughts. No one spoke. Only the night sounds of the distant animals and the crackling of the fire could be heard. Juliana watched the expression on Jeremiah's face. He seemed lost in the memory of his friend.

"When I heard Jed had died," he went on, "it was like I had lost a brother. He was young. Only thirty-three. He died at the hand of the Comanche. He was trying to find water—on this very trail—for himself and his friends." Jeremiah's eyes looked sad.

"I tell you about Jed, my friends, because it was this man who showed me who God is. The first time I ever heard the story of Christmas was from this book, read by Jed's own voice.

"And it's in his memory that I read you the story now." Jeremiah leafed through the Bible until he found the book of Saint Luke, then in a tone that held power in its simplicity, he read the words.

"And it came to pass in those days, that there went out a decree from Caesar Augustus, that all the world should be taxed," he began, and continued reading the story of Mary and Joseph and the babe who was born in the manger.

Juliana had heard the story read many times through her childhood, but somehow it was different this night. When Jeremiah read, "And, lo, the angel of the Lord came upon them, and the glory of the Lord shone round about them...," she looked out into the star-spangled night. Wonder filled her heart as she realized that these were the same stars. It was the same sky. Could God be the same God? A God so personally interested in the affairs of mankind that he sent his Son to earth?

Jeremiah read on, "And the angel said unto them, Fear not: for behold, I bring you good tidings of great joy, which shall be to all people."

All people? She thought about the phrase. It didn't say just those shepherds, or just those people who lived at the time of Jesus' birth.

"For unto you is born this day in the city of David a Saviour, which is Christ the Lord." Jeremiah read on, but the phrase "*all* people" settled into her mind. That meant her.

She would think about it later, she decided. After all, she had everything she needed. She glanced up at Parker. His eyes met hers. He took her hand and squeezed it gently, a warm smile on his face. Yes, she decided. She had everything she needed. Someday she would think about God. About his Son, Jesus. But not today. Not now. She smiled at Parker.

A few minutes later, Sun stepped to Jeremiah's side. She was dressed in a white buckskin dress, beaded and fringed. She wore moccasins and leggings of the same design. Her raven hair was plaited into one long braid that hung down her back. Juliana thought she had never seen her look so beautiful.

When Sun spoke to the gathering, her voice was soft. "I know a little of what it is like to give up a child," she said.

"Seventeen summers ago, Jeremiah and I had a baby. We named him Jedediah after our friend. Little Jed grew up strong and wise. I taught him about the Mandan. His father taught him trapping and as much book learning as he could.

"One day I told our child about what had happened to my people—his people, the Mandan. That only a few are left because of disease. Our son decided that he wanted to help his people. He wanted to study medicine to become a doctor.

"Three summers ago I said goodbye to Jed. Jeremiah took him to St. Louis to live with a doctor and learn medicine. I have seen him only once since."

She paused, her blue eyes dark with emotion. "When my child left our home, it seemed that the sun went out of my life. Though he was grown, my arms still feel empty. When he goes to the Mandan villages, he may die of the same disease that killed thousands of my people."

Sun's eyes searched those in the crowd. It seemed to Juliana that she looked directly at her when she spoke again. "God sent his only Son to a lonely death on a cross. He knew when he sent him that he would be despised, hated, mocked." Her eyes filled with tears. "I do not know—even as much as I love my people—that I can let my son give his life for them." Again, she paused. There was not a sound from the listeners.

"But God loved the world so much that he gave his only Son so that whoever believes in him can live forever. The baby that Mary laid in the manger was so much more than a simple child born to a young couple in a faraway place. That baby was God's Son, sent to save us, to bring us to himself."

After Sun finished speaking, a few moments of silence fell over the group, then an old trader began to sing a carol. Others joined in, softly, reverently, without the instruments. When it was quiet again, Callie stood and, holding a glowing coal with cooking tongs, lit each of the candles on the piñon Christmas tree.

In a blaze of light, the fiddle player began *O Come, All Ye Faithful*, and the travelers again lifted their voices in song.

"This is the best Christmas ever!" Callie declared that night as they prepared for bed.

Juliana gave her sister a hug. "It's even better than you know, Callie." Then she told her about Parker James and their talk on the hill.

Callie's joy was written on her beaming freckled face. After wishing each other "Merry Christmas," Juliana turned out the lantern and drifted to sleep, lost in loving thoughts of Parker James.

✎☙

For the next two weeks, the caravan moved slowly toward Santa Fe and the end of the trail.

The weather stayed clear, though cold. The buffalo were scarce now, and fewer bands of Indians trailed behind. The oxen seemed despondent in their weariness. They moved with effort, ribs showing, backs bonier than when they had left Westport. They moaned and bawled less often, seeming to conserve even that effort.

Juliana and Parker ate supper together each night. They sat together at the evening fire, enjoying the storytelling and song. Sometimes they visited with Jeremiah and Sun. Often, Callie tagged along, teasing Parker in a bantering tone. She told him more than once that she'd always wanted a big brother and that it was nice that Juliana had finally gotten her one for Christmas.

The night before they were to pull into Santa Fe, Juliana and Parker sat near the night fire long after everyone else had left for bed.

"Juliana," he said, holding her hand and searching her eyes. "I have to leave you tomorrow—just for a short time. The train will break up after we pull into Santa Fe. My job here is done." He glanced around the sleeping camp.

She tilted her head, watching him closely. There was pain in his eyes. "It has to do with my assignment from the government." He had already explained his connection to Cookingham and the undercover work for the U.S. Government. This new development didn't come as a surprise.

"I had wondered when you'd tell me," she said quietly. "I figured you still had work to do for them."

He smiled, grateful for her understanding. "I need to leave for La Sal tomorrow. Right after we get into Santa Fe." He went on to tell her of the danger that Governor Charles Bent had placed himself in by moving from Santa Fe to La Sal. "He's in the middle of an area controlled by the Oñate family. Francisco de Oñate is Graves's dupe. He follows orders. But even if Bennett has captured Graves, Francisco de Oñate may act without him." His expression was serious. "I've got to get Bent and his family out of La Sal."

"Do you know when the Mojada will act?"

"Our guess is mid-January. There's a local celebration called a *fandango* around then. A carnival of sorts. Brings people swarming into La Sal from the outlying provinces. The Mojada usually attend as well."

"Perfect timing."

Parker nodded. "Yes. If I can get there before it begins, I can get Bent out."

Juliana sighed. "What are your chances?"

His eyes held hers. She could see worry in them. "Not good. If Graves gets there before I do, the Mojada won't wait for the carnival."

"When will I see you? When will I know that you're all right?"

"I want you and Callie to go with Sun and Jeremiah to their cabin in the *Sangre de Cristos*. You'll be safe there. As soon as I can, I will come for you."

"How soon?"

There was a sadness in Parker's eyes that worried Juliana. He gathered her into his arms. "I don't know, darling. I don't know." He pulled back and tilted her face toward his. "But remember, I will come to you as soon as I can." He smiled gently. "I don't want to be away from you one moment longer than I have to."

He kissed her and she melted into his arms, never wanting to leave their warmth and strength. How could she let him go— even for a short time? "Oh, Parker," she whispered. "I can't stand the thought of being away from you. Without you—" Her voice choked. She felt desperately sad, desperately lonely. "If anything should happen to you—"

He put his fingers on her lips. "Sh-h-h, my darling." Then he kissed her cheeks where the tears had slipped from her eyes. He covered her mouth with his. "My beloved," he whispered, "I love you."

They sat talking into the night. The fire died to glowing coals, then turned to cold ashes. Juliana trembled, more from the dread that had settled inside than from the cold.

Parker held her close as he slowly walked her back to her tent.

❧

The following morning, the wagon train wound its way down the mesa and neared the dusty town of Santa Fe, passing winter-brown fields of corn and wheat. Small adobe houses came into view. Flocks of sheep grazed peacefully in the fields. As the caravan passed, families called out greetings, and the children ran along the wagon sides. Some of the drivers threw trinkets, grinning at the squeals of delight.

As they neared Santa Fe, the bullwhackers cracked their whips louder, urging their teams to move faster. By now everyone rode in their wagons. Juliana had heard an old bullwhacker say it was too late to save the oxen now. "Might as well ride into town in style," he'd said with a wink.

As soon as the first wagons rolled into town, the drivers stood, whooping and hollering, calling out to each other with shouts of laughter. Juliana noticed that their skin had been scrubbed clean and their hair was slicked back and shiny. They were dressed in odd-fitting but, Juliana supposed, their best Sunday suits.

Young Santa Feans in their colorful dresses stood at the side of the road, cutting their black eyes toward the drivers, which caused an even greater hoopla.

Most of the bullwhackers had tied new pieces of leather to their whips, and they popped the air above the oxen, making more noise than a gunfight. Each seemed to be trying to outperform the others with the sharp cracks and fancy twists of their whips.

"*Los Americanos!*"—"*Los Carros!*"—"*La entrada de la caravana!*" came the shouts as the train passed by. Crowds of women and little children ran to the wagons and followed as the traders and bullwhackers popped their whips and moved their teams along.

Most of the wagons pulled into an area near warehouses, and the business of unloading began. The *remuda* was corralled nearby.

Juliana halted her wagon outside one of the larger adobe buildings where Parker had driven his wagons for unloading.

He was saddling the Appaloosa and turned to greet her as she jumped down from the wagon. Callie stayed on the wagon's bench.

Juliana and Parker spoke for a few minutes about the days ahead. Again he reminded her he would see her in a few days at Sun and Jeremiah's place. Then he said it was time to leave.

"This is goodbye then?" She fought to keep her voice from breaking.

He nodded. "Juliana, remember that no matter what happens—I love you. I will always love you." He touched her face gently, then bent to kiss her.

For a moment Juliana couldn't speak. She just held him with her gaze, memorizing everything about him. The color of his eyes in the sunlight. The way he brushed his hair back from his forehead with his fingers. The way he looked at her.

She blinked back her tears. "Please hurry back to me, my love," she finally whispered.

He nodded, then swung into the Appaloosa's saddle and pulled his felt hat low over his forehead. He nodded again, then reined the horse northward.

Twenty-Two

Two days later, Juliana and Callie sat near the morning camp fire, sipping coffee with Sun and Jeremiah. The four had left Santa Fe the previous day and were heading up into the high country, the mountains of the *Sangre de Cristo*, to the cabin that would be Sun and Jeremiah's home. The two young women would be staying there while they waited for Parker James to return.

A light snow had just begun to fall from an ashen sky when a lone horseman rode into camp. The *caballero* was dressed in black and rode a gray horse, its dark saddle trimmed in tooled silver.

He spoke first in his native language, then after a short exchange in Spanish with Jeremiah, switched to English.

"I am looking for *Señorita* St. Clair."

"I am she." Juliana stood, with Callie right behind her.

The rider, still atop the gray, reached into his saddlebag. "You are needed," he said. Then he handed Juliana a small leather pouch.

She took it from his hand, her head tilted in puzzlement.

"I need you to come with me," the horseman said, as she opened the pouch.

Juliana untied the leather thong and reached into the pouch with her fingers. The object inside fit too tightly to remove, so she tipped the pouch into her palm.

A gold watch fell into her hand. A gold pocket watch. She turned it over. Parker's initials were inscribed on the case.

Her heart seemed to stop. "Where did you get this?" she breathed hoarsely.

"He needs you to come, *señorita*. He is injured. He sent me to get you. To bring you to him. It is not far from here. But you must come now. Come quickly."

"Is it bad?"

"Yes, *señorita*. He needs you to come now. There is not much time."

"Please. How badly is he hurt?" Her voice was desperate. "Oh, please tell me."

The gray danced sideways, as if impatient. "Just get your things. I will take you to him."

Juliana nodded. "Of course." She bit her lip. She felt like crying, but there was no time. Parker needed her. She had to get to him. "Of course I'll come," she repeated.

Callie stepped up beside her. "Julie, I'll come with you."

The horseman shook his head. "No," he said. "Only the *señorita*."

"No, no." Juliana interrupted. "I want my sister to come with us."

He shrugged. "Have it your own way, *señoritas*."

Minutes later, after a hurried goodbye to Sun and Jeremiah, Juliana and Callie mounted Sir Galahad and Darley, their quickly packed satchels strapped to the saddles.

Just before they rode from camp, Jeremiah placed a folded piece of paper in Juliana's hand. "Directions to our cabin," he explained. "Remember you are always welcome there. Come soon. We will be praying for you."

Juliana nodded, grateful for his words. "Pray for Parker," she said, her voice breaking. "Pray that he's all right—that I'll reach him in time."

Jeremiah, with Sun at his side, squeezed Juliana's hand. "We will." His clear eyes met hers. "Don't worry about your wagon. We can manage getting both to our place."

Juliana was touched by their thoughtfulness. "Thank you." She released his hand.

"God is with you, child," Sun whispered. "Remember that, Juliana. There is never a time that you are out of his thoughts."

Juliana nudged Sir Galahad with her heels and the horse bolted forward. Soon the three riders were moving swiftly across the mesa, Callie and Juliana side by side, the *caballero* slightly in front, leading the way.

They rode without stopping for nearly three hours due north into increasingly rough terrain. The temperature hovered near freezing, with the light snow sometimes turning into sleet and rain, then back to snow. The sky remained the color of ashes, darkening as the day wore on.

The *caballero* followed no path or road that Juliana could see. He didn't speak after they left Sun and Jeremiah. From time to time he glanced back at them as if to make sure they still followed.

Juliana's thoughts did not stray from Parker. Though her face stung from the exposure to the snow and sleet, she dwelt only on the man she loved and getting to him. Quickly. He needed her. That's all that mattered. She urged the gray forward, her heart aching in despair.

A short time after noon, the *caballero* led them through a

small village. A few dozen adobe houses were scattered around a central square where several larger adobes faced. An uneasy silence greeted them as they slowed the horses to a walk. Very few people were on the streets. Those who were stared at Juliana and Callie with what seemed to be open hostility and insolence.

Juliana was struck by the contrast to their arrival in Santa Fe a few days earlier, where the people had poured into the streets in celebration. She nudged Sir Galahad forward until she was beside the *caballero*.

"Where are we?" She looked over at the man, noticing that his eyes mirrored the expression of the people on the street.

"La Sal, *señorita.*" His black eyes held hers, unblinking. "Welcome to Fort La Sal." The *caballero* nodded toward a small adobe building set apart from the central plaza. Stark and the color of desert sand, the structure was perfectly square except for an arched facade that held a plain white cross at its highest point. A thick adobe wall circled the building, with a heavy wooden gate at its center.

"That is where the *capitán* waits. In the *iglesia.*"

They dismounted just outside the wall, and the *caballero* pointed to the wooden gate. "Someone will meet you inside," he said simply. "I will take your horses to the stable."

Juliana nodded and, with Callie at her side, entered the small courtyard and walked to the tall double doors of the church.

She knocked at the door. Within seconds it was opened by another man dressed like the *caballero* who had led them there.

"*Señorita,*" he said, with a slight bow. "You have been expected."

"Please." Juliana looked earnestly at the man. "Please take me to *Señor* James."

"Follow me." He led them into a small, dark foyer, then turned to Juliana. "You, *señorita,* may enter the sanctuary. You will be met there." He nodded, indicating the direction. Then to Callie, "Please, come with me. I will show you where to put your things."

Callie smiled gratefully at the man as he took the satchels and she followed him down a hall, away from Juliana.

Juliana took a deep breath and opened the door leading to the sanctuary. The light was dim, but in a few moments her eyes had adjusted. The small room was empty except for the dark wooden pews lining the aisle and the ornate, colorful altar at one end. Candles glowed at the altar's base.

She walked to the altar and stood, wondering why she had been sent to this room. Where was Parker? Why would he—or someone else—want to meet her here?

For several minutes Juliana waited in the quiet of the place, feeling strangely uncomfortable. Something was wrong. The place, perhaps. Or the eerie silence. She shivered, wondering why it struck her so.

The doors behind her opened and she turned. The figure walking toward her at first was shrouded in darkness. It wasn't until he had almost reached the place where she stood that Juliana could see his face. Matthias Graves.

She looked at him in confusion. "What are you doing here?" Though the chill traveling down her back made her realize that she already knew.

He smiled and reached for her hand. "Darling," he said, his dark eyes appraising her. "You are as beautiful as ever. I have missed you."

Juliana pulled her hand away. "Matt, why?—" she managed to stammer. "Why have you brought me here?"

He chuckled. "Darling! Don't tell me you have forgotten. We are going to be married."

"Matt—after what has happened—" She stopped. Surely he

understood. Surely he didn't think she would still consider marriage. "Matt, I can't marry you."

He cocked his head, the smile frozen on his handsome face. "Can't?" he repeated, an eyebrow raised. "Can't?"

"You lied to me, Matt. You lied about everything. Who you are. What you are. What you have planned. I can't marry you. I won't marry you."

He didn't answer, just stared at her with those cold, dark eyes. Juliana could see the candle flames behind her reflected in them.

Then his lip curled on one side. "Ah, but you are wrong, my darling. You will marry me." He took her hand again, squeezing it tightly, painfully, between his fingers so that this time she couldn't pull away. "You see, Juliana, you really do not have a choice. We will be married in the morning. A priest is on his way."

"You can't hold me here against my will, Matt. You can't do this." Though as she said the words, Juliana knew that she was wrong. No one knew where she and Callie were. Even if they did, she was sure he had guards—probably an army—simply awaiting his command.

Juliana forced a softness, a conciliatory tone, into her voice. "Why do you want to do this, Matt?" She looked straight into his eyes. "You don't love me. I know that you don't. Why do you insist on pursuing it?

He laughed. "You have not guessed, have you, Juliana?" He laughed softly again. "I met someone once in Washington whose wife had moved him into powerful political circles."

Juliana looked at him, not understanding what he was getting at.

"John C. Frémont. You've heard of him? Explorer? Map-maker?" He raised an eyebrow.

"Of course. I know him. I've met his wife. His father-in-law is a friend of my uncle's." As soon as the words left her lips,

Juliana knew where Graves was leading. But she asked anyway. "What does this have to do with me?"

"Actually, it has more to do with the uncle you speak of than with you. As governor of New Mexico, it will be a great boost for me to have a wife with Washington connections. Your uncle has the president's ear. With his niece standing by this governor's side, who in the U.S. would dare lift a finger to depose me?

"You see, I thought of it as soon as you told me about your dear Uncle Caleb Benedict. You did not even have to call him Senator Benedict for me to know who your uncle was. Anyone who has been around Washington circles knows of his power and influence.

"I, of course, thought of Jessie Benton Frémont and how she influenced her father, Senator Benton, and President Polk on behalf of her husband." He laughed again, an affected, knowing chuckle, obviously delighted with his plan. "Without her, he would not have set foot past his own front yard on behalf of the U.S. government."

He dropped Juliana's fingers and cupped her face in his hands. "It is simple, my dear. You can do the same for me."

"My uncle and I have had a falling out. You know that. He does not care about me—where I am, or who I will marry."

"I have already decided what to do about that. You are going to send him a letter of apology, telling him of your new life and the wonders of what you have seen in New Mexico. You will tell him, of course, all about me, your new husband." He smiled into her eyes. "I have taken the liberty of composing this letter for you. You need only copy it in your own hand."

Juliana backed away from him. "I will not. I will not marry you. I will not do as you say." Her voice was low, angry.

The smile left his face. "It is up to you, of course. But maybe I should tell you what will happen to your sister if you do not."

And he proceeded to tell her in great detail what would happen to Callie.

"You wouldn't. You wouldn't dare!" Juliana hissed.

"Who is here to stop me?"

Juliana lifted her chin and looked at him, her gaze steady. "Your plan will never work," she said.

A sinister smile curled one side of his lip. "Again I ask, who is here to stop me?"

"You underestimate me, Matthias." Juliana straightened her shoulders, refusing to let her fear show.

He laughed and reached for her hand. She pulled it away. "That is why I love you, Juliana. You are a strong woman. You are a fighter." He laughed again. The sound was brittle. "It will also be a pleasure to teach you what it means to obey. It is time you had someone teach you that." He reached for her chin and tilted her face toward his.

Juliana slapped him.

He stepped back, his hand moving to strike her. Then he thought better of it and let his hand drop. For a moment he did not speak, then his lip curled again.

"I think you need time to think over your choices, my dear. We will discuss this again in the morning. I fully expect you to see things my way—either before or after my men come for your darling sister."

Moments later, Juliana was ushered by one of Graves's men to a small cell-like room at the back of the church. Callie stood near the only window and turned as Juliana stepped in. The room was bare except for a weathered altar table at its center.

The heavy door slammed behind her, followed by the sound of a crossbar locking into place on the outside.

"Julie, what's happened?" Callie moved to her side.

"No one's told you?"

Callie shook her head. "No. I was shoved in here. Then someone locked the door. That's all. What's going on?"

"It's Matthias Graves, Callie. Parker's not here—at least I don't think he is." It suddenly occurred to Juliana that Parker might have been captured too. How else would Graves have gotten his pocket watch? "It was a trick. Just to get us here."

"But, why? Why would Matt want to do that after all that has happened?"

"He wants to marry me, Cal." Juliana went on to explain all that Graves had said.

"What are we going to do?"

"We've got to get out."

Callie looked around the room. "There's not much daylight left. I've already searched every bit of space for a way to escape. The window's too small. I don't see how we can escape."

Juliana began searching the walls, touching the adobe bricks, feeling for loose stones or mortar. "Keep searching, Callie. We've got to find something. Anything. We've only got until morning."

"That's when he's planned the marriage?"

Juliana nodded. "He says a priest is on the way."

They searched in vain. The walls were solid. Juliana thought they might enlarge the window by scraping the adobes around it, but the bricks were as hard as granite. Her fingers bled after just a few minutes of trying.

With a sigh she sat on the floor next to Callie. The light was fading fast.

Callie squinted her eyes at the walls, then looked up at the ceiling. "Julie, what are those brown spots?" Her gaze focused on the altar table, then back to the ceiling. "They're everywhere." She wrinkled her nose. "I hate to say this, but they look like blood. Splatters of blood."

Juliana stood and inspected the table, then touched the spots on the walls. She smiled softly. "They are, Callie." She touched a few more, then looked back to her sister. "I had forgotten until just now. But I think I know what they are."

She studied the splatters again. "Maurice Dupree once told me about the *Penitentes*. Did you ever hear him speak of them?"

Callie shook her head.

"He said that there was a secret society that formed in Spanish America in the sixteenth century. They called themselves the *Los Hermanos de Penitencia*, or the *Penitentes*. They've been active in New Mexico for at least fifty years."

"What do they do?" Callie sounded like she didn't really want to know.

"Dupree said that he saw the procession once in the town of Tomé. It was around Easter, I think—someone had been chosen to carry a large heavy cross. The man was stripped, and the cross, weighing about a hundred pounds, was strapped to his back. His face was covered so that no one knew who he was. He was beaten and whipped as he carried the cross."

Callie shuddered.

"Then a whole parade of people followed the man with the cross, flagellating themselves with cactus."

"Flagellating?"

"Beating."

"Oh, Julie. That's awful."

Juliana looked around the room again. "Dupree told me that the society has gotten out of hand in New Mexico. It isn't sanctioned by the Church. So the *Penitentes* meet in secret—probably in a room like this—and beat themselves. Beat each other."

"With cactus?"

Juliana nodded. "That's why the tiny splatterings of blood on the walls, the ceiling."

Callie looked thoughtful. "Why do they do it?"

"Because they think that's the only way God will forgive them for anything they've done wrong. They try to purify themselves through doing penance."

"That doesn't sound like the same God that Sun and Jeremiah know."

"Because their God is one of love?"

Callie nodded. "And he wants love from us. I heard Sun reading from Jed Smith's Bible one morning. I don't remember the exact words, but she read something about God wanting us to love him with all our heart and mind and soul. To love our neighbors as ourselves. And that those things are more important to God than offerings or sacrifices."

By now the light in the room had faded to near darkness. Juliana thought about Callie's words and was reminded of the comfort Sun found in her relationship with her God. Rather than fearing him as the *Penitentes* must, she trusted God the way a small child trusts a beloved father.

She remembered the unseen Presence who had been in the room the night that Callie had been injured, the way Sun had spoken to him as a friend. What were the words she had used when speaking to him about Callie? *You love her this moment as if she is the only child, the only one, in your world.*

And she had asked her Friend to touch Callie with the power that raised Jesus from the dead.

Juliana remembered how that night, as she fell asleep, she had thought about those words, and wondered what it would be like to be loved by a God like this. A God of power and might. Yet a God of tender mercies, one who could love you as if you were the only one in his kingdom.

She also thought about Christmas night, how she had looked out into the brilliant night sky as Jeremiah read the story of Christ's birth. Wonder had filled her heart as she thought of the angels who had appeared from the same heavens that she looked into that night.

And when Jeremiah read, *I bring you good tidings of great joy, which shall be to all people,* she had thought about the phrase, *all people.* It struck her that the good news wasn't just for those shepherds, or just for those people who lived at the time of Jesus' birth.

Juliana also remember the thoughts that had followed: *She would think about it later,* she had decided. *After all, she had everything she needed.* Then she had looked up at Parker and felt her newly discovered love for him well up inside.

She had everything she needed. Juliana thought of the words now. How empty they seemed.

She thought about human love. She didn't know whether the man she loved was alive. Or if she would ever see him again. Their love for each other was wonderful. But it wasn't all she needed. It wasn't even close.

And she thought about God. A God who never changed but remained the same. Yesterday, today, throughout eternity. A God of power and might and love and wisdom. A Friend who required love, not sacrifice. A Friend who would be with her always.

She *did* need him. How foolish to think that she didn't. With all her heart she was crying out to the God who loved her as if she were the only one in the world.

The room had completely darkened now.

"Juliana," Callie said after a few minutes, "I'm scared."

"Callie, I want to tell you what happened the night you were hurt." Juliana related all that had happened the night Callie was unconscious. When she had finished, she said, "Callie, I'm not sure how to do this. I've never prayed before. But let's ask God to be with us and bring us comfort. No matter what happens—that he'll just be with us."

Callie nodded and held Juliana's hand as she whispered a simple prayer.

"I don't know quite how to talk to you," Juliana began, "but we really need you to be here with us. We're scared. We're not sure how to get ourselves out of this. And we need your help. I know you've been with us, helping us all along—only we haven't realized it.

"But now we need you even more. The night Callie was so sick I felt that you were in that tent with us—could you be with us in the same way? Could you comfort us the same way you did me that night?"

Afterward, they sat in the dark, though it didn't seem as dark and frightening as it had before.

"I feel different," Callie said after a bit. "Not so alone."

"I know. He's really here with us, Callie. I know he is." Again, the memory of their father holding her in his lap, reading to her, came back to her. She asked Callie if she remembered their Bible storybook with the picture of Jesus blessing the children. Callie nodded, telling Juliana she remembered the feel of their father's strong arms as he carried her up the winding stairs and tucked her in bed.

"That's what it feels like now, Juliana. Like Jesus' arms are around me, holding me safe."

They spoke of other memories of their father and Stonehaven, then of their wagon trip and Sun and Jeremiah. Juliana spoke of Parker, telling Callie some of her dreams of the special wedding they had planned, the house they wanted to build near Sun and Jeremiah.

Finally, the conversation turned back to Matthias Graves and their imprisonment.

"It's too bad the *Penitentes* don't pick Matt for their next flagellation rites." Callie looked up at the ceiling, now barely visible.

Juliana followed her gaze. "I wonder when the next rites are," she mused. "Some of this blood looks fresh—like they hold the rites fairly often."

"I wonder how they get in here." Callie still stared at the ceiling. "If their self-flagellation isn't sanctioned by the Church, they surely don't waltz in the front door."

"You may be right. Maybe there's another entrance, a passageway someplace."

"But we checked everywhere."

"Only down here." Juliana's gaze swept the ceiling. "Help me move the table."

They pushed the table to the wall, then both of them stood on it, feeling the individual bricks, up and down, as far as they could reach. They moved the table around the room, checking every inch of wall space. Still there was nothing.

The young women again sat down on the floor, disappointed.

"I wonder if they'll bring us supper," Callie said.

"What a time to think about food."

"No. I'm wondering—if we do find a way out—shouldn't we wait until they think we're sleeping?"

"You're right." She paused. "Of course, it won't matter if we can't get out anyway."

"Jules," Callie mused after a while, "what about the ceiling? What's it made of?"

"Those crossbeams are called *vegas.*"

"It looks like there are sticks behind the *vegas.*"

"There are." Juliana tilted her head, wondering where Callie was going with this. "Willows. Then on top of those, two feet of mud."

Callie studied the ceiling, though by now it could barely be seen in the darkness. "What if—"

Juliana jumped up. "What if there's no mud on top of some of the willows?"

Callie nodded. "And if that's the way the *Penitentes* get in, there's bound to be a way down from the roof."

They had just moved to the table when they heard footsteps outside the door. The heavy bar was lifted, and the door opened. One of the *caballeros* brought in a tray of food, set it down, and left without speaking.

As soon as the door had again latched, Juliana and Callie climbed onto the table and began searching for loose willows.

"It's here. I've found it." Juliana could feel the willows give way. The cool night air met her fingertips. "But we'd better wait. Let them come take our dishes. We'll pretend to sleep, then be off."

The next few hours passed slowly. The supper tray was removed. The young women waited impatiently.

The shouts of voices in the plaza drew Juliana to the window. She listened for a few minutes, then noticed a glow in the night sky above the courtyard wall.

"Callie, come look," she whispered. The flickering light seemed to be taking the form of torches barely visible above the wall. Soon they heard voices growing louder, angrier.

"I hear Indians," Callie whispered. "Listen, they're calling out—I hear screams and war whoops."

"The Mojada," Juliana breathed. "It's the uprising, Callie. The uprising's finally begun. We've got to get out now—before it gets worse."

Callie nodded. "I know."

"Are you ready?"

Callie had already moved toward the table. Juliana stood next to her, and together they moved the willows away from the *vegas*, until the opening was large enough to squeeze through. Callie crawled through first, then Juliana pulled herself upward and found herself on the roof. They carefully replaced the willows.

Still on the church roof, they turned to face the plaza. Indians on horseback tore through the plaza. People had been dragged from their beds and were being slaughtered in front of their homes. Mothers, fathers, little children.

In other places, torches were thrown into houses and families ran for their lives into the streets, only to be butchered by the waiting Mojada.

"Oh, Julie," Callie cried.

Screams of terror pierced the air, growing louder with each new onslaught. Juliana started to turn away, unable to watch, when a rider on an Appaloosa caught her eye.

"Callie, look. It's Parker!" Juliana grabbed her sister's hand.

There were three riders with him. They rounded the corner, heading toward the church.

Then, from a side street, a band of Mojada rode screaming to the attack. Rifles and knives in hand, they fell upon Parker and his companions like wild animals upon prey.

"There are too many." Juliana's voice caught with a sob. "He doesn't have a chance."

As they pulled him from his horse, she thought for one wild instant that he had looked in her direction, that he had seen her standing on the roof.

"Oh, no! Please, no," she breathed. "They've killed him. They've killed Parker."

Twenty-Three

Two days later, Juliana and Callie rode into a mountain meadow high in the *Sangre de Cristos*. The thin winter sun had slipped behind the forest of tall pines to the west, and the meadow was shrouded in the shadows of dusk.

"I see the cabin. There—" Callie pointed. "Almost hidden at the far end."

Juliana nodded.

As they drew closer, the log structure seemed to welcome them with its lighted windows and curling chimney smoke.

When Sun opened the cabin door to them, Juliana fell into her arms. "Parker's been killed," was all she could manage. The Indian woman held Juliana in her arms, rocking her, as Juliana wept.

A few minutes later, Jeremiah, who had been tending the animals, joined them. While Sun served them stew from her fire, Callie related all that had happened.

Juliana sat in an old rocker, staring at the fire, unable to join in the conversation, unable to think of anything except the horror of watching Parker pulled from the Appaloosa and slaughtered before her eyes.

For days she sat in front of the fire, sometimes weeping, but most of the time sitting silently, staring into the flames. Callie tried to speak with her but stopped after Juliana looked up and told her in a tired voice that she wanted to be alone.

A week passed and Juliana began walking alone in the meadow. For hours at a time she wandered in and out of the piñon forest, lost in thoughts of Parker. The loneliness overwhelmed her. She had loved him so much. She still loved him and couldn't let him go.

Thoughts of God haunted her, especially how she had felt his nearness the night that she and Callie had spoken their simple prayers. Bitterness welled up inside her. She felt betrayed. Empty. Cold. How could a loving God, someone she thought was her friend, take Parker from her?

❧

Sun Jones watched Juliana with a heavy heart. She wanted to reach out to her young friend, to comfort her, but it wasn't yet time. So Sun waited and prayed.

The day following Juliana and Callie's arrival, Sun had pondered the events that the young women had relayed. When they told of Parker's death at the hands of the Mojada, Sun asked pointed questions about what they had actually witnessed.

That night she told Jeremiah of her doubts: "I have seen Indian raids. I know the chaos of the wild moments. Some can be left for dead only to survive. I do not want to raise Juliana's hopes. But Miah, could you go to Fort La Sal and see if you can find our friend?"

Without Juliana or Callie knowing, Jeremiah had done her bidding, only to return two days later with sadness written on his face. He shook his head sadly. "I'm sorry, Morning Sun. But there is no trace of him. Those who were killed in the uprising were buried in a mass grave. No one has seen Parker James since the night the Mojada attacked."

But Sun could not rid her mind of her thoughts about Parker. She loved the young man like a son. She had prayed for him during their journey across the plains. She found it impossible to stop praying for him now.

She prayed for him in each waking moment. "Father, if he is alive, be with him now. Let him know you are there beside him. That you will never leave him," she whispered, even as she went about her chores. "May he look to you. May he find comfort in your arms."

As she watched Juliana's aimless wanderings, she prayed for the young woman to be healed. "Let her find peace in you," she prayed. "And help me know when to speak. Let your words be my words."

❧

One morning, several weeks later, when spring had finally come to the high meadow, Sun looked out at the pale green grasses. Nearly overnight the locust trees and the velvet mesquite had borne their soft blossoms, the colors of a mountain sunrise. The sunlight danced on the dew, and in the distance a meadowlark began its sweet song, followed by that of a mockingbird.

Sun knew in her bones that at last it was time to speak.

Juliana rose and, as had become her pattern, pulled on her cape, and silently walked from the cabin. This morning, though, she heard footsteps behind her.

Sun smiled as Juliana turned toward her.

"May I walk with you today?"

Juliana nodded.

"I would like to show you something. It is over here." Sun led her to a copse of velvet mesquite across the meadow. "Stand very quietly. Do not move."

They waited a short time, then Juliana heard the low clucking of a quail. It ran along the ground from underneath the brush, looking quickly around, then clucked softly again. Soon several more large quail appeared, followed by a covey of young.

Juliana smiled as the tiny birds scattered in all directions. The adult quail tried to keep up with them, running, clucking, calling out to their young ones. After the covey scratched for food, then headed to a stand of locust trees, Sun took Juliana's hand. They walked on a path near the meadow's edge.

Sometimes they stopped and Sun would tell of a certain plant, how it was used for food or seasoning. Again and again she pointed out new growth on plants that had appeared dead through the winter.

Sun picked a tender lilac branch and handed it to Juliana. "Just weeks ago, this branch had no leaves," she said. "Then the leaves came. Soon fragrant blossoms will burst from these buds."

They stopped near a fence that Jeremiah had begun building a few weeks earlier. Juliana leaned against a mesquite post and looked out across the meadow. It blazed in a profusion of color. The winter browns and grays and whites had gone. In their place, the grasses, the wildflowers, the butterflies and dragonflies, rising on wing against the sun, spoke of life. Renewed life.

Juliana turned to Sun, understanding even before her friend spoke what she had tried to say without words.

"All life includes death, Juliana," she began, her voice soft. "But death leads to another life. A life that never ends." She reached for a twig from an oak. The twig held new leaves, tender green, shining in their newness. "If we had stood here just days ago, we might have thought this tree was dead. There were no signs of life. No green." She gestured to the magnificent oak, alive with spring color. "But now it lives.

"You have grieved for Parker. You have died a death of your own as you thought of your loss. Your winter has been as bleak and dead as that of this oak." Her eyes held Juliana's tenderly. "Though you have not known it, there is something in you, a part of you that waits for spring. That waits to live again."

Juliana didn't speak, but waited for Sun to go on, feeling a sense of peace begin to settle into her soul.

"Juliana, Callie told me about your words about God that night in the church. She said you prayed, asking him to be with you."

Juliana nodded. "Yes, I thought of him as my friend. I asked him to comfort us."

"Did he?"

"Yes."

"But you have been angry with him for betraying you, for deserting Parker?"

"Yes." Juliana looked away from Sun's piercing blue eyes.

For a moment, Sun did not speak. The sounds of the meadow surrounded them. It seemed to Juliana almost like music, low and soft.

Sun looked up at the towering oak, seemed to study it a moment, then fixed her gaze again on Juliana. "If God lives in you, Juliana, new life begins inside. It is different than just having him *with* you. All things become new. Just as new life comes to an oak or a field of meadow grasses in the spring, new life begins in you when you give your life to him. When you ask him to live within you."

Something inside Juliana quickened at her words. But the

desperate loneliness, the feeling of bitterness and loss, seemed too deep and entrenched. How was it possible for God to bring new life to that place?

For a few minutes longer, Sun spoke of God's love and presence and care. Before she left Juliana alone, she hugged her gently. "Remember, child, God loves you as if you were the only one in the world to love. That will never change."

Juliana nodded, feeling the sting of tears behind her eyes. Sun walked away, back toward the cabin, leaving Juliana alone with her thoughts.

Juliana watched the sun rise higher in the purple mountain sky. The shadows of the towering pines disappeared. The meadow became a blaze of sunlight. She lifted her eyes to the heavens and began to speak to God.

She told him the bitter, angry thoughts held too long in her breaking heart. She spoke to him of Parker, her love for him, and her grief that she felt would never end. She told God how she missed her father. And her home. Feelings poured from her, feelings she had kept inside about Stonehaven and their forced departure. She told him everything as if he stood beside her, listening to every word, caring about every feeling.

When Juliana had finished, a sense of peace had begun to warm that place inside of bitter cold. "I need you, Father," she whispered. "I want to give my life to you." She raised her eyes to the oak beside her. She looked at its strong trunk, rising to the heavens, the tender new life sprouting forth in its leaves. "Give me new life," she breathed to her Lord. "Please live in me."

Juliana stood for a moment, while the sunlight bathing the meadow paled in comparison to the light and warmth that flooded her being. She raised her face, feeling fresh tears trace down her cheeks, feeling a sense of nearly overwhelming awe from a Presence within her.

She looked around the meadow. Everything seemed new, fresh, clean. New life abounded.

She saw a deer with two spotted fawns leap across the grasses. She smiled. That was the way she felt inside.

She lifted her heart, her voice, in praise to her Lord.

As Juliana walked back toward the cabin a short time later, she thought about Parker's death. It struck her that if God had allowed him to live, she might have continued thinking that he was all she needed. She might not have known the deep peace that had settled into her soul.

Twenty-Four

Two weeks later, a few hours before sunset, Juliana carried her paints, a canvas, and an easel to the far side of the meadow. It was the first time she had wanted to paint since before arriving in New Mexico.

She had chosen late afternoon so that she would have greater contrasts of light and shadow as she painted. She had also hoped to catch a glimpse of deer coming to a spring near the edge of the forest. She had seen them several times on her walks along the small stream and wanted to set up her easel to quietly await their arrival.

As she made her preparations, Juliana thought about the events of recent days. She and Callie had decided to build a cabin down the hill from Sun and Jeremiah. Callie was delighted at the prospect, though she still talked of someday going home to Stonehaven. Her sister couldn't let go of the feeling that their uncle had betrayed them, perhaps had cheated their father and caused him to lose the plantation.

Juliana told Callie that she had no interest in returning to Stonehaven. That part of her life was over. She wanted nothing more than to buy land in the meadow near Sun and Jeremiah and build a home of her own. Maybe from time to time she would travel to other parts of the West to paint, but she planned always to return to her beloved mountain meadow.

Callie, though, with fire in her eyes, declared she still planned to someday return and take what was rightfully theirs. She would reclaim Stonehaven—by herself, if necessary.

Jeremiah and Sun promised to help with building the cabin. Jeremiah said he would call on some of his fellow trappers to help fell pines of the right size and roll them into place.

They also said they expected their son Jed home sometime soon. They had received a letter from him, telling that Dr. Hill was allowing him to leave for a visit west. They figured he would arrive sometime in the late spring or early summer.

With the house-raising and homecoming, the mountain air seemed alive with expectation. Juliana felt it, rejoiced in it, as she dabbed the paints on her palette.

The deer she had anticipated—a magnificent buck, a doe, and two fawns—stepped silently through the thicket and into view. Without a sound, Juliana began to sketch with charcoal, minimizing her movement, almost not daring to breathe. She worked swiftly, concentrating only on the graceful forms before her, hoping they wouldn't bolt before she had finished. She glanced from canvas to deer and back again, with no thought in her mind except the beauty of the four creatures.

Juliana sketched the buck's antlers, the tilt of his head, the light in his eye. Lost in her work, she didn't see a rider approaching the cabin across the meadow. She didn't see the man remount after a brief visit to the cabin and kick the horse to a gallop across the meadow, riding toward her as swiftly as a prairie wind.

Then, suddenly, she heard the beat of horse's hooves. At the same time, the deer leapt into a stand of mesquite.

She turned in annoyance. The brush and palette slipped from

her hands as she watched the approaching rider.

The setting sun slanted into her eyes, obscuring her view. The light was behind him and she couldn't see the horse's color or the man's face because of the night shadows.

He rode closer. She watched him intently, afraid to believe what her heart told her was true. She noticed the way he sat in the saddle, the way he brushed his hair from his forehead with his fingers.

She held her breath as the rider drew nearer.

No. It couldn't be, she told herself. Parker was dead. She had seen him pulled from his horse. She had seen the glints of knives, heard the report of gunfire. It couldn't be.

Juliana shielded her face with her hand, biting her lip, waiting, hoping.

Then she could see his face. His beautiful face.

With a cry she ran to him, almost before he had slid from the Appaloosa's back.

Parker picked her up in his arms, lifting her off her feet. "Oh, my beloved," he cried, as he buried his face in her neck.

Juliana wrapped her arms around him, then backed away slightly, holding his face in her hands. "How?—" she began, then stopped, overcome by tears. She drew a shaking breath. "I thought you were dead. I saw it happen."

"You were there?"

She nodded slowly. "Yes."

He drew her closer, held her for a time without speaking. She could feel his heart pounding.

"I was in La Sal that night. Matt held Callie and me captive in the church. We got out. When we were on the roof, I saw you riding toward us—I saw the Mojada. I thought—" Her voice broke again.

"Oh, Juliana," he whispered. "I'm so sorry. I had no idea." He searched her eyes. "Did Graves hurt you?"

"No."

He sighed. "Cookingham arrested him that night. Graves and his cohorts have been taken to Fort Leavenworth. They'll be tried for treason."

"What happened to Charles Bent? And his family?"

Parker's face saddened. "I didn't reach them in time." He shook his head. "There was a massacre—" His voice dropped.

Then he pulled her close again, holding her tightly. "I've missed you. My precious Juliana, how I've missed you." His voice was husky with emotion. Then he began to tell of his ordeal. During the attack he had fallen unconscious. The Mojada had left him for dead. That night his body had been piled with the others awaiting burial.

"Cookingham found me the next day. Carried me away from town to the home of a family he knew. They nursed me back to health."

Juliana reached up to touch a scar along the side of his forehead. She gently pulled his face toward her and kissed the place.

"There were times I thought I wouldn't make it. There was a darkness, Juliana, a swirling darkness that held me. A fear as strong as death itself. I couldn't get out of it."

Juliana took his hand and held it close while he spoke. "Then it seemed that Someone else was with me in that place. A Light that dispelled the darkness. I can't explain it." His clear eyes held hers. "I just knew God was with me." He was quiet a moment. "He brought me comfort, greater than any I had ever known.

"Juliana, there is so much I have to tell you. I've been angry with God for years. I know I don't deserve his love. Yet he was there—a Presence so real I could have touched him. I didn't want to leave that place where I had found him.

"Then, suddenly, I knew. I knew that he was with me always. Everywhere. Not just in that place. And he has been with me all along. Even when I was shaking my fist in anger, he was there, loving me. Waiting for me to acknowledge him, to turn to him again."

Parker's voice softened. "Then the darkness left, and I knew that I would live. All at once I wanted to live. I *had* to live. To be with you. To marry you. To spend a lifetime with you."

He traced his fingers along her forehead, her cheeks, her lips. "I remembered your eyes. I've always thought they were the color of a mountain lake. And I pictured them in my mind. I thought about the way you tilt your chin in wonder, in curiosity."

He drew Juliana again into his arms. "I love you. Oh, Juliana. I love you." And he kissed her.

Juliana laughed softly, love and joy filling her to overflowing. As he bent to kiss her again, the glow from the fading sunset touched his face. It struck her that there were no shadows, only light. And love.

Dear Reader:

The seed of *Westward's* plot took root when I visited beautiful New Mexico for the first time. I walked across the "Fort La Sal" (the real-life Taos) plaza, visited the house where Governor Charles Bent was killed during the Taos Uprising, and saw the splatters of *Penitente* blood in a centuries-old adobe church. I could "see" Juliana St. Clair and Parker James in this setting. I knew that this place had to be the backdrop for their story.

My husband Tom (a history professor) and I are fascinated by the study of old emigrant trails—the Oregon-California Trail, the Old Spanish Trail, and the Santa Fe Trail. We've spent hours on these trails, searching for wagon traces, reading journals of early explorers and travelers (such as Jedediah Smith and Susan Magoffin), trying to find the sites of the events they describe.

When I began writing *Westward*, I had just finished reading Susan Magoffin's diary telling of her honeymoon spent on the Santa Fe Trail in 1846 with her husband (a caravan owner much like Parker James). Young, lively, curious, Susan describes her travels with a contagious enthusiasm. After reading her enchanting account, I *had* to place Juliana and Callie in a trading caravan on that trail.

As Juliana and Parker, Callie, Sun and Jeremiah came to life in *Westward*, and I (almost as an outside observer) watched them in their timeless struggles and failures and triumphs, I was reminded of my own life's journey. A journey that has its own adventure and drama. A journey in which God interacts with me, loving, forgiving, guiding, always walking beside me.

I can't respond to every letter I receive, although I love hearing from my readers. Please know how deeply I appreciate your support. May God be with you on your own life's journey.

Blessings always,

Amanda MacLean

Amanda MacLean
c/o Palisades
P.O. Box 1720
Sisters, Oregon 97759

You met Callie in *Westward*.

Now her story continues in *Stonehaven*.

Even as she works to win back Stonehaven, the undauntable Callie St. Clair turns her former home into a station on the Underground Railroad. She plays a dangerous and duplicitous role: a southern belle enjoying the grandeur of the pre-Civil War South—and "Nashtara," the mysterious leader of the Natchez Underground.

Callie can't reveal her true identity—even to the man she loves—and faces losing him forever.

Don't miss *Stonehaven!*

Watch for it this August in a
Christian bookstore near you.